DECODING THE TALMUD'S EXEGETICAL PROGRAM

From Detail to Principle
in the Bavli's Quest for Generalization

Babylonian Talmud
Tractate Shabbat

SOUTH FLORIDA STUDIES IN THE HISTORY OF JUDAISM

Edited by
Jacob Neusner
William Scott Green, James Strange
Darrell J. Fasching, Sara Mandell

Number 67
DECODING THE TALMUD'S
EXEGETICAL PROGRAM
From Detail to Principle
in the Bavli's Quest for Generalization

by
Jacob Neusner

DECODING THE TALMUD'S EXEGETICAL PROGRAM

From Detail to Principle
in the Bavli's Quest for Generalization

Babylonian Talmud
Tractate Shabbat

by
Jacob Neusner

Scholars Press
Atlanta, Georgia

DECODING THE TALMUD'S EXEGETICAL PROGRAM

From Detail to Principle
in the Bavli's Quest for Generalization

©1992
University of South Florida

Publication of this book was made possible by a grant from the Tisch Family Foundation, New York City. The University of South Florida acknowledges with thanks this important support for its scholarly projects.

Library of Congress Cataloging in Publication Data
Neusner, Jacob, 1932-
    Decoding the Talmud's exegetical program: from detail to
principle in the Bavli's quest for generalization: Babylonian
Talmud Tractate Shabbat/ by Jacob Neusner.
        p. cm. — (South Florida studies in the history of Judaism;
no. 67)
    Includes index.
    ISBN 1-55540-804-4
    1. Talmud. Shabbat—Criticism, interpretation, etc. 2. Mishnah.
Shabbat—Criticism, interpretation, etc.   I. Title. II. Series:
South Florida studies in the history of Judaism; 67.
BM506.S27N48 1993
296.1'25—dc20   92-39001
                                                      CIP

Printed in the United States of America
on acid-free paper

Table of Contents

Preface

The description of so vast and influential a piece of writing as the Talmud of Babylonia, a.k.a. the Bavli, requires a variety of approaches. I have taken two, the one analytical and formal, the other philosophical and synthetic. First, I wanted to know about the document's paramount formal traits, with special reference to its rhetorical and logical rules. In a sequence of monographs I have demonstrated beyond any reasonable doubt the simple and obvious fact that the Talmud of Babylonia is a commentary to the Mishnah not only in external form but in inner construction and composition. These monographs are as follows: *The Rules of Composition of the Talmud of Babylonia: The Cogency of the Bavli's Composite* (Atlanta, 1991: Scholars Press for South Florida Studies in the History of Judaism); *The Bavli's One Voice: Types and Forms of Analytical Discourse and Their Fixed Order of Appearance* (Atlanta, 1991: Scholars Press for South Florida Studies in the History of Judaism); *How the Bavli Shaped Rabbinic Discourse* (Atlanta, 1991: Scholars Press for South Florida Studies in the History of Judaism); *The Bavli's Massive Miscellanies: The Problem of Agglutinative Discourse in the Talmud of Babylonia* (Atlanta, 1992: Scholars Press for South Florida Studies in the History of Judaism); *Sources and Traditions: Types of Composition in the Talmud of Babylonia* (Atlanta, 1992: Scholars Press for South Florida Studies in the History of Judaism); culminating in *The Bavli's Primary Discourse: Mishnah Commentary, its Rhetorical Paradigms and their Theological Implications in the Talmud of Babylonia Tractate Moed Qatan* (Atlanta, 1992: Scholars Press for South Florida Studies in the History of Judaism).

The synthetic inquiry builds upon the results of the analytical. Specifically, now that such monographs as *The Bavli's One Voice* have presented me with firm formal evidence of the cogency of the Talmud of Babylonia, I have to address the task of finding out whether the substance of the Talmud as a commentary to the Mishnah was as cogent and systematic as the form. And this has led me to seek for generalizations: traits of mind, propositions and viewpoints, characteristic of many passages, though expressed in abstract form in none of them. This work is necessarily slow, since it involves sifting vast stretches of the Talmud. So, asking whether the Talmud's commentary to the Mishnah is episodic or systematic, I have constructed a number of experiments on that question, in particular.

This one is the fourth and last in a sequence of monographs pursuing the same line of inquiry, the norms of the Bavli's reading of the Mishnah. The earlier monographs are as follows: [1] *The Bavli's One Statement: The Metapropositional Program of Babylonian Talmud Tractate Zebahim Chapters One and Five* (Atlanta, 1991: Scholars Press for South Florida Studies in the History of Judaism); [2] *The Law Behind the Laws: The Bavli's Essential Discourse* (Atlanta, 1992: Scholars Press for South Florida Studies in the History of Judaism); and [3] *The Bavli's Intellectual Character: The Generative Problematic in Bavli Baba Qamma Chapter One and Bavli Shabbat Chapter One* (Atlanta, 1992: Scholars Press for South Florida Studies in the History of Judaism). This monograph is the logical next step, beyond the inquiry into the generative problematic. I shall explain in the introduction what I learned there which drew my attention to the somewhat different inquiry I pursue here. In the concluding chapter I set forth the reason that I regard the present inquiry as a failure in that the results are negative. I did not set out to prove a point, but I did want to find out whether my hypothesis could yield promising results. My four probes show that the results are not promising at all, because in all instances my cases are not subject to demonstrable generalization. All I have are examples, but they exemplify only themselves. Of course, a negative result (or a null hypothesis, in this instance the two are the same) proves as important as a positive one; for me, it dictates the next stage in my inquiry into how the Bavli forms a cogent documentary statement, as, in formal terms, I have shown that it does. The upshot is simple. All of this monographic work, of course, is suggestive and interesting, but inconclusive. The results justify no generalizations. Until the entirety of the Talmud of Babylonia has been characterized, in proportion and in detail, the suggestions I have made in the four monographs on what I think the exegetical dynamic and moving force for the Bavli's dialectic consists of are merely plausible.

Now I am sure that characterization of the whole must begin in the systematic, not merely episodic, comparison of the two Talmuds, which I began in my *Judaism: The Classical Statement. The Evidence of the Bavli* (Chicago, 1986: University of Chicago Press). But that work was only a first step, and even now I cannot say for sure what I conceive the right moves to be. Nor am I persuaded that for the purposes of my program of inquiry – now moving into its fourth decade, for I began in 1960 and I

have walked a single, continuous, and generally straight path since then,
– I have to characterize the document in a whole and final way.

A brief prospect of my program will explain what I need to know to
find out what I want to understand. All of these works are part of a
much larger program of inquiry into the transformation of Judaism from
philosophy to religion to theology. The literary evidence of the Judaism
of the Dual Torah, from the Mishnah through the second of the Talmuds,
for me yields a picture of a highly philosophical book, the Mishnah,
standing at the outset; a quite different kind of writing, which I
characterize as religious, comes to the fore in the Talmud of the Land of
Israel and associated Midrash compilations, as I showed through the
analysis of category formation worked out in my *Transformation of
Judaism* (Champaign-Urbana, 1992: University of Illinois Press). I see the
third and final phase as one of the synthesis of these two opposites, the
re-presentation of religion in the medium of philosophy, which is to say,
the presentation of Judaism as theology; this was done by the Talmud
and associated writings.

My complete translation of both Talmuds now nearly entirely in
press, for reasons now abundantly set forth, I plan the next phase of this
rather protracted project as follows:

> *The Torah in the Talmud. A Taxonomy of the Uses of
> Scripture in the Talmud of Babylonia in Comparison
> with the Talmud of the Land of Israel.*

> *The Bavli and the Yerushalmi. A Systematic Comparison. I.
> The Problem and a Preliminary Probe: Bavli and
> Yerushalmi to Mishnah-Tractate Niddah.*

> *The Bavli and the Yerushalmi. A Systematic Comparison. II.
> Bavli and Yerushalmi to Selected Mishnah Tractates
> in Moed.*

> *The Bavli and the Yerushalmi. A Systematic Comparison. III.
> Bavli and Yerushalmi to Selected Mishnah Tractates
> in Nashim.*

> *The Bavli and the Yerushalmi. A Systematic Comparison. IV.
> Bavli and Yerushalmi to Selected Mishnah Tractates
> in Neziqin. Conclusion: Does the Bavli Establish an
> Autonomous Discourse?.*

> *The Definition of Judaism. From the Yerushalmi's Religion to
> the Bavli's Theology. The Autonomous Discourse of
> the Bavli and its Associated Midrash Compilations.*

> *The Traits and Program of the Normative, Dual Torah in Conclusion.*
>
> *The Bavli and the Denkart. A Comparison of the Systemic Statements of Judaism and Zoroastrianism.*
>
> *From Old Order to New: Judaism, Zoroastrianism, Islam at the End of Antiquity.*

The critical position of the Bavli translation, on the one side, and of these monographs aimed at the systematic description of the Bavli, on the other, is clear from that program. I have no reason to doubt that I shall reach my goal and find out what I wish to know.

JACOB NEUSNER

Distinguished Research Professor of Religious Studies
UNIVERSITY OF SOUTH FLORIDA
Tampa, St. Petersburg, Sarasota, Lakeland, Fort Myers

735 Fourteenth Avenue Northeast
St. Petersburg, Florida 33701-1413 USA

1

Introduction

To understand the issues I raise here, readers will require a brief review of prior results. Those familiar with the two principal monographs summarized below will prefer to move directly to section III of this chapter.

I. The Bavli's One Statement. The Metapropositional Program of the Babylonian Talmud

The Talmud not only makes specific points but also – at a number of points – conducts discourse at a higher level of abstraction, one that I call metapropositional. Specifically, I hold that when analyses of a variety of problems yield diverse propositions that as a matter of fact turn out to say the same one thing about many diverse things, that one thing said in many ways about many things forms not a proposition but a metaproposition. It is a proposition that derives from all subsets of propositions and states in an abstract and general way – whether explicitly or merely by indirection – the one proposition contained within many demonstrations of propositions. We know that we have identified the metapropositional program of a writing when we can say what we think is at stake, in the most general terms, in a variety of specific syllogisms and turn out to be saying the same thing again and again. We may test our hypothetical metaproposition by asking whether, in those many things, we may identify any other proposition to define the stakes of a demonstration; or whether some other encompassing proposition may serve as well as the one we propose over as broad a range of data as we examine. Where may we expect to find not only propositions but a statement that coheres throughout: a statement in behalf of all propositions? A coherent legal system, for one example, not only sets forth rules for diverse circumstances but, through the rules, also may lay out a philosophy of the social order, an account of what is always fair

1

and just; then all of the cases, each with its generalization, turn out to repeat in different ways a single encompassing statement.

So, too, while the author of a document makes statements about a great many subjects, a well-crafted document by a strong-minded writer will find the author saying much the same thing about all things. Then the key to good writing will be the power to make the same point again and again without boring the reader or belaboring the obvious. Indeed, an important and truly well-conceived piece of writing addressed to a long future will precipitate productive debates about not only details but what that some one thing said in many ways is meant to propose. Great writing leaves space for readers. That is the mark of a strong argument, a well-crafted formulation of a considered viewpoint, the expression of a deeply reflected upon attitude, or, in intellectual matters, a rigorously presented proposition. To find out what we might imagine some one thing a writer may say about many things, we ask simply, "What is at stake if this point is validated?" or simply, "If so, so what?" If time and again we find that treatment of a given subject yields as its final and most general and abstract point a proposition that turns out also to emerge from an unrelated treatment of some other subject, altogether, then we have what I call a metaproposition, meaning, a proposition that transcends a variety of propositions and that occurs in all of them.

Obviously, defining the metapropositional statement that an author repeatedly sets forth involves an element of eisegesis – and even subjectivity. That is invariably a starting point. On the one side, others may see some other metaproposition that circulates throughout a piece of writing, different from one that I might proposed. On the other, still others may perceive no metaproposition at all. How to test a thesis on the metaproposition of a diverse piece of writing? One irrefutable demonstration is that a single rhetoric prevails, for that legitimates asking whether saying everything in some one way, writers also say one thing about many things. To define that some one thing, and to find out whether or not a proposed metaproposition in fact circulates throughout such a writing, first of all, a massive survey must show where, how, and why one proposes that one and same proposition that – according to a proposed metaproposition – an author persists in setting forth in the context of a great many diverse discussions. If it can be shown that most, or even all, of a large and various corpus of writing turns out to be saying that one thing through its treatment of a great many things, then one is justified in claiming to have set forth that proposition beyond the propositions that animates a document. It is the one that the authors have composed the document to set forth and in a vast number of ways to demonstrate. But let me forthwith turn to the two problems just now noted. What about the possibility that another metaproposition may be shown to inhere, different from the one that as a matter of hypothesis is set forth at the outset? Or what if a proposed metaproposition is not shown to be present at all? Then the experiment has failed. And how are we going to test the validity of two or more proposed metapropositions, and so to know whether the metaproposition that is suggested is the right one? The answer lies in a detailed demonstration that the proposed metaproposition is the best one possible one, in the context of a variety of possibilities, to encompass the data at hand. And God lives in the details.

My case that the Talmud contains metapropositions, not just proposals about this and that, derives from Bavli Zebahim Chapter Five, which yields two important facts. First, monotonously set forth in the treatment of Mishnah-tractate Zebahim 5:3ff. to the end, nearly the entire chapter addresses the question of the connection between rules recorded in the Mishnah and rules presented in Scripture. The metaproposition that encompasses the numerous specific propositions is simple: How do we make connections between rules and their point of origin? Every time we ask, "What is the source [in Scripture] for this statement?" we find an answer that is left to stand. So one fundamental and ubiquitous metaproposition of the Bavli may be set forth in this language:

1. It is important to link laws that occur in one source to those that occur in another.
2. Among the compilations (components of "the one whole Torah of Moses, our rabbi," in later mythic language) that enjoy canonical status (in our language), the premier is Scripture.
3. So whenever we find a statement of a rule in the Mishnah and ask for its source, the implicit criterion of success will be, "the rule is founded on language of Scripture, properly construed."
4. So, consequently, the proposition implicit in numerous propositions, common to them all and holding them all together, is this: all rules cohere, and the point of origin of nearly all of them is the written part of the Torah revealed by God to Moses at Sinai.

And yet we cannot then assign to the authorship of our chapter and the numerous other chapters in which a principal, recurrent concern and point of generative tension is the link of the law (contained in the Mishnah or other Tannaite compilations) to the law (contained in Scripture) and its particular wording merely the task of saying explicitly what the framers of the Mishnah occasionally said and commonly implied. For there is a second metaproposition in the cited chapter, and it does not pertain to so general an issue as the ubiquitous one now well represented. It is the issue of the nature and structure of thought; at stake is the demonstration that metapropositions in the Bavli are not only particular to the problem of the documentary provenance of rules – Scripture forms the basis of nearly all rules; all rules harmonize, at their foundations in abstract principles, with all other rules. The metapropositional program turns out, as I shall now show through a reprise of my findings concerning the pertinent propositions of the Bavli's reading of Mishnah-tractate Zebahim 5:1-2, to be so abstract as vastly to transcend rules and their generalizations and harmonies, rising to the height of principles of thought that guide the intellect in contemplation of all being and all reality.

To grasp the metapropositional program that, in my view, defines the stakes of discourse, let me specify what I conceive to be the counterpart program, pertaining not to connecting rules to Scripture, but rather, connecting principle to (consequent) principle: how thought really takes place, which is, not in a stationary pool but in a moving stream. To state the result up front: the Mishnah portrays all things at rest, a beautifully composed set in stasis, a stage on which nothing happens. The Bavli portrays all things in motion, a world of action, in which one thing leads to some other, and nothing stands still. All of this is accomplished in a shift in the received mode of thought, and the shift is set forth in the metaproposition, fully exposed, in the reading of two paragraphs of the Mishnah. We now consider what I conceive to be the counterpart program to the one that, in my view, the Bavli's sages inherited from the Mishnah and spelled out in tedious and unending particulars. To understand what is fresh and important in the Bavli's metapropositional program concerning the nature of thought, we have to call to mind what they inherited, for what they did was to impose the stamp of their own intellect upon the intellectual heritage that the Mishnah had provided for them.

To set forth the basic theory of the framers of the Mishnah on how thought takes place, which is to say, how we may understand things and know them, we must recall a simple fact. The Mishnah teaches the age-old method of scientific thought through comparison and contrast. Like things follow like rules, unlike things, the opposite rules; and the task of thought is to show what is like something else and therefore follows the rule that governs that something else, or what is unlike something else and therefore follows the opposite of the rule that governs that something else. So the Mishnah's mode of thought establishes connections between and among things and does so, as is clear, through the method of taxonomy, comparison and contrast, list making of like things, yielding the rule that governs all items on the list.

List making places on display the data of the like and the unlike and implicitly (ordinarily, not explicitly) then conveys the rule. The Mishnah is then a book of lists, with the implicit order, the nomothetic traits of a monothetic order, dictating the ordinarily unstated general and encompassing rule. And all this why? It is in order to make a single statement, endless times over, and to repeat in a mass of tangled detail precisely the same fundamental judgment. The framers of the Mishnah appeal solely to the traits of things. List making then defines way of proving propositions through classification, so establishing a set of shared traits that form a rule which compels us to reach a given conclusion. Probative facts derive from the classification of data, all of which point in one direction and not in another. A catalogue of facts, for example, may be so composed that, through the regularities and indicative traits of the entries, the catalogue yields a proposition. A list of parallel items all together points to a simple conclusion; the conclusion may or may not be given at the end of the catalogue, but the catalogue – by definition – is pointed. All of the catalogued facts are taken to bear self-evident connections to one another, established by those pertinent shared traits implicit in the composition of the list, therefore also bearing meaning and pointing through the weight of evidence to an inescapable conclusion. The discrete facts then join together because of some trait common to them all. This is a mode of classification of facts to lead to an identification of what the facts have in common and – it goes without saying, an explanation of their meaning.

If I had to specify a single mode of thought that establishes connections between one fact and another, it is in the search for points in common and therefore also points of contrast. We seek connection between fact and fact, sentence and sentence in the subtle and balanced rhetoric of the Mishnah, by comparing and contrasting two things that are like and not alike. At the logical level, too, the Mishnah falls into the category of familiar philosophical thought. Once we seek regularities, we propose rules. What is like another thing falls under its rule, and what is not like the other falls under the opposite rule. Accordingly, as to the species of the genus, so far as they are alike, they share the same rule. So far as they are not alike, each follows a rule contrary to that governing the other. So the work of analysis is what produces connection, and therefore the drawing of conclusions derives from comparison and contrast: the *and,* the *equal.* The proposition then that forms the conclusion concerns the essential likeness of the two offices, except where they are different, but the subterranean premise is that we can explain both likeness and difference by appeal to a principle of fundamental order and unity. To make these observations concrete, we turn to the case at hand. The important contrast comes at the outset. The high priest and king fall into a single genus, but speciation, based on traits particular to the king, then distinguishes the one from the other. Now if I had to specify the deepest conviction at the most profound layers of thought, it is that things set in relationship always stand in that same relationship. The work of making connections and drawing conclusions produces results that are fixed and final. If we establish a connection between one set of things and another, that connection forms the end of matters – that, and not a series, by which the connection between A and B serves as a guide to a movement from C to A via B, that is, as we shall now see, the formation of not a connection but a series of things that are connected only to one another, but not to other components of the same series – which is to say, a series. To put matters very simply, if A is like B, and B is like C, then is C like A? And if we entertain the possibility of a series, then, *what are the rules of connection that form the links of the results of comparison and contrast?* In other words, in the aftermath of classification comes not hierarchization but movement, this thing in relationship to that, that in relationship to the other, all things in movement, nothing at rest. So, if a series is possible, then how is a series composed? That is the question answered by the Bavli, the question no one in the Mishnah asked, because the Mishnah's framers contemplated a world at rest, and the Bavli's, a world in motion.

Now that the Mishnah's position is in hand, we revert to my claim that the Bavli's own statement in the chapter under discussion concerns the nature of thought. Let us first of all review the points that are made and the sequence in which they are set forth. We begin with the point of intersection:

1. It is important to know how to connect rules to Scripture.
2. The principles that governing the making of connections to Scripture are those that govern making connections not between words and words ("the hermeneutical principles") but rather between one thing and something else, that is, defining a genus and its species; so when we know how to compare and contrast, find what is like something else and what is different from something else, we know how to conduct the passage from rules to Scripture.
3. Exegetical rules tell us how to form classes of things in relationship to Scripture.
4. Dialectical rules tell us how to move from one class of things to another class of things.

No. 2 then marks the point of departure, and Nos. 3 and 4, the remarkable shift in the passage. We go not only from rule to generalization, or from case to principle. That, to be sure, takes place and forms an everywhere present metaproposition, as the tedium of the remainder of the chapter showed us. Rather, we go from thinking about things and their connections (comparison and contrast) to thinking about thought itself. So what I have represented as the rules of dialectical thinking – not merely argument! – turns out to tell us how thought happens; the Bavli's reading of Mishnah-tractate Zebahim 5:1-2 forms a fundamental exercise of thought about thinking. For, when we review the principal steps in the sustained and unfolding inquiry, we realize that, in particulars and in detail, the framers of the passage have set forth a profound essay on thought. In the terms just now given, if A=B, and B=C, then does C=A? Is a series possible? Are there limits to the extension of a series? And on what basis do we construct a series? Do the media of linkage between A and B, that is, A=B, have to be the same as those that link B to C, for C to stand in the series that A has begun? These abstract questions have to become concrete before the sense of matters will emerge. So let us now review the sequence of points that represent the inquiry into the making of connections, which is to say, the Bavli's metapropositional statement on the character of a series. For it is the series, first this, then that, finally the third thing, and the rules that govern the movement from this, to that, to the third thing, that defines what is the center of deep thought in the Bavli's reading of the specified Mishnah paragraphs. My account of this matter in detail does not require review for the present purpose.

It remains only to state that the metapropositional program contributed by the Bavli's framers concerns how series are made, which is to say, whether connections yield static or dynamic results, which is to say, at the deepest layers of intellect, how thought happens. The importance of this observation for the next step is obvious. Once we know that, in general, the framers of the Bavli want to know how a list becomes a series, we address the further question: What, exactly, is a series? My answer is, a series is a set of lists that are brought into relationship with one another. Let me explain.

II. The Bavli's Intellectual Character.
The Talmud's Generative Problematic

By "the intellectual character" of a document, I mean the program of thought and inquiry that brings about the writing of that document. My claim is very straightforward. The Bavli constitutes an intellectual document, not merely an informative one; second the intellectual program of the document, replicated in countless details but everywhere uniform, can be identified and defined. This second point sets the stage for the present work. The Bavli is more than a merely informative document, important parts of which set forth information and explanation. The Bavli is also a highly intellectual piece of writing, important parts of which also identify problems and solve them; more to the point, those parts use information as a medium for the investigation of propositions that vastly transcend concrete data. The Bavli is both concrete – everywhere, all the time, always very concrete – but it is also abstract; it is practical but also speculative; it is detailed but, in many ways (though not everywhere) also cogent. The description of the Bavli's intellectual character requires me to spell out this claim for abstraction and intellectual vigor and transcendence: Why is the Bavli a statement, not merely a compilation of information? Much of the Bavli consists of explanations of words and phrases of the Mishnah; identification of scriptural bases for the Mishnah's rules, discovery of the authority behind an unattributed law, and similar problems of an essentially factual nature. But the Bavli is a richly argumentative document. It not only presents facts. It also solves problems. But how do the framers of the Bavli's large-scale composites know a problem from a fact, and what tells them that a problem requires attention? By that I mean, what constitutes the problematic of the document, its philosophical hermeneutic? The Mishnah exegetes of the Bavli proposed to take the two-dimensional chess of the Mishnah and to transform it into a three-dimensional game: changing the game from chess on a flat board to cubic chess defines the generative problematic of the Bavli.

The Mishnah concentrates on the correct classification of things. The Bavli takes up the issue of the relationships between and among what has been classified, adding to a simple classification system of the Mishnah's other, fitting classificatory grids (hence: 'mixed grids'). The Mishnah's mode of thought therefore is static, the Bavli's, dynamic; the Mishnah addresses a world at rest, the Bavli, calls that same world into motion. The meaning of these simple descriptive statements will emerge in these pages. For in this monograph I try to show that, in a variety of entirely unrelated topics, when the framers of the Bavli move beyond the labor of Mishnah exegesis and amplification, they address a single question over and over again. This they do at a great many points, though two will suffice to state my proposal.

The question that occupies the authors of analytical compositions and composites concerns the interplay of classifications of things that form the same thing, which is to say, in taxonomic terms, of the species of a genus. A given genus is made up of various species. Each of these species, by definition, exhibits distinctive traits. When brought into relationship with other species of the same genus, how the various species interrelate, by reason of the distinctive taxonomic traits characteristic of each, allows us to compare like to like and identify points of unlikeness, or to compare unlike to unlike and discover points of commonality. In so doing, we probe deeper into the concrete laws that govern each of the species of a common genus. So this labor of dialectical comparison and contrast aims at moving ever more profoundly into the depths of the law. We see not only how laws form law, but also, how law generates laws: the unity of the law in its diversity, the power of diversity, too, to emerge out of unity.

At the most profound and abstract layer of discourse, what gives the Bavli its dynamic and power of dialectic is this question of how to sort out the diverse ways in which different things form the same thing. That is not what occupies the framers of the Mishnah and shapes the character of their inquiry into any given topic, but it is a question that depends upon their work and forms the logically consequent inquiry. So while what generates inquiry and shapes analysis of things in the Mishnah is the taxonomic question, what does the same for the heirs of the Mishnah in the Bavli is the result of that taxonomy. A single process unfolds, but in clearly differentiated steps – just as the very presentation of the Bavli as a commentary and secondary amplification of the Mishnah is meant to indicate even in visual form. A simple analogy, drawn from music, will show what is at stake. The Mishnah may be compared to Ravel's "Bolero," saying the same thing over and over again, pretty much in the same way, varying only the subject matter (in this, the analogy fails, being unfair to the brilliance of the Mishnah authorship, for Ravel says the same thing in the same way and never changes the musical counterpart to his subject matter). The Bavli then may be compared to a Beethoven or a Bruckner symphony, in which the same simple idea is reworked in countless variations, so that the whole exhibits both a rich complexity and also an essential simplicity.

The meaning of "generative problematic" then is very simple. When I address any topic whatever, is there something I want to know about that topic that is pretty much the same as what I want to know about any and every topic? In the Mishnah and in the Bavli, the answer to that question is affirmative. If I bring to bear a problem that provokes inquiry and focuses my attention on one thing, rather than some other, then that is what generates my work: makes me curious, requires me to answer a question (particularly of an analytical, not merely descriptive) character. By "problem" we may mean a variety of things, but by "problematic" only one: what persistently provokes curiosity and demands inquiry. The "generative problematic" then is that abstract problem that over and over again, in a variety of concrete settings, tells me what I want to know about this, that, and the other thing: which, for there to be a generative problematic, must always be the same thing.

What is at stake in identifying the generative problematic of the Bavli? The answer is simple. I have maintained that the Bavli forms a coherent statement, that, wherever we are, we know why we are told the things that we are told, and what makes one thing cohere with some other, and all things with all other things. Now that conception is hardly fresh; to the contrary, just as the framers of the Bavli's Mishnah commentary rightly took for granted that all the laws of the Mishnah and of sources of equivalent authority harmoniously cohere, so all those who have studied the Bavli have understood the same premise as the beginning of all inquiry. So in general mine is a classic question: How does the document cohere? But, of course, in particular, my question is my own. To my knowledge, only a very few of those for whom the Bavli formed a principal component of the Torah ever asked in terms so abstract as these precisely what the document is all about.

Let me turn to a concrete example of what I mean by alleging that the Bavli takes the simple grid of the Mishnah and adds a second, third, and even a fourth dimension to it: two, three, or four grids placed into relationship with one another. Only then will the further work of the present experiment find its proper context.

The thesis for testing is simple. When the Bavli's framers look at a passage of the Mishnah, one fundamental problem that will engage their attention is how the taxa of the Mishnah passage intersect with other taxa altogether. If the Mishnah paragraph (or chapter or tractate) classifies data within a given grid, the authors of the Bavli's sustained response to that paragraph will ask about other grids, proposing to place one grid atop the other, or, more accurately, to see how the two grids fit together. When the exegesis of words and phrases, sources and authorities, comes to an end,[1] then what sustains the Bavli's framers' interest in their work is a fascinating intellectual problem: turning two-dimensional into three-dimensional chess. That simple, but abstract, definition of matters demands a concrete example, and we turn forthwith to that task. My one sample of what I mean brings us to a clear, taxonomic statement: four generative classifications of causes of damages and their subdivisions. The Mishnah paragraph invites a secondary exercise in taxonomy, which is why I present it as my initial case. The relevance of what we are about to examine to the thesis I wish to propose is simple. Since I maintain that

---

[1] I have defined that matter in *The Bavli's Primary Discourse: Mishnah Commentary, Its Rhetorical Paradigms and Their Theological Implications in the Talmud of Babylonia Tractate Moed Qatan* (Atlanta, 1992: Scholars Press for South Florida Studies in the History of Judaism).

what has prompted the framer of the composite before us to ask the questions we address, rather than some others, is a sustained and systematic interest in how various classes of things relate to one another. This leads to the inquiry into how considerations extrinsic to these classes of things turn out to affect the definition and relationship of the classes of things onto which they are brought to bear.

1:1

A.   [There are] four generative classifications of causes of damages: (1) ox (Ex. 21:35-36), (2) pit (Ex. 21:33), (3) crop-destroying beast (Ex. 22:4), and (4) conflagration (Ex. 22:5).

B.   [The indicative characteristic] of the ox is not equivalent to that of the crop-destroying beast;

C.   nor is that of the crop-destroying beast equivalent to that of the ox;

D.   nor are this one and that one, which are animate, equivalent to fire, which is not animate;

E.   nor are this one and that one, which usually [get up and] go and do damage, equivalent to a pit, which does not usually [get up and] go and do damage.

F.   What they have in common is that they customarily do damage and taking care of them is your responsibility.

G.   And when one [of them] has caused damage, the [owner] of that which causes the damage is liable to pay compensation for damage out of the best of his land (Ex. 22:4).

The first statement alerts us to the exegetical program of the Bavli's authorship at hand: Are there secondary causes of damages? And, if there are, how do the damages of the secondary or derivative class compare to those of the primary or generative one: clearly an exercise in secondary taxonomy.

I.1   A.   Four generative causes of damages:

B.   *Since the framer of the passages makes reference to* **generative causes,** *it is to be inferred that there are derivative ones as well.* Are the derivative causes equivalent [in effect] to the generative causes or are they not equivalent to them in effect?

C.   *We have learned with reference to the Sabbath:* **The generative categories of acts of labor** [prohibited on the Sabbath] **are forty less one** [M. Shab. 7:2A]. *Since the framer of the passages makes reference to* **generative categories,** *it is to be inferred that there are derivative ones as well.* Are the derivative categories equivalent to the generative categories or are they not equivalent to them?

D.   *Well, there is no difference between one's inadvertently carrying out an act of labor that falls into a generative category, in which case he is liable to present a sin-offering, and one's inadvertently carrying out an act of labor that falls into a derivative category of labor, in which case he is also liable to present a sin-offering. There is no difference between one's deliberately carrying out an act of labor that falls into a generative category, in which*

> case he is liable to the death penalty through stoning, and one's
> deliberately carrying out an act of labor that falls into a derivative category
> of labor, in which case he is also liable to the death penalty through
> stoning.

E. So then what's the difference between an act that falls into the generative
    category and one that falls into the derivative category?

F. The upshot is that if one simultaneous carried out two actions that fall into
    the class of generative acts of labor, or two actions that fall into the
    classification of a derivative category, he is liable for each such action,
    while, if he had performed simultaneously both a generative act of labor
    and also a derivative of that same generative action, he is liable on only one
    count.

G. And from the perspective of R. Eliezer, who imposes liability for a
    derivative action even when one is simultaneously liable on account of
    carrying out an act in the generative category, on what basis does one
    classify one action as generative and another as derivative [if it makes no
    practical difference]?

H. Those actions that are carried out [even on the Sabbath] in the building of
    the tabernacle are reckoned as generative actions, and those that were not
    carried out on the Sabbath in the building of the tabernacle are classified as
    derivative.

Clearly, the starting point of the reading of this Mishnah paragraph
is precisely what I have claimed; we shall not find surprising the
secondary development of the same point, specifically, a survey of other
cases in which we have primary or generative and secondary or
derivative taxa, and how the latter relate to the former.

I.2 A. With reference to uncleanness we have learned in the Mishnah: **The
         generative causes of uncleanness [are] (1) the creeping thing, and
         (2) semen [of an adult Israelite], [2B] and (3) one who has
         contracted corpse uncleanness, [and (4) the leper in the days of his
         counting, and (5) sin-offering water of insufficient quantity to be
         sprinkled. Lo, these render man and vessels unclean by contact,
         and earthenware vessels by [presence within the vessels'
         contained] air space. But they do not render unclean by carrying]
         [M. Kel. 1:1].** And their derivatives are not equivalent to them, for
         while a generative cause of uncleanness imparts uncleanness to a
         human being and utensils, a derivative source of uncleanness
         imparts uncleanness to food and drink but not to a human being or
         utensils.

What is important is the comparison of derivative classes; this
question emerges only from the prior and primary interest in showing
how the Mishnah's classes yield further ones. This same work now
proceeds at a secondary level of complication.

I.8 A. Biting: *Does this not fall into the classification of a derivative of tooth?*

B. *Not at all, for what characterizes injury under the classification of tooth is that there is pleasure that comes from doing the damage, but biting is not characterized by giving pleasure in the doing of the damage.*

I.9 A. Falling, and kicking: *Do these not fall into the classification of derivatives of foot?*

B. *Not at all, for what characterizes injury under the classification of foot is that it is quite common, while damage done by these is not so common.*

What is important in what follows is the introduction of altogether fresh considerations, that is to say, things that affect the taxa now defined, but that at the same time complicate our original taxonomy. Specifically, we want to know how the issue of intentionality interrelates with the generative classifications we have in hand: Does this form a further, autonomous point of differentiation? Here is a fine case of how the Bavli builds its inquiry by introducing one grid after another: this set of distinctions made complicated by the next, still more by the third, and so onward.

I.10 A. *Now, then, as to those derivatives that are not equivalent to the generative causes [from which the derivatives come], to which R. Pappa made reference, what might they be? Should we say that he makes reference to these? Then how are they different from the generative cause? Just as horn is a classification that involves damage done with intent, one's own property, and one's responsibility for adequate guardianship, so these, too, form classifications that involve damage done with intent, one's own property, and one's responsibility for adequate guardianship. So it must follow that the derivatives of horn are equivalent to the principal, the horn, and R. Pappa must then refer to tooth and foot.*

I.15 A. *What is the derivative of the generative category of tooth?*

B. If for its own pleasure the cow rubbed itself against a wall and broke it, or spoiled produce by rolling around in it.

C. *What distinguishes damage done by the tooth* [as a generative category] is that it is a form of damage that gives pleasure to the one that does it, it derives from what is your own property, and you are responsible to take care of it. *Well, in these cases too, one may say the same thing, namely, here we have* a form of damage that gives pleasure to the one that does it, it derives from what is your own property, and you are responsible to take care of it.

D. *It must follow that the derivative classes of the generative category of tooth are equivalent to the generative category itself, and when R. Pappa made his statement, he must have referred to the generative category of foot.*

I.16 A. *What is the derivative of the generative category of foot?*

B. If the beast while moving did damage with its body or hair or with a load on it or with a bit in its mouth or with a bell around its neck.

C. *What distinguishes damage done by the foot* [as a generative category] is that it is a form of damage that is very common, it derives from what is your own property, and you are responsible to take care of it. *Well, in these cases too, one may say the same thing, namely, here we have* a form of damage that is very common, it derives from what is your own property, and you are responsible to take care of it.

D. *It must follow that the derivative classes of the generative category of foot are equivalent to the generative category itself, and when R. Pappa made his statement, he must have referred to the generative category of pit.*

I.17   A. *Then what would be derivatives of the generative category of pit?*

B. *Should I say that the generative category is a pit ten handbreadths deep, but a derivative is one nine handbreadths deep, Scripture does not make explicit reference to either one ten handbreadths deep nor to one nine handbreadths deep!*

C. *In point of fact that is not a problem, since the All-Merciful has said, "And the dead beast shall be his" (Ex. 21:34). And, for their part, rabbis established that a pit ten handbreadths deep will cause death, one only nine handbreadths deep will cause only injury, but will not cause death.*

D. *So what difference does that make? The one is a generative classification of pit when it comes to yielding death, the other an equally generative classification yielding injury.*

E. *So R. Pappa's statement must speak of a stone, knife, or luggage, left in the public domain, that did damage.*

F. *How then can we imagine damage of this kind? If they were declared ownerless and abandoned in the public domain, then from the perspective of both Rab and Samuel, they fall into the classification of pit.* [3B] *And if they were not declared ownerless and abandoned in the public domain, then from the perspective of Samuel, who has said,* "All public nuisances are derived by analogy to the generative classification of pit," *they fall into the classification of pit, and from the perspective of Rab, who has held,* "All of them do we derive by analogy to ox," *they fall under the classification of ox.*

G. *What is it that characterizes the pit? It is that* to begin with it is made as a possible cause of damage, it is your property, and you are responsible to watch out for it. *So of these, too, it may be said,* to begin with it is made as a possible cause of damage, it is your property, and you are responsible to watch out for it. *It therefore follows that the derivatives of pit are the same as the pit itself, and when R. Pappa made his statement, it was with reference to the derivatives of the crop-destroying beast.*

I.18   A. *So what can these derivatives of the crop-destroying beast be anyhow? From the perspective of Samuel, who has said,* "The crop-destroying beast is the same as tooth [that is, trespassing cattle]," *lo, the derivative of tooth is in the same classification as tooth [as we have already shown], and from the perspective of Rab, who has said,* "The crop-destroying beast is in fact the human being," *then what generative categories and what derivatives therefrom are to be identified with a human being! Should you allege that a human being when awake is the generative classification, and the human being when asleep is a derivative, have we not learned in the Mishnah:* Man is perpetually an attested danger [M. B.Q. 2:6A] – *whether awake or asleep!*

B. *So when R. Pappa made his statement, he must have referred to a human being's phlegm or snot.*

C. *Yeah, well, then, under what conditions? If the damage was done while in motion, it comes about through man's direct action, and if it does its damage after it comes to rest, then, whether from Rab's or Samuel's* perspective, it falls into the classification of pit. And, it must follow, the offspring of the crop-destroying beast is in the same classification as the crop-destroying beast, so when R. Pappa made his statement, he must have been talking about the derivatives of fire.

I.19 A. *So what are derivatives of fire? Shall we say that such would be* a stone, knife, or luggage, that one left on one's roof and was blown off by an ordinary wind and caused damage? *Then here, too, under what conditions? If the damage was done while in motion, then they fall into the category of fire itself. For what characterizes fire is that it derives from an external force, is your property, and is yours to guard, and these, too, are to be described in the same way, since each derives from an external force, is your property, and is yours to guard. And, it must follow, the offspring of fire are in the same classification as fire, so when R. Pappa made his statement, he must have been talking about the derivatives of fire.*

I.20 A. *Foot? Surely you're joking! Have we not already established the fact that the derivative of foot is in the same classification as the generative classification of foot itself.*

B. *At issue is the payment of half damages done by pebbles kicked by an animal's foot, which we have learned by tradition.*

C. *And why is such damage classified as a derivative of foot?*

D. *So that compensation should be paid only from property of the highest class possessed by the defendant.*

E. *But did not Raba raised the question on this very matter? For Raba raised this question, "Is the half-damage to be paid for damage caused by pebbles to be paid only from the body of the beast itself or from the beast property of the owner of the beast?"*

F. *Well, that was a problem for Raba, but R. Pappa was quite positive about the matter.*

G. *Well, if it's a problem to Raba, then from his perspective, why would pebbles kicked by an animal's foot be classified as a derivative of foot?*

H. *So that the owner in such a case may be exempted from having to pay compensation where the damage was done in the public domain [just as damage caused by the generative category, foot, is not to be compensated if it was done in the public domain].*

The main point is now clear. There is no understanding the passage at hand unless we realize that the Mishnah has given us a taxic structure, which the Bavli has dissected and reconstructed. This is accomplished by the introduction of successive distinctions, some of them invited by the original grid, some not, and the exegetical task in the reading of the Mishnah is to raise distinctions the Mishnah statement has not raised, and so to compose what I called a cubic chess game. This long discussion prepares us for the task at hand. For having shown in a rather general way that the Bavli's exegetes take a grid and bring it into juxtaposition with another grid – or two or three or four more – I have to demonstrate a further point: that this is the fundamental mode of reading the Mishnah that characterizes the Talmud's authors. And that brings us to the present work.

III. Decoding the Talmud's Exegetical Program

All of this is much too general, since we have no idea of how large a role the analysis of intersecting grids plays in the exegetical program of the Bavli. Now that I claim to have identified in rather general terms what I conceive to be the generative problematic of the Bavli, it is my task to show in great detail how that problematic stimulates detailed reading of the larger part of an entire document. What I wish to know is this: How in detail can we see the working of my general notion that the Bavli's framers form of a two-dimensional grid a cubic one, that is, bringing into relationship two, three, or even four taxic structures and uncovering their interstitial relationships? To what extent is a sizable sample of the Bavli accurately characterized by my allegation as to its intellectual quality? And, of great interest, what proportions of the document are formed in the way I claim they are, and what proportions are not? For that purpose I turn to some of the longer chapters of Bavli-tractate Shabbat. We shall consider in rich detail how they respond to the Mishnah tractate under discussion and ask whether we can identify patterns of thought that underlie the particular inquiries at hand, with close attention to my specific claim on how a cogent exegetical program guides thought on concrete exegetical problems.

2

Bavli Shabbat
Chapter Three

Folios 36B-47B

I propose for the sake of inquiry to maintain that a principal source of exegetical interest for the Bavli's framers derives from their larger task, which is to bring to bear upon the two-dimensional grid of the Mishnah classification scheme third, fourth, or even fifth dimensions: further sets of distinctions or grids, to be brought into relationship with the Mishnah's initial classification scheme. More concretely, are there issues that will be introduced into the reading of a Mishnah paragraph, so that the exegetical progress will be dictated by those extrinsic issues, which yield a new and more profound sense for the potentialities of the Mishnah rule? The answers to these questions can be found only by a close reading of a sizable sample of the document. Since in *The Bavli's Intellectual Character: The Talmud's Generative Problematic*, I dealt with Bavli-tractate Shabbat Chapter One, I decided to continue the examination of that wonderful tractate.

In the examination that follows, I want to find out two things. First, can I discern the presence of a set of issues that alert the framers of the Bavli's exegesis of the Mishnah to potentialities for generalization and abstraction that inhere in a given rule? And if there are such issues, can I catalogue and even characterize them for the chapters under discussion? In other words, is there a set of premises not expressed in the Mishnah and not articulated by the Bavli's framers at any given passage, which (in the view of the Talmudic exegetes of the Mishnah) are addressed to what the Mishnah does say and which account for the the Talmud's necessarily consequent exegesis of the Mishnah? And what are those issues? In the concluding chapter I catalogue the results and review them.

Second, and equally interesting, approximately what proportion of the discussion as a whole is taken up by the interplay of the Mishnah's grid with this other, abstract grid? How much of the chapter as a whole comprises the exposition of the mixed grid, the interstitial exercise compounded by the introduction of one, then another set of interstices? And how much of the chapter would I characterize in some other way altogether?

To answer these two questions at the same time is simple. First, I present the bulk of a given discussion for the present chapter, so that readers may see precisely how I read a given discussion and why I think the moving force of the discussion derives from a premise not in the Mishnah passage but invited by it in some way or another.[1] In the concluding chapter I catalogue all the instances of premises or propositions imputed at the deepest structure of analysis to a given Mishnah problem. Second, to show the proportions of the chapter occupied by what I claim is the Talmud's exegetical program, I shall divide the discussions that follow into columns, presenting at the left-hand column the exposition of the passage in terms of two or more grids, at the right-hand column the presentation of what I regard in the light of the monographs summarized in the preceding chapter, as mere, inert information.

How about composites? Here I am most interested in the amplification of the abstract principle brought to bear upon a concrete passage, so I give the greater part of a composite that expands upon the initiative that carries us from detail to principle. On the other hand, composites in the right-hand column, which presents mere information, are presented only in a very brief way. Since my reference system is uniform, readers can readily consult my complete translation to see what I have omitted.

My comments will be limited to the identification of premises or principles, distinctions introduced into the Mishnah rule, and observations on the character of the materials on the right-hand column as well. For the treatment of M. 3:1, I give the complete passages; beyond

---

[1] I have no argument to offer on whether, if a premise of discourse is introduced by the Talmud's exegetes, that is because it was already there in the Mishnah's statements; or whether the Talmud's exegetes "may" or "must" have had a tradition that such and such an abstract issue inhered in such and such a concrete rule. These are not questions we can settle, there being no evidence pertinent to them. So I shall ignore them.

that point, I shall abbreviate the right-hand column's materials, which contain nothing of much interest to us.

3:1

A. A double stove which [people] have heated with stubble or straw –

B. they put cooked food on it.

C. [But if they heated it] with peat or with wood, one may not put [anything] on it until he has swept it out,

D. or until he has covered it with ashes.

E. The House of Shammai say, "Hot water but not cooked food [may one put on it on the eve of the Sabbath]."

F. And the House of Hillel say, "Hot water and cooked food."

G. The House of Shammai say, "[On the Sabbath] they take off [hot water placed thereon], but they do not put it back."

H. And the House of Hillel say, "Also: they put it back."

The long opening exposition does not seem to me to contain any points accessible of generalization. All I am able to discern is an exposition of the wording and sense of the Mishnah rule.

I.1 A. [But if they heated it with peat or with wood, one may not put [anything] on it until he has swept it out, or until he has covered it with ashes:] *The question was raised: Since the language used is,* one may not put, does it mean, he may not put back, but it is permitted to keep it there, and that is the case even if the stove is not swept out or covered with ashes, *in consequence of which the authority of the unassigned ruling must be Hananiah?*

B. *For it has been taught on Tannaite authority:* Hananiah says, "Any food that is cooked to such an extent that it can have been eaten by Ben Derusai [that is, a third cooked] – it is permitted to keep it on the stove [on the Sabbath], even though it is not swept clear of cinders or sprinkled with ashes."

C. *Or perhaps we have learned the Mishnah's rule only in respect to keeping the food there, but that is permitted only if the oven is swept* or covered with ashes, and not otherwise. Then how much the more so would that be the rule as to putting it back!

D.   *Come and take note of how matters are formulated in two clauses of our Mishnah paragraph:*

E.   **The House of Shammai say, "Hot water but not cooked food [may one put on it on the eve of the Sabbath]."**

F.   **And the House of Hillel say, "Hot water and cooked food."**

G.   **The House of Shammai say, "[On the Sabbath] they take off [hot water placed thereon], but they do not put it back."**

H.   **And the House of Hillel say, "Also: they put it back."**

I.   *Now, if you should say that the sense of our Mishnah rule pertains to keeping the food there, then there is no problem, for that is the sense of the formulation,* **A double stove which [people] have heated with stubble or straw, they keep a pot on it. If it was heated with peat or with wood, they keep a pot on it until he has swept it out, or until he has covered it with ashes. And what do they keep on it? The House of Shammai say, "Hot water but not cooked food [may one put on it on the eve of the Sabbath]." And the House of Hillel say, "Hot water and cooked food."** *And just as they dispute concerning keeping a pot on the dish, so do they differ on putting it back, in which case,* **The House of Shammai say, "[On the Sabbath] they take off [hot water placed thereon], but they do not put it back." And the House of Hillel say, "Also: they put it back."** *But, by contrast, what our Mishnah tells us concerns* putting the pot back, *then this is how we shall have to read it:* **A double stove which [people] have heated with stubble or straw,** they put a pot back on it. If it was heated with **peat or with wood,** they do not put a pot back on it until he has swept it out, or until he has covered it with ashes. And what do they put back on it? **The House of Shammai say,** "Hot water but not cooked food [may one put on it on the eve of the Sabbath]." And the House of Hillel say, "Hot water and cooked food." *[Then comes the language:* The House of Shammai say, "[On the Sabbath] they take off [hot water placed thereon], but they do not put it back." And the House of Hillel say, "Also: they put it back" – *but what need do I have for this further formulation [since we've just said "but not a dish"]?*

J. [37A] *In point of fact, I shall say to you that the way in which we are to understand our Mishnah rule is indeed*, putting the pot back, *but the formulation of the passage is flawed, and this is how it is to be read:* A **double stove** which [people] have heated with stubble or straw, they put a pot back on it. If it was heated with peat or with wood, they do not put a pot back on it until he has swept it out, or until he has covered it with ashes. But they may leave a pot on it, even if he has not swept it out or covered it with ashes. And what do they put back on it? **The House of Shammai say,** "Hot water but not cooked food [may one put on it on the eve of the Sabbath]." **And the House of Hillel say,** "Hot water and cooked food." *And as to this question of replacing, of which I have spoken [that it is permissible to do so if the stove is swept out], that is not the position of both parties but the topic of* a dispute between the House of Shammai and the House of Hillel,

for the House of Shammai say,
"[On the Sabbath] they take off
[hot water placed thereon], but
they do not put it back." And
the House of Hillel say, "Also:
they put it back."

K.   *Come and take note of what* R.
Helbo said R. Hama bar Guria
said Rab said, "They have stated
that rule only with respect to the
top of the stove, but as to the
space within it, it is forbidden."
*Now, if you say that the sense of the
statement of the Mishnah is,* to put
the pot back, *then that is in line
with the formulation before us, which
distinguishes the top of the oven from
the inside of it. But if you maintain
that what is at issue in our Mishnah
rule is keeping the pot there, then
what difference is there between the
inside of the oven and the top of it?*

L.   *But what makes you think that R.
Helbo makes reference to the opening
part of the Mishnah paragraph? In
point of fact, he refers to the
concluding part, namely:* And the
House of Hillel say, "Also: they
put it back." And said R. Helbo
said R. Hama bar Guria said Rab,
"They have stated that rule only
with respect to the top of the
stove, but as to the space within
it, it is forbidden."

M.   *Come and take note:* Two double
stoves that are paired, one of
them having been swept out and
had its ashes covered, and one of
them not having been swept out
and had its ashes covered – they
keep something on the one that
has been swept out and had its
ashes covered, and they do not
keep anything on the one that
has not been swept out and has
not had its ashes covered.

N.   And what is it that they keep on
it?

O.   "The House of Shammai say,
'They do not keep anything at all
on it.' And the House of Hillel

say, 'They keep on it hot water but not cooked food.' If one removed the cooking pot, all concur that he should not put it back," the words of R. Meir.

P. R. Judah says, "The House of Shammai say, 'Hot water but not cooked food. And the House of Hillel say, 'Hot water and cooked food.' If he removed it from the stove, the House of Shammai say, 'He should not put it back.' And the House of Hillel say, 'He may put it back'" [T. Shab. 2:13A-K].

Q. *Now, if you take the view that the sense of our Mishnah paragraph is,* to keep the pot there, *then there is no problem, for with whom does our Mishnah paragraph agree? It is R. Judah. But if you say that what we learn concerning* putting the pot back, *then who can be the authority of our Mishnah, since it is neither R. Judah nor R. Meir? If it were R. Meir, there would be a problem in respect to the House of Shammai on one count, and the House of Hillel on two.* [Freedman: The House of Shammai in the Mishnah paragraph permit hot water to be kept there even if it is not swept or covered with ashes; here they permit nothing. In the Mishnah paragraph the House of Hillel permit hot water and a dish to be kept there even if the oven is not swept out, but here if it is swept out, hot water only may be kept there and nothing if it is not swept; in the Mishnah the House of Hillel say that the pot can be put back on an oven that is swept; here, all concur that it may not be put back.] *If it were R. Judah, then there is a problem with the stove that is swept or covered over with ashes.* [Freedman: Here nothing may be kept there, in the Mishnah either hot water alone or a dish also

may be kept there according to
the two Houses, respectively.]

R.   *In point of fact, I shall tell you: What*
we have learned in our Mishnah
paragraph concerns putting the pot
back. *And our Tannaite authority*
concurs with R. Judah in one matter
and differs from him in another. He
concurs with R. Judah in one point,
that is, in regard to hot water and
a dish, and removing and putting
them back. *But he differs from him*
in another, for while our Tannaite
authority maintains that one may
keep a pot there, and that is so
even if the oven is not swept out
nor covered with ashes, *R. Judah*
takes the position that in the case of
one that is swept out or covered with
ashes, it is permitted to do so, but if
not, it is not permitted to do so.

I.2   A.   *The question was raised: [As to an*
oven that is not swept out or covered
with ashes,] what is the law on
leaning a pot against it? *As to*
putting it inside or on top, it is
forbidden, but leaning against it
would be permitted, or perhaps
there's no difference?

B.   *Come and take note:* **Two double**
stoves that are paired, one of
them having been swept out and
had its ashes covered, and one of
them not having been swept out
and had its ashes covered – they
keep something on the one that
has been swept out and had its
ashes covered – *and that is so even*
though heat reaches it from the other
stove [and our problem is parallel, so
one may do so].

C.   *But maybe that case is exceptional;*
since it is at a higher level, the air
affects it. [Freedman: The pot
stands on the stove and is
surrounded by air, which cools it,
and therefore the heat from the
other stove is disregarded; but
leaning against an unswept stove
without air interposing may still
be forbidden.]

D. *Come and take note of what* R. Safra said R. Hiyya said, "If one covered the stove with ashes, but it blazed up again, one may lean a pot against it, keep a pot on it, remove a pot from it and put it back. *This proves that even leaning a pot against the oven is permitted only when it is covered with ashes, not otherwise.*

E. *But, according to your reading of matters, what about the language,* remove a pot from it? *Does that mean, only if it is covered with ashes, but not otherwise? [Since that is impossible,] you have to understand, the framer speaks of* removing the pot *on account of* putting it back; *so here, too, he speaks of* leaning the pot *on account of* keeping it there. [Freedman: Yet covering it with ashes may not be required for leaning.]

F. *But how are the cases parallel? In that case, both taking the pot away and putting it back involve a single location, so there you may well say that the Tannaite framer of the passage has made reference to taking it because he wishes to speak of putting it back. But here, leaning the pot speaks of one location, while keeping the pot on the stove speaks of a different location!*

G. *So what's the upshot?*

H. *Come and take note:* A stove that is heated with peat or wood – one may lean a pot against it, but not keep it there unless the stove is swept out or covered with ashes. If the coals have merely died down, or well beaten flax is put on the oven, it is as though it is covered with ashes [T. Shab. 2:11]. [Freedman: Thus for leaning it need not be swept out.]

I.3 A. Said R. Isaac bar Nahmani said R. Oshayya, "If one covered up a stove with ashes but it blazed up again, one may keep on the stove hot water that had already been sufficiently heated, or a cooked dish that had already been sufficiently cooked."

B.   [37B] *This proves that* if something shrinks through cooking, but is improved thereby, it is permitted.

C.   *That case is different, since he covered it with ashes.*

D.   *If so, what's the point?*

E.   *It was necessary to make that statement to deal with the case of the fire's blazing up again. What might you have supposed? Since the fire has blazed up, it reverts to its original state [and the dish may not be kept there]. So we are informed that that is not the case.* [Freedman: By covering it with ashes, the cook showed he did not desire any further shrinkage.]

I.4 A.   Said Rabbah bar bar Hannah said R. Yohanan, "If one covered the stove with ashes but it blazed up again, they may keep on the oven hot water that had been sufficiently heated or a cooked dish that had been sufficiently cooked, and even if they are broom coals" [that keep their heat longer than other coals and don't go out so quickly (Freedman)].

B.   *This proves that* if something shrinks through cooking, but is improved thereby, it is permitted.

C.   *That case is different, since he covered it with ashes.*

D.   *If so, what's the point?*

E.   *It was necessary to make that statement to deal with the case of the fire's blazing up again.*

F.   *Yeah, I know, you just said so.*

G.   *It was necessary to make that statement to deal with broom coals.*

I.5 A.   Said R. Sheshet said R. Yohanan, "On a stove that one heated with peat or wood one may keep hot water that had not been sufficiently heated or a cooked dish that had not been sufficiently cooked. If one removed these things, one may not put them

back until he sweeps the oven or
covers it with ashes."

B. *He takes the view that for our*
Mishnah paragraph, we learn the
reading, put back; but as to
leaving a pot there, it is permitted
to do so even if the oven is not
swept out or covered with ashes.

I.6 A. *Said Raba, "We have learned for the*
Mishnah formulation both items,
namely, with respect to keeping
something on the stove, we have
learned as a Tannaite statement:
They do not put bread into an
oven at dusk, nor cakes on the
coals, unless there is time for
them to form a crust [even] on
the top surface while it is still
day [M. 1:10B-C]. *It follows then*
that if there is time for them to form a
crust, it is permitted to keep it there,
even though the oven is not swept
out.

B. *"In regard to putting it back, we*
have learned in the Mishnah: And
the House of Hillel say, 'Also:
they put it back.' *So the House of*
Hillel permit it only if the oven is
swept or covered with ashes, but not
if it is neither swept nor covered with
ashes." [Freedman: So what need
is there for Yohanan's statement?]

C. *So R. Sheshet has told us how a close*
reading of the Mishnah yields that
very point. [Sheshet holds that the
Mishnah rule refers to replacing
the pot (Freedman).]

I.7 A. Said R. Samuel bar Judah said R.
Yohanan, "On a stove that one
heated with peat or wood one
may keep a cooked dish that has
been cooked sufficiently, or hot
water that has been heated
sufficiently, and that is so even if
the thing shrinks and improves
thereby."

B. *Said one of the rabbis to R. Samuel*
bar Judah, "But lo, both Rab and
Samuel have said, 'If it shrinks and
is improved thereby, it is
forbidden'!"

C. *He said to him, "So don't I know that said R. Joseph said R. Judah said Samuel, 'If it shrinks and is improved thereby, it is forbidden'? When I made that statement to you, it was in accord with the authority of R. Yohanan that I said it to you [that it is permitted]."*

D. Said R. Uqba of Mesene to R. Ashi, "You, who are located near Rab and Samuel, act in accord with Rab and Samuel. We shall act in accord with R. Yohanan."

I.8 A. *Said Abbayye to R. Joseph, "What is the law as to keeping a pot on the stove [if it is not swept out]?"*

B. *He said to him, "Lo, for R. Judah they keep it on the stove and he eats it."*

C. *He said to him, "Except for R. Judah, for, since he would be in danger if he didn't eat hot food, it is permitted for him even on the Sabbath, but what about the likes of thee and me?"*

D. *He said to him, "In Sura they keep it on the stove. Now R. Nahman bar Isaac is fastidious, and yet for him they keep it on the stove and he eats it."*

I.9 A. *Said R. Ashi, "I was standing in the presence of R. Huna, and they kept a fish pie on the stove for him and he ate it. But I don't know whether that was because he takes the view that if it shrinks but it is good for it, it is nonetheless permitted to eat it, or if it was because, since it contains flour pastes, it shrinks and that is bad for it."*

B. Said R. Nahman, "If it shrinks and it is good for it, it is forbidden, if it shrinks and it is bad for it, it is permitted."

C. *The governing principle is this: whatever contains flour paste shrinks and it is bad for it, except for a turnip stew, which contains flour paste but shrinks and improves. And that is so only if it has meat. But if there is no meat, it shrinks and it is bad for it.*

> *And even if there is meat in it, this rule applies only if the meal is not intended for guests, but if it is intended for guests, it shrinks and it is bad for it [since it will be cut up in large chunks, and shrinking causes deterioration].*
>
> D. *Date papa, pounded grain, and a dish of dates shrink and that is bad for them.*

As I said at the outset, what I see in the foregoing is a sequence of very specific issues, none of them susceptible of generalization; I find no principle that can serve a case other than the kind before us. In what follows, by contrast, we find an issue that may pertain to a broad variety of cases. It is the effect of forgetting the law and doing what is prohibited. To what degree is such forgetfulness penalized, and to what degree do we impose a penalty even when a deed is utterly inadvertent (or issue a precautionary decree on that account, which is the same thing). There is an issue subject to application in countless areas of the law. But it does not strike me as a very provocative question.

I.10 A. *They asked R. Hiyya bar Abba,* [38A] "[Freedman: on the view forbidding the keeping of food on an unswept stove,] if one forgot a dish on the stove and cooked on the Sabbath, what is the rule?"

B. *He shut up and said nothing. The next day he went out and expounded for them,* "One who cooks on the Sabbath – [if he does so] unintentionally, he may eat [the food he has prepared]; [but if he does so] intentionally, he may not eat [the food] [M. Ter. 2:3D-F]. *And there is no difference."*

C. *What is the meaning of, And there is no difference?*

D. *Both Rabbah and R. Joseph said, "It is to make a lenient ruling, namely, if one cooked, he has deliberately carried out a deed, so he may not eat; but in this case that you raise for me, in which he has done no concrete deed, even if it was deliberate, he may eat the food."*

E. *R. Nahman bar Isaac said, "It is to issue a prohibition, namely, it is in the case of cooking in particular, in which case someone is unlikely to practice deception, that, if one did so unintentionally, he may eat; but in this case, in which it is entirely likely that someone will practice deception, even if it is a case of inadvertence too, he may not eat the food."*

F.   *An objection was raised:* "If someone forgot a pot on the stove and it cooked on the Sabbath, if this was inadvertent, he may eat the food; if this was deliberate, he may not eat the food. Under what conditions? In the case of hot water that was not sufficiently heated or a dish that was not sufficiently cooked. But as to hot water that was sufficiently heated or a cooked dish that was sufficiently cooked, whether this was inadvertent or deliberate, he may eat the food," the words of R. Meir.

G.   R. Judah says, "In the case of hot water that was sufficiently heated, it is permitted, because it shrinks and it is bad for it; in the case of a cooked dish that was sufficiently cooked, it is forbidden, since it shrinks and that is good for it. And in the case of anything that has been boiled down and for which such treatment is an improvement, for instance, cabbage, beans, or boiled meat, it is prohibited; but in the case of anything that has been boiled down and for which such treatment is not good, it is permitted" [T. Shab. 2:14A-N].

H.   *Now the Tannaite formulation in any event covers the matter of a dish that was not sufficiently cooked. Now that clearly poses no problem to R. Nahman bar Isaac: the passage before us speaks prior to the enactment of the precautionary decree, the formulation of R. Nahman's view of R. Hiyya bar Abba's statement is prior to the*

enactment of the precautionary
measure. But from the perspective of
Rabbah and R. Joseph, who explain
the matter so as to yield a permissive
ruling, if this was prior to the
precautionary measure, there is a
problem with the rule governing a
deliberate action [it is supposed to be
forbidden but he says it is permitted
to eat that food], and if it was after
the precautionary decree, then even
the rule covering inadvertent cooking
presents a problem.

I. Yes, that's a problem.

I.11 A. So what's this precautionary ruling
anyhow?

B. Said R. Judah bar Samuel said R.
Abba said R. Kahan said Rab, "In
the beginning, they would say:
'He who cooks on the Sabbath, if
this was inadvertent, may eat the
food; if this was deliberate, he
may not eat the food; and the
same rule applies to forgetting
[food cooking on the stove].'
When a great many people began
deliberately to leave food on the
stove, saying, 'we forgot,' they
went and imposed an
extrajudicial penalty on the one
who forgets food on the stove
[saying that, too, may not be
eaten]."

I.12 A. One statement of R. Meir's
contradicts another statement of his,
and one statement of R. Judah's
contradicts another statement of his.
[Freedman: Meir has forbidden a
dish even if sufficiently cooked;
here he permits it; Judah permits
a dish sufficiently cooked; here he
forbids it.]

B. One statement of R. Meir's doesn't
contradict another statement of his,
the one statement pertains to the rule
to begin with, the other, after the fact.
[One may not leave a dish on the
stove even if it was sufficiently
cooked prior to the Sabbath; if he did
so, it is permitted to eat the food.]

C.   *One statement of R. Judah's doesn't*
      contradict another statement of his:
      one statement refers to an oven that
      had been swept out or covered with
      ashes [in which case the dish is
      permitted], the other not.

I.13   A.   *The question was raised: If one*
             violated the law and left a dish on the
             stove, what is the rule? Did rabbis
             impose an extrajudicial penalty or is
             that not the case?

       B.   *Come and take note of what* Samuel
             bar Nathan said R. Hanina said,
             "When R. Yosé went to
             Sepphoris, he found hot water
             that had been left on the stove on
             the Sabbath, and he didn't forbid
             it to them; he found eggs that had
             been overcooked and shrunk, and
             he forbade them to them." *Now*
             that obviously refers to the Sabbath
             day itself?   [So there was no
             extrajudicial penalty.]

       C.   No, it refers to the Sabbath to
             come [that he told them not to
             leave the eggs on the stove in the
             future].

I.14   A.   *It is to be inferred that* when eggs
             are shrunk and go on shrinking,
             that is good for them.

       B.   *True, for* said R. Hama bar
             Hanina, "once I was a guest along
             with Rabbi in a certain place, and
             they brought us eggs shrunk to
             the size of crab apples, and we ate
             lots of them."

I see nothing in the next unit that yields a generalization or bears
implications for any legal topic beyond the one before us.

II.1   A.   **And the House of Hillel say,**
             "Also: they put it back":

       B.   Said R. Sheshet, "From the
             perspective of him who says,
             [38B] 'They put it back,' that is so
             even on the Sabbath."

       C.   And also R. Oshayya takes the
             view, "They put it back, that is so
             even on the Sabbath." *For* said R.
             Oshayya, "Once we were
             standing before R. Hiyya the

Elder, and we brought up for him a kettle of hot water from the lower to the upper story, we mixed the cup for him, and then we put the water back, and he didn't say a word to us."

D. Said R. Zeriqa said R. Abba said R. Taddai, "That rule applies only if the pot of hot water is still in hand, but if he set it down on the ground, it is then forbidden to put it back on the stove."

E. *Said R. Ammi, "R. Taddai did this for himself, but this is what R. Hiyya said R. Yohanan said, 'Even if he set the pot of hot water down on the ground, it is permitted to put it back on the stove.'"*

II.2 A. *There was a dispute on this matter between R. Dimi and R. Samuel bar Judah, both of them speaking in the name of R. Eleazar.*

B. One of them said, "If the pot of water is still in hand, it is permitted to put it back on the stove; if it is on the ground, it is forbidden."

C. And the other said, "If he put the pot of water on the ground, it is also permitted to put it back on the stove."

D. *Said Hezekiah in the name of Abbayye, "As to your statement, 'If it is still in hand, it is permitted to put it back on the stove,' we have made that statement only in a case in which he intended to put it back on the stove, but if he didn't intend to put it on the stove, it is forbidden to do so."* It follows that with reference to having put the pot of hot water down on the ground, even though one had the intention of putting the pot back on the stove, it is forbidden to do so.

E. *There are those who say: said Hezekiah in the name of Abbayye, "As to your statement, 'If it is still in hand, it is permitted to put it*

back on the stove,' we have made
that statement only in a case in
which he did not intend to put it
back on the stove, but if he did
intend to put it on the stove, it is
permitted to do so." *It follows that
with reference to having the pot of
hot water yet in hand,* even though
one had no intention of putting
the pot back on the stove, it is
permitted to do so.

II.3   A.   *R. Jeremiah raised this question:* "If
one hung the pot up on a staff,
what is the law? If he put the pot
on a bed, what is the law?"

      B.   *R. Ashi raised this question:* "If one
emptied the water from kettle to
kettle, what is the law?"

      C.   *So who knows.*

I.1, 2+3-4, 5-10+11-12, 13-14 raise secondary exegetical questions
prompted by the formulation of the Mishnah rule. The discussions are
sustained and show us deeper issues inhering in our Mishnah paragraph
and in versions of its wording. The entire composite works well only in
the context of Mishnah exegesis; out of that context, the whole (though
not all of the parts) would be incomprehensible. II.1-2+3 amplify the
rule of the cited passage of the Mishnah paragraph. In the sections that
follow I shall give only an abbreviated sample of the materials in the
right-hand columns. There also is no reason to comment on those
materials; readers will see for themselves why, in my view, these in no
way yield generalizations, but only rules restricted to the cases to which
they pertain.

3:2

A.   An oven which [people] have heated with stubble or with straw –
one should not put anything either into it or on top of it.

B.   A single stove which [people] have heated with stubble or with
straw, lo, this is equivalent to a double stove.

C.   [If they heated it] with peat or with wood, lo, it is equivalent to an
oven.

I.1   A.   An oven which [people] have
heated:

      B.   *R. Joseph considered explaining,*
"...into it or on top of it are *meant
literally, but as to leaning a pot
against it, that is acceptable."*

      C.   *Objected Abbayye,* "A single stove
which [people] have heated with

stubble or with straw, lo, this is equivalent to a double stove. [If they heated it] with peat or with wood, lo, it is equivalent to an oven – and therefore forbidden. *Lo, if it were like a double stove, it would be permitted. Now with what case do we deal here? Should we say that reference is made to the top? Then, again, under what circumstances? Should we say it is not swept out or covered with ashes? But would use of the top of a stove be permitted if the stove is not swept or covered with ashes? So it must mean leaning a pot against the stove, and yet the ruling is,* [If they heated it] with peat or with wood, lo, it is equivalent to an oven – and therefore forbidden!"

D.   *Said R. Adda bar Ahbah, "Here with what object do we deal?* It is with a single stove that was swept out or covered with ashes, and an oven that is swept out or covered with ashes. *Thus:* Lo, it is equivalent to an oven *means, even though it is swept or covered with ashes, use of the top is forbidden; but if it were comparable to a double stove, then if swept or covered with ashes, it would be acceptable [and permitted]."*

I.2   A.   *It has been taught on Tannaite authority in accord with the position of Abbayye:*

I.3   A.   *Said R. Aha b. Raba to R. Ashi, "As to the stove that is treated here, what is it like? Is it comparable to a double stove, then even if it is heated with stubble or straw, too, [use of it should be permitted, if it is swept out or covered with ashes], and if it is comparable to an oven, then it should not be permitted even if heated with stubble or raked out!"*

I.4   A.   *What is the definition of a stove and what is the definition of a double stove?*

3:3

A.   They do not put an egg beside a kettle [on the Sabbath] so that it will be cooked.
B.   And one should not crack it into [hot] wrappings.
C.   And R. Yosé permits.
D.   And one should not bury it in sand or in road dirt so that it will be roasted.

3:4A-E

A.   M'SH S: The people of Tiberias brought a pipe of cold water through a spring of hot water.
B.   Sages said to them, "If [this was done] on the Sabbath, [the water] is in the status of hot water which has been heated on the Sabbath [itself].
C.   "It is prohibited for use in washing and in drinking.
D.   "[If this was done] on the festival day, [the water] is in the status of hot water which has been heated on the festival day.
E.   "It is prohibited for use in washing, but permitted for use in drinking."

I.1   A.   [They do not put an egg beside a kettle [on the Sabbath] so that it will be cooked:] *The question was raised:* If one roasted it, what is the rule?
       B.   Said R. Joseph, "If one roasted it, he is liable to a sin-offering."
       C.   *Said Mar b. Rabina, "So, too, we have learned as a Tannaite rule:* [39A] "Whatever is put into hot water on the eve of the Sabbath – they soak it [again] in hot water on the Sabbath. And whatever is not put into hot water on the eve of the Sabbath – they [only] rinse it in hot water on the Sabbath, except for pickled fish, small salted fish, and Spanish tunny fish, for rinsing them is the completion of their preparation [for eating] [M. Shab. 22:2]."
       D.   *That proves the point.*
II.1   A.   And one should not crack it into [hot] wrappings. And R. Yosé permits:
       B.   *And as to that which we have learned in the Mishnah:* They put a cooked dish in a cistern so that it may be preserved, and [a vessel containing] fresh water into foul

water to keep it cool, and cold water into the sun to warm it up [M. Shab. 22:4A-C], *may we say that this represents the position of R. Yosé but not of rabbis?*

C. *Said R. Nahman, "If the dish is left in the sun, all parties concur that that would be permitted; if the dish is put into an object heated by fire, all parties concur that it would be forbidden [to keep people from roasting directly on fire]. Where there is a disagreement, it concerns an object heated by the sun [for example, a cloth]. One master holds that we forbid an object heated by the sun on account of one heated by fire, the other that we make no such precautionary decree."*

III.1 A. And one should not bury it in sand or in road dirt so that it will be roasted:

B. *Why shouldn't R. Yosé take a dissenting position here too?*

C. Rabbah said, "He would regard it as a precautionary decree, lest one come to bury it in hot ashes."

D. R. Joseph said, "It is because he may move the dirt from its place [which may not be done on the Sabbath, and Yosé would concur]."

E. *What would be a practical point of difference between these two explanations?*

F. At issue would be crushed earth. [Here Joseph's reason is null and it would be permitted, since there would be no danger that he would have to scoop out more dirt; Rabbah's consideration pertains.]

IV.1 A. M'SH S: The people of Tiberias brought a pipe of cold water through a spring of hot water. Sages said to them, "If [this was done] on the Sabbath, [the water] is in the status of hot water which has been heated on the Sabbath [itself]. It is prohibited for use in washing and in drinking. [If this was done] on the festival day, [the water] is in the status of hot water which has been heated on the festival day. It is prohibited for use in washing, but permitted for use in drinking:

B. *[As to the prohibition of the water for use in washing,] to what is reference made here? Should I say that it is to washing the entire body? But is it forbidden to use in that connection only hot water heated on the Sabbath, though hot water heated on Friday would be permitted? But hasn't it been taught on Tannaite authority:* as to hot water heated on Friday, on the next day one may wash with it one's hands, face, and feet, but not his entire body. *So it must refer to washing one's hands, face, and feet. Then I point to the concluding clause:* [If this was done] on the festival day, [the water] is in the status of hot water which has been heated on the festival day. It is prohibited for use in washing, but permitted for use in drinking. *So are we going to have to conclude that the unattributed Mishnah rule accords with the position of the House of Shammai [which would be highly irregular]? For we have learned in the Mishnah:* The House of Shammai say, "[On a festival day] a person may not heat water for his feet, unless it is also suitable for drinking." But the House of Hillel permit [M. Bes. 2:5A-C]*!*

IV.2 A. Said Rabbah bar bar Hannah said R. Yohanan, "The decided law is in accord with R. Judah."

B. *Said to him R. Joseph, "So did you hear this in so many words, or have you received this tradition on the basis of mere inference?"*

C. *What would be the inference?*

D. Said R. Tanhum said R. Yohanan said R. Yannai said Rabbi, "In any case in which you find two authorities at odds and one taking a mediating position, the decided law accords with the position of the one who takes the mediating position, except in the case of the catalogue of lenient rulings that pertain to rags [catalogued at B. Shab. 29A], in which case even though R. Eliezer takes the strict position and R. Joshua the lenient, with R. Aqiba mediating, the decided law does not accord with the mediating position. *The reason is, first, because R. Aqiba was a mere disciple. And, furthermore, lo, [40A] R. Aqiba retracted in favor of R. Joshua."*

E. *So anyhow, what does it matter if it is by inference?*

F. *Maybe [Yohanan's rule] applies only to what is in the Mishnah, but not what is reported in a Tannaite formulation external to the Mishnah.*

G. *He said to him, "At any rate I heard it in so many words."*

Here is a most valuable generalization, having to do with the negotiation of conflicted opinions as these are preseved in the authoritative writings.

IV.3 A. *It has been stated:*

B. As to hot water heated on Friday –

C. Rab said, "On the next day one may use it for washing his entire body, limb by limb."

D. Samuel said, "Sages have permitted washing with it only the face, hands, and feet."

IV.4 A. *Said R. Joseph to Abbayye, "Did Rabbah act in line with Rab's ruling?"*

B. *He said to him, "I don't know."*

C. *What led him to raise the question? He obviously didn't act in accord with his position, for after all, Rab had been refuted!*

D. *He hadn't heard these refutations.*

IV.5 A. Our rabbis have taught on Tannaite authority:

B.   A bath the holes of which one
     stopped up on the eve of the
     Sabbath [to preserve the steam] –
     at the end of the Sabbath one
     may wash therein forthwith. If
     he stopped up the openings on
     the eve of the festival, one may
     go in on the festival itself and
     sweat, then go out and take a
     bath in cold water.

IV.6   A.   *What is the sense of* w h e n
            transgressors became numerous?

IV.7   A.   *Said Raba, "Someone who violates a
            rule made on the authority of rabbis –
            it is permitted to call him a sinner."*

IV.8   A.   They may stroll through the
            baths of large cities and have no
            scruple [that one is suspect of
            going through in order to sweat]:

       B.   Said Raba, "That is in large cities
            in particular, but not in villages.
            How come? *Since they are tiny
            bathhouses, the heat in them is
            enormous   [and   will   cause
            sweating]."*

IV.9   A.   *Our rabbis have taught on Tannaite
            authority:*

       B.   A person may warm up at a big
            fire, go out and wash in cold
            water, on condition that he
            doesn't first rinse off in cold
            water and then warm himself at
            the fire, because if he does so, he
            also heats up the water that is on
            his body.

IV.10 A.   *Our rabbis have taught on Tannaite
            authority:*

       B.   One may warm a sheet and put it
            on his belly.

       C.   But he may not put a hot water
            bottle on his belly on the
            Sabbath [T. Shab. 3:7A-B].

       D.   This   is   forbidden   even   on
            weekdays, since it's dangerous.

IV.11 A.   *Our rabbis have taught on Tannaite
            authority:*

       B.   One may bring a jug of water
            and put it near a bonfire, not to
            warm it up but to temper the
            cold.

IV.12 A. *The question was raised: As to the initial Tannaite authority, what is his opinion on oil?*

B. *Rabbah and R. Joseph both say, "It is a permissive position."*

C. *R. Nahman bar Isaac said, "It is a restrictive position."*

IV.13 A. Said R. Judah said Samuel, "All the same are oil and water: if the hand shrinks back from touching it, it is forbidden to put them in front of a fire to reach that temperature, but if the hand doesn't, it is permitted."

IV.14 A. Said R. Isaac bar Abedimi, "Once I followed after Rabbi into the bathhouse, and I wanted to place a cruse of oil for him in the bath [to heat it up for his use]. But he said to me, 'Take some water in a second utensil [into which boiling liquid has been poured, but not a utensil containing the liquid directly heated by the fire] and put the oil into that.'"

IV.15 A. *Said Rabina, "From that story one may infer that* one who cooks food in the hot water of Tiberias on the Sabbath is liable. *For the case involving Rabbi took place after the decree* [that forbade sweating in an artificially heated bath, so it must have been in the thermal bath at Tiberias (Freedman)], *yet he said to him,* 'Take some water in a second utensil [into which boiling liquid has been poured, but not a utensil containing the liquid directly heated by the fire] and put the oil into that.'"

IV.16 A. *Said R. Zira, "I personally saw R. Abbahu swimming in a bath, but I don't know whether or not he lifted up his feet [actually swimming, or merely bathing]."*

IV.17 A. *And said R. Zira, "I personally saw R. Abbahu put his hand near his 'face down there' [penis], but I don't know whether he touched or not."*

IV.18 A. *R. Zira was avoiding R. Judah, for [the former] wanted to go up to the*

> Land of Israel, while R. Judah held, "Whoever goes up from Babylonia to the Land of Israel violates a positive commandment, for it is said, 'They shall be brought to Babylonia and there they shall be until the day that I remember them, says the Lord' (Jer. 27:22)."

3:4F-G

F. A miliarum which is cleared of ashes – they drink from it on the Sabbath.
G. An *antikhi* [boiler], even though it is clear of ashes – they do not drink from it.

> I.1 A. *What is the meaning of* a miliarum which is cleared of ashes?
>
>   B. *A Tannaite statement:* It has water inside and coals outside.
>
> II.1 A. *What is the meaning of* an antikhi [boiler]?
>
>   B. *Rabbah said, "It is a utensil suspended between two fireplaces [of heated bricks]."*

3:5A-C

A. A kettle [containing hot water] which one removed [from the stove] –
B. one should not put cold water into it so that it [the cold water] may get warm.
C. But one may put [enough cold water] into it or into a cup so that [the hot water] will cool off.

The issue that follows gives us a fine example of how through a particular case a principle of broad general interest and applicability is set forth. It is whether the effect of an action affected by the intention of the person who does it. Here it is expressed in this language: If there is a result that is not intentional, the act is permitted [on the Sabbath]. The upshot is that we take an action to bear consequences only if it is done with full intentionality.

I.1 A. What's the sense of this statement?

     B. *Said R. Adda bar Matena, "This is the sense of the statement:* A kettle [containing hot water] from which one removed hot water – one should not put a little cold water into it so that it [the cold water] may get warm. But one may put a lot of cold water into it or into a cup so that the hot water will cool off."

C. [41B] But by doing so, doesn't he harden the metal of the pot [Freedman: by pouring cold water into it while it is hot? This is itself forbidden on the Sabbath.]

D. *This represents the position of R. Simeon, who has said, "If there is a result that is not intentional, the act is permitted [on the Sabbath]."*

E. *Objected Abbayye, "But does the language before us in the Mishnah say,* A kettle [containing hot water] *from which one removed hot water? What it says is,* A kettle [containing hot water] which one removed [from the stove]!"

F. *Rather, said Abbayye, "This is the sense of the sentence:* A kettle [containing hot water] which one removed [from the stove], which contains hot water — one should not put a little cold water into it so that it [the cold water] may get warm. But one may put a lot of cold water into it or into a cup so that the hot water will cool off. But if water is poured out of a boiler, one may not pour any water at all into it, because this hardens it. *And it represents the position of R. Judah, who has said, 'If there is a result that is not intentional, the act nonetheless is forbidden [on the Sabbath].'"*

I.2 A. Said Rab, "This rule permits only tempering the water, but if the intent is to harden the metal, the act is forbidden."

B. And Samuel said, "It is even permitted to do so in order to harden the metal."

C. *Yeah, well, if to begin with, the intent is to harden the metal, can this possibly be permitted? Rather, if there was such a statement, this is what has to have been said:*

D. Said Rab, "This rule permits only a case in which there is a sufficient quantity for tempering the water, but if there is enough to harden the metal, the act is forbidden."

E. And Samuel said, "It is even permitted to do so if there is enough [42A] to harden the metal."

F. *Is that to say, then, that Samuel concurs with the theory of R. Simeon? But didn't* Samuel say, "People may extinguish a lump of fiery metal in the street so that it will not do any harm to the public, but not a burning piece of wood"? *Now if you take the view that he is in accord with R. Simeon, then he should permit extinguishing even a coal of burning wood.*

G. *In respect to a matter in which there is no intentionality he concurs with R. Simeon, but in respect to an act of labor which is not required for its own sake he concurs with R. Judah* [and that is why he permits the unintentional putting out of fire on the altar but forbids unintentionally putting out a burning piece of wood (Freedman)].

H. Said Rabina, "Therefore if there is a thorn in the public domain, one may carry it away in stages of less than four cubits; *but if it is in the neglected portions of public domain, it is permitted to do so over even a great distance.*"

The principle is not expounded, merely introduced and, one may suppose, illustrated or applied. We cannot point to this passage as a stunning example of how a deeper principle has generated the Bavli's treatment of a Mishnah paragraph or its exposition of ideas of some other order entirely. This item is interesting because of its point, not because of its position in a vast hermeneutical system and structure.

II.1 A. But one may put [enough cold water] into it or into a cup so that [the hot water] will cool off:

B.   *Our rabbis have taught on Tannaite authority:*

C.   "One may put hot water into cold water, but not cold water into hot water," the words of the House of Shammai.

D.   And the House of Hillel, "Whether it is hot water into cold or cold water into hot, it is permitted to do so. Under what circumstances? In the case of a cup of water for drinking [since one doesn't want to heat it up to a high degree]. But in the case of a bath, hot into cold is permitted, but not cold into hot."

II.2   A.   *R. Joseph considered stating, "As to a basin, it is in the category of a bath."*

B.   *Said to him Abbayye, "R. Hiyya set forth a Tannaite rule: As to a basin, it is not in the category of a bath."*

II.3   A.   *In the initial premise that it is in the category of a bath, and said R. Nahman, "The decided law accords with R. Simeon b. Menassayya," then is there no washing whatsoever in hot water on the Sabbath?* [Even if water is heated on Friday, cold water has to be added to temper the heat, and Simeon forbids doing so (Freedman/Rashi).]

II.4   A.   *Said R. Huna b. R. Joshua, "I saw Raba, that he wasn't meticulous about utensils [putting hot into cold water, cold into hot], because R. Hiyya set forth as a Tannaite rule:* one may pour hot water into cold or cold into hot."

3:5D-G

D.   The pan or pot which one has taken off the stove while it is boiling –

E.   one may not put spices into it.

F.   [42B] But he may put [spices] into [hot food which is] in a plate or a dish.

G.   R. Judah says, "Into anything may one put [spices], except what has vinegar or fish brine [in it]."

I.1 A. *The question was raised: Does R. Judah refer to the first clause [D-E], yielding a lenient ruling* [Spices may not be put into the original utensil, right off the flame; Judah permits, except if it has vinegar or brine (Freedman)], *or to the second clause [F], yielding a strict ruling* [spices are permitted in a secondary utensil, no matter the contents; Judah excepts the specified items (Freedman)]?

B. *Come and take note of what has been taught on Tannaite authority:* R. Judah says, "Into all stew pots and boiling pots that are boiling, one may put spices, except into one that contains vinegar or brine" [he refers to the initial utensil].

I.2 A. *R. Joseph considered stating, "Salt is in the category of spices: it boils in the initial utensil but not in the second one* [that is, the utensil on the flame, not the one into which the broth is then poured]."

B. *Said to him Abbayye, "R. Hiyya set forth the Tannaite rule:* Salt is not in the category of spices, for it boils even in the second utensil."

3:6A-D

A. [On the Sabbath] they do not put a utensil under a lamp to catch the oil.

B. But if one put it there while it is still day, it is permitted.

C. But they do not use any of that oil [on the Sabbath],

D. since it is not something which was prepared [before the Sabbath for use on the Sabbath].

I.1 A. Said R. Hisda, "Even though they have said, 'They do not put a utensil under chickens to collect the eggs,' nonetheless, one may turn a utensil over an egg so that it not break."

B. *Said Rabbah, "What's the operative consideration in the mind of R. Hisda? He takes the view that* a chicken ordinarily drops her eggs on a compost heap but not on sloping ground. *Sages permit* [moving a utensil to care for something that itself may not be handled, as in this egg (Freedman)] in a predictable situation of saving something [for example, from being trampled on the compost heap], but they didn't permit one to do so in an unusual situation [for example, from rolling down a slope (Freedman)]."

C. *Objected Abbayye, "But didn't the sages permit saving something in an unusual situation? Hasn't it been taught on Tannaite authority:* If one's jug of wine in the status of produce that is untithed but is liable for tithing broke on his roof, he may bring a utensil and put it underneath the roof [he cannot handle the wine itself, which cannot be used; this situation is unusual; but sages permit saving the produce nonetheless]?"

D. *At issue here are new jugs, which do commonly burst.*

E. *An objection was raised:* **They put a utensil under a lamp to catch the sparks [M. 3:6H].**

F. *Sparks are also commonplace.*

G. **[43A]** *An objection was raised:* They may put a dish over a lamp so that the beams won't catch fire.

H. *In low houses, fires of that sort are commonplace.*

I. *An objection was raised:* And so, if a beam was broken, they may hold it up with a bench or bed staves.

J. *That speaks of new planks, which routinely split.*

K. *An objection was raised:* On the Sabbath they may put a utensil under a leak in the roof.

L. *In new houses roof leaks are commonplace.*

M. *Said R. Joseph, "This is the operative consideration behind the ruling of R. Hisda:* It is because he deprives the utensil of its status as a utensil [that had been ready for use, thus revising the purpose for which that utensil is to serve for that Sabbath]."

N. *Objected Abbayye,* "If one's jug of wine in the status of produce that is untithed but is liable for tithing broke on his roof, he may bring a utensil and put it underneath the roof."   [Freedman: On the Sabbath the produce may not be made fit for use through designating its dues; neither it nor the utensil that receives it may be handled; so that, too, loses its status as being generally fit; but the act is permitted.]

O. He said to him, "So far as the Sabbath is concerned, produce that is liable for tithing but not yet tithed is deemed ready for use on the Sabbath, for if someone violated the law and designated the tithes, it is regarded as properly prepared for use."

P. *An objection was raised:* **They put a utensil under a lamp to catch the sparks [M. 3:6H].**

Q. Said R. Huna b. R. Joshua, "Sparks are intangible."

R. And so, if a beam was broken, they may hold it up with a bench or bed staves.

S. *That means it is placed in a loose way [and not placed firmly], so if he wants, he can take it away.*

T. They put a utensil under drippings on the Sabbath.

U. That speaks of drippings that can be used.

V. They may turn over a basket before fledglings so that they can go up and down [to and from the hen coop]. [The utensil now no longer serves as it was supposed to prior to the Sabbath and ceases to fall into its designated category.]

W. *He takes the view that* it is still permitted to handle the basket.

X. *But it has been taught on Tannaite authority:* That is only when the fledglings are on it.

Y. *But it has been taught on Tannaite authority:* When the fledglings are not on it, it is forbidden.

Z. Said R. Abbahu, "This is what it means: If they were on it throughout twilight; *since in any case in which it was forbidden to handle the basket at twilight, it is forbidden to handle it throughout the Sabbath"* [but if the basket were put there on the Sabbath itself, it had been fit for handling at twilight, so it may be moved when birds aren't on it (Freedman)].

AA. Said R. Isaac, "Just as they do not put a utensil under a chicken to receive its egg, so they don't turn a utensil over the egg so that it won't be broken."

BB. *He takes the view that* it is still permitted to handle the basket only for the sake of something that itself may be handled on the Sabbath.

CC. *All the prior objects were addressed to him, and at each point he replied, it is a case in which its place was required [in which case a utensil may be moved, and when it is moved, it may be utilized for the stated purposes].*

DD. *Come and take note:* All the same are an egg born on the Sabbath and one born on a festival: they may not be handled, either for covering a utensil or for holding up the legs of a bed; but a utensil may be turned over it so that the egg won't be broken.

EE. *Here, too, it is a case in which its place was required [in which case a utensil may be moved, and when it is moved, it may be utilized for the stated purposes].*

FF. *Come and hear:* They spread a mat over stones on the Sabbath.

GG.   [This applies in the case of] rounded stones, *which are fit for a toilet.*

HH.   *Come and hear:* They spread a mat over bricks on the Sabbath.

II.   *[This refers to] bricks that were left over from building, which are fit for sitting on.*

JJ.   *Come and hear:* They spread a mat over a beehive on the Sabbath.

KK.   When it is sunny, [this is to protect the hive] from sun; when it is rainy, [it is to protect the hive] from rain.

LL.   But [in either case] it is on the condition that the individual does not intend [the mat] to catch [the bees].

MM.   Here with what situation do we deal? It is because of the edible honey it contains.

NN.   *Said R. Uqba of Mesene to R. Ashi, "This makes sense for when it is sunny, [43B] at which time there is honey [in the hive]. But when it is rainy, [for example, in winter, at which time there is no honey in the hive], what can one say [to explain why one is permitted to cover the hive]?"*

OO.   *It is necessary [to teach that the hive may be covered even when it is rainy] for the case of those two honeycombs [that the hive's owner places in the hive during the winter, as food for the bees]. [Even in the winter the hive thus contains food so it may be covered.]*

PP.   *[The honey in the hives in the winter is not set aside for human consumption.] But he has not designated those two honeycombs [for consumption on the Sabbath]! [They therefore are not in the status of food, and the hive should not be covered by reason of their presence.]*

QQ.   *[This is a case in which] he had [at one point] considered [using] them [himself]. [These honeycombs therefore are in the status of food and, by reason of their presence, the hive may be covered.]*

RR. *Well, if he had not given thought to making use of them, what is the law?*

SS. *[In this case] it is forbidden [for him to cover the hive, even though it contains honey].*

TT. *[If so, then] rather than teach, "On* the condition that he does not intend [the mat] to catch [the bees]," *he should draw a distinction [within the rule for when it is rainy, cited at L] and should teach for its case:* Under what condition does this pertain, [that one may cover the hive when it is rainy]? When he considered [i.e., designated, the honeycombs in the hive for his own use]. But if he did not consider them [for himself], it is forbidden [to cover the hive with a mat, since it contains no food that the person may eat on the Sabbath].

UU. *Here is what the framer of the passage means to say [by phrasing matters as they stand]:* Even though he has considered them [for his own use, he may cover them] so long as he does not intend [the mat for the purpose of] catching [bees].

VV. Which authority stands behind the rule? It cannot be R. Simeon, who rejects the conception of not using what has not been designated prior to the Sabbath for use on the Sabbath. It cannot be R. Judah, for so far as he is concerned, what matters if one doesn't intend to capture the bees, since he holds that an unintentional act is forbidden anyhow. [Freedman: Since covering blocks the bees' exit, he does in fact capture them, even if he did not intend to.]

WW. *In point of fact, it represents the position of R. Judah, and what is the meaning of the phrase,* on condition that one not intend to capture the bees? *It means, he must not arrange it like a net, but must leave an opening so that the bees are not automatically caught?*

XX.   [The following returns to the original question, Why should one be permitted to cover the hive when it is rainy, that is, in winter, when the hive does not contain honey. Ashi here explains that the Tannaite rule in fact does not permit covering the hive in winter – when it contains no honey – at all.] R. Ashi said, *"Does [this rule] teach,* [One may cover a beehive on the Sabbath] in the sunny season [that is, summer] and in the rainy season [that is, winter]? [No! Rather, it teaches that one may cover it] 'When it is sunny because of the sun and when it is rainy because of the rain.' [The rule thus refers not to summer and winter, but to] the days of the months of Nissan and Tishré, [roughly March and September], when there is sun and rain and there is honey [in the hive]."

YY.   *[Reverting to BB,] said R. Sheshet to them, "Go and tell R. Isaac, 'R. Huna has already set forth your ruling in Babylonia. For said R. Huna, "They may make a partition around a corpse for the sake of the living, but not for the sake of the dead."'"*

ZZ.   *What's the sense of that statement?*

AAA. *Said R. Samuel bar Judah, and so, too, did Shila Mari teach as a Tannaite statement:* "If a corpse is lying in the sun, two men come and sit at its side. If they feel hot from the ground's heat, each may bring a couch and sit on it. If they feel hot from overhead, they may bring an awning and spread it above them. Then each one sets up his couch, takes his leave and goes along, with the result that a

screen for the corpse turns out to
have been set up en passant."

The exposition through a series of cases does not address the
fundamental principle but only tests it against decided law. What
follows is another example of working out the issue, does one do what is
ordinary forbidden in an extraordinary manner, so as to accomplish a
licit goal? And if so, how is this done.

I.2   A.   *It has been stated:*
      B.   A corpse lying in the sun –
      C.   R. Judah said Samuel [said], "One
           may turn it over from one bier to
           the next [until it comes to
           shade]."
      D.   R. Hanina bar Shelamayya said in
           the name of Rab, "One puts a loaf
           of bread or a child on it and
           carries it [on account of carrying
           those items, which it is
           permissible to carry."
      E.   *Well, if there should be a loaf or a*
           child available, all parties concur that
           it is permitted to do as Rab has said.
           Where there is a dispute, it is when
           these are not available. The one
           authority takes the view that moving
           by indirection [changing over from
           bier to bier] is classified as moving
           and so is forbidden, the other, that it
           is not classified as moving.
      F.   *May we say that the same issue is*
           subject to dispute among Tannaite
           authorities?
      G.   They do not save a corpse from a
           fire on the Sabbath.
      H.   Said R. Judah b. Laqish, "I have
           heard that they do save a corpse
           from a fire on the Sabbath" [T.
           Shab. 13:7F-G].
      I.   *Now how shall we imagine this case?*
           If there is a loaf of bread or child at
           hand, then what stands behind the
           position of the initial Tannaite
           authority [since it is perfectly correct
           to save the corpse in that way]? But
           if there is no loaf of bread or child at
           hand, then what explains the position
           of R. Judah b. Laqish? So isn't what
           is at issue the status of moving
           sideways, with one master taking the

> view that that is classified as moving
> [therefore forbidden], the other that it
> is not classified as moving [therefore
> is permitted]?

J. Not at all. *All concur that sideways
moving is classified as moving. And
this is the operative consideration
behind the ruling of R. Judah b.
Laqish: since a person is distressed
about the corpse,* [44A] *if you don't
permit him to move it, he will turn
out extinguishing the fire itself.*

K. Said R. Judah b. Shila said R. Assi
said R. Yohanan, "The decided
law in connection with the corpse
is in accord with R. Judah b.
Laqish."

II.1   A. But they do not use any of that
oil [on the Sabbath], since it is
not something which was prepared [before the Sabbath for
use on the Sabbath]:

B. *Our rabbis have taught on Tannaite
authority:*

C. The leftovers of the oil in the
lamp is forbidden.

D. R. Simeon permits it.

3:6E-F

E. They carry a new lamp, but not an old one.

F. R. Simeon says, "On the Sabbath any sort of lamp do they carry,
except for a lamp that actually is burning."

Another recurrent principle is whether or not one may touch on the
Sabbath what one may not use. That is certainly a problem that pertains
to a broad variety of cases. In the most general terms, it represents
whether and how we erect barriers against the possible violation of the
law, by preventing even the possibility of violating the law.

I.1   A. *Our rabbis have taught on Tannaite
authority:*

B. "They carry a new lamp but not
an old one," the words of R.
Judah.

C. R. Meir says, "On the Sabbath
any sort of lamp do they carry,
except for a lamp one actually lit
on that very Sabbath."

D. R. Simeon says, "On the Sabbath
any sort of lamp do they carry,

      except for a lamp that actually is burning.

E.   "If he put it out, it is permitted to carry it."

F.   But as to a cup, dish, or lantern which they extinguished – one should not move them from their place.

G.   And R. Eleazar b. R. Simeon says, "One may take a supply of oil from a lamp that is going out and a lamp that is dripping, and even at the moment that the lamp is burning" [T. Shab. 3:13A-E, 3:14A].

What is in play in what follows is a subordinate expression of the foregoing: how are we going to be reminded of the status of an object, for example, may we or may we not handle it? How are we going to deal with the issue, expressed in very minor matters, of how to assess, therefore cope with or even govern, one's intentionality?

I.2   A.   *Said Abbayye, "R. Eleazar b. R. Simeon concurs with his father [Simeon] in one matter but differs from him in another. He concurs with his father [Simeon] in one matter, in that he does not accept the principle that what cannot be handled on the Sabbath also may not be touched on the Sabbath. But he differs from his father on another matter, for while his father holds that if the lamp has gone out, it is permitted, if not, it is not permitted, while he maintains that even if it is not out, one may do so."*

I.3   A.   But as to a cup, dish, or lantern which they extinguished – one should not move them from their place:

B.   *What distinguishes these objects?*

C.   *Said Ulla, "This last clause carries forward the view of R. Judah."*

D.   *Objected Mar Zutra to this proposition, "If so, what is the sense of But?!"*

E.   *Rather, said Mar Zutra, "In point of fact that phrase belongs to R. Simeon, but R. Simeon permits handling only in the case of a small lamp, in which one is concentrating on it* [Freedman: thinking that the oil won't last long and when it goes out I will use the lamp], *but in the case of these, which are large, he is not thinking about them."*

F. *But hasn't it been taught on Tannaite authority:* The leftovers of the oil in the lamp is forbidden. R. Simeon permits it?

G. *In that case the dish is comparable to a lamp, in this case, it is comparable to a cup.*

I.4 A. Said R. Zira, "A plain candlestick that one kindled on that very Sabbath – in the view of him who permits [Meir] is forbidden [Freedman: because it burned on that Sabbath, that is, the lamp was employed on that Sabbath for burning and one may not light a lamp on the Sabbath itself], in the view of him who forbids [Judah, speaking of an old lamp, which is repulsive] is permitted [Judah rejecting the prohibition of what is forbidden by reason of a decree]."

B. *Does that then imply that R. Judah accepts the principle that something may be forbidden for use on the Sabbath on account of being repulsive, but rejects the principle that something may not be handled on the Sabbath because of a prohibition? But has it not been taught on Tannaite authority:* R. Judah says, "All metal lamps may be handled, except for a lamp that was lit on that Sabbath"?

C. *Rather, if the statement was made, this is how it was formulated:* Said R. Zira, "A plain candlestick that one kindled on that very Sabbath – all parties concur that it is forbidden. If it was not lit on that day, all parties concur, it is permitted."

I.5 A. Said R. Judah said Rab, "A bed that was singled out for use for money may not be moved about on the Sabbath." [Freedman: Mere designation renders it forbidden, even if money was not actually put on the bed.]

B. *An objection was raised by R. Nahman bar Isaac,* "They carry a new lamp, but not an old one! [44B] *Now if a lamp, that was made for that very purpose, if not lit may be handled, a bed, which was not made for the purpose of holding money, all the more so should be available for handling [if money is not actually located thereon]!*"

C. *Rather, if such a statement was made, this is how it has to have been made:* Said R. Judah said Rab, "A bed that was singled out for use for money – if one put money on it, it may not be moved about on the Sabbath. If one did not put money on it, it is permitted to move it about. If one did not single it out for use for money, if there is money on it, it is forbidden to move it about; if there is no money on it, it is permitted to move it about – but that is so only if there was no money on it at twilight." [If there were money on it at twilight, it couldn't be handled then, and what cannot be handled at twilight cannot be handled for the whole of the Sabbath (Freedman).]

D. *Said Ulla,* "*Objected R. Eleazar:* Its [a chest's] device [trundle] – when it may be slipped off, it is not connected to it, and is not measured with it, and is not afforded protection with it in the tent of the corpse, and they do not drag [the trundle] on the Sabbath when there are coins in it [the chest] [M. Kel. 18:2A-B]. *Lo, if there is no money on it, it is permitted to be handled, and that is the case even though money may have been on it on the eve of the Sabbath.*"

E. *That represents the position of R. Simeon, who rejects the law that that which may not be used on the Sabbath may not be handled thereon.* [Freedman: Nonetheless, since money may not be handled for any purpose at all, he concedes that the trundle may not be rolled when there is actually money on it now.] *But Rab concurs with R. Judah.* [45A] *And that stands to reason that Rab concurs with R. Judah. For* Rab said, "Before the Sabbath they may leave a lamp on a palm tree on the Sabbath. [Freedman: The lamp will burn during the Sabbath; there is no fear that he will take and use it if it goes out, thus using what is attached to the soil; since it was forbidden for use at twilight, it is forbidden for use for the whole of the Sabbath.] But they may not leave a lamp on a palm tree on a festival day. [Freedman: Then one may remove it from the tree and replace it, using the tree itself, which is forbidden.]" *Now if you maintain that Rab accords with R. Judah, that explains why he differentiates between the Sabbath and a festival day, but if you maintain that he concurs with Simeon, then what difference does it make to me whether it is a Sabbath or a festival day?*

F. *But does Rab concur with R. Judah? And isn't it so that they asked Rab, "What is the law on carrying a Hanukkah lamp off from before Magi on the Sabbath," and he said to them, "Well and good."* [Judah would not permit handling the lamp on the Sabbath.]

G. *A ruling made under emergency conditions is exceptional [and he would not ordinarily have permitted doing so]. For lo, said R. Kahana and R. Ashi to Rab, "Is that really the law?" He said to them, "Well, it's* o.k. to rely on R. Simeon in an emergency."

I.6   A.   *R. Simeon b. Laqish asked R. Yohanan, "As to wheat that one sowed in the soil or eggs under a chicken, what is the law [on taking them on the Sabbath for use, the wheat not having taken root, the egg not having addled]? When R. Simeon rejects the prohibition in a case in which on one's own action one has not rejected an object* [here, when one sows wheat in the ground or puts an egg under the fowl, he has rejected it for the interim (Freedman)], *but in a case in which one has rejected the object through one's own action, he will affirm that it is forbidden to handle such a [self-designated, repulsive] object on the Sabbath? Or maybe he makes no such distinction?"*

   B.   *He said to him, "R. Simeon accepts the principle that what is not designated for use on the Sabbath is forbidden for handling on the Sabbath only in the case of oil in a lamp when the lamp is burning, since, at that point, the oil is both designated for carrying out the religious duty [of the Sabbath lamp] and it also is at that moment set apart because of a prohibition* [putting out a lamp on the Sabbath, which one may not do; that prohibition renders the oil inaccessible while the lamp is burning (following Freedman's reading and explanation)]."

   C.   *Well, then, does he not hold that where something is singled out only to carry out a given religious duty, that alone would suffice to render handling that thing forbidden? And hasn't it been taught on Tannaite authority:* [If] one properly roofed over the Sukkah and beautified it with hangings and sheets and also hung up in it nuts, peaches, pomegranates, bunches of grapes, and wreaths of ears of corn, it is valid. [But] one should not eat of any of these, even on the last day of the festival. But if one made a stipulation concerning them that he would eat of them on the festival, it is entirely in accord with what he has stipulated [T.: permitted to do so] [T. Suk. 1:7G-I]? *And how do you know that this represents the position of R. Simeon? Because R. Hiyya bar Joseph repeated before R. Yohanan the following Tannaite statement:* [On a festival day] they do not take pieces of wood from [the walls or roof of] a hut, but [they take wood] from that which is adjacent to it [M. Bes. 4:2A]. But R. Simeon permits. And they concur in regard to the Sukkah that was built for that festival in particular that it is forbidden to do so on the festival [should that hut collapse, its wood may not be used during the whole festival, having been designated to carry out the religious duty of a Sukkah for that festival]. But if he made a stipulation in that regard, it is entirely in accord with what he has stipulated. [So the foregoing concurs with Simeon.]

D.   *What we mean to say was,* parallel to the oil in the lamp; since it was singled out to carry out its religious duty, it was also singled out in respect to the prohibition affecting it. [The former consideration suffices.] So, too, it has been stated: said R. Hiyya bar Abba said R. Yohanan, "So far as R. Simeon is concerned, the principle that on the Sabbath one may not touch what one may not use applies only to a case parallel to one involving oil in a burning lamp: since the oil has been singled out to carry out that religious duty, it has been singled out also to be subject to the prohibition applying to it."

I.7 A. Said R. Judah said Samuel, "So far as R. Simeon is concerned, the principle that on the Sabbath one may not touch what one may not use applies only to drying figs and grapes." [Freedman: When they are spread out to dry, they cease to be fit for food until fully dried; hence they are certainly rejected as food, and even Simeon admits the prohibition here.]

B. *Nothing else? But what about what has been taught on Tannaite authority:* [If prior to a festival] one was eating grapes, had some left over, and brought them up to the roof to make from them raisins, or [if he was eating] figs, left some over, and brought them up to the roof to make from them dried figs – he may not eat of them [on the festival] unless he designates them [for festival use] while it is still daylight, before the start of the holy day. And this you find [is the law] for peaches, quinces and all other types of fruit? *Now who can be the authority behind this rule? Should I say it is R. Judah? But if in a situation in which by one's own action one has not rejected use of something, the thing nonetheless is forbidden for use on the Sabbath, in a case in which by one's own action, one has done so, all the more so will he concur! So isn't it R. Simeon's position [in which case he invokes the stated principle in more than the instance specified above].*

C. *In point of fact it stands for R. Judah's view, but it was necessary to specify that that is the case even when one was actually eating the fruit. For it might have entered your mind to suppose that, since one was going along and eating the fruit, it was not necessary that he designated the produce for eating on the*

Sabbath. So we are informed that, since he has brought up the residue to the roof, he has given up regarding the produce as useful [and so it is subject to the same prohibition].

I.8   A.   *R. Simeon bar Rabbi asked Rabbi,* [45B] "According to R. Simeon, what [is the law whether or not on a festival day one may eat] burst figs?"

B.   [And, indicating that Rabbi does not require prior designation, Rabbi] said to [Simeon b. Rabbi], "R. Simeon requires that food be set aside for festival use only in the case of dried figs and raisins." [These foods were edible but now have been set aside for drying. The owner himself purposely imposed upon them the status of a nonedible. If he wishes to make them available for festival use, accordingly, prior to the holy day, he must indicate his intention to eat them. But in most other cases, Simeon does not require designation of food for festival use. The assumption is that Rabbi reports this perspective because it is his own opinion, not simply that of Simeon.]

C.   *But doesn't Rabbi accept the principle that what may not be used on the Sabbath may not be handled? Haven't we learned in the Mishnah:* **They do not give drink to field animals or slaughter them [on a festival day, since they are not deemed set aside as food]. But they give drink to and slaughter household animals, [which are deemed set aside for festival use]** [M. Bes. 5:7D-E]? *And hasn't it been taught on Tannaite authority:* **What are the field animals and what are the household animals? Field animals are those that go out to pasture at Passover and come back in the first quarter, [that is, in the rainy season]. And what are the household** animals? Those that go out and pasture outside the Sabbath boundary but come back and spend the night within the Sabbath boundary. Rabbi says, "Both of these [types of animals], are household animals. Rather, what are field animals? Those that go out and graze in [the distant] pastures and do not return to town either in the sunny season or the rainy season" [T. Y.T. 4:11]?

D. [The apparent contradiction between Rabbi's opinion at F, in which he requires prior designation, and his understanding of Simeon's position, I, which states that in most cases no designation is required, is resolved.] *If you wish I can say that these [field animals], too, are comparable to dried figs and raisins, [such that even Rabbi holds that they require prior designation if they are to be used on a festival day].* [Like the figs and raisins, the animals should automatically be ready and available as food. But they have been removed from the person's home, such that they no longer are deemed ready for consumption. They are a special case in which designation is required.] *And if you wish I can reason that [Rabbi] made his statement, according to the opinion of R. Simeon, even though this is not his own [view].* [Unlike Simeon, whose opinion he reports, Rabbi always requires food to be set aside for use on a festival day]. *And if you wish I can explain that [Rabbi does not require prior designation, as indicated, but that he] reported the law according to the view of rabbis, thus: "In my opinion food to be used on a holy day need not be set aside prior to the start of that day. But even you, [who require prior setting aside], should agree with me that [animals that] go out to pasture at Passover and come back in the first quarter are household animals!" But the rabbis said to him, "No! These are field animals!"*

I.9   A.   Said Rabbah bar bar Hannah said R. Yohanan, "They said: the law accords with R. Simeon."

        B.   *But did R. Yohanan make any such statement? And lo, a certain elder of Qirvayya, and some say, from Sirvayya, addressed this question to him:* "What is the law on handling a fowl nest on the Sabbath?" And he said to him, "Is it made for anything other than chickens?" [It is designated for what may not be handled on the Sabbath and therefore is forbidden; Simeon would not take that view in that case.]

        C.   *Here with what situation do we deal? It is a case in which the nest contains a dead bird [which even in Simeon's view may not be handled].*

        D.   *Well, now, that poses no problem to Mar bar Amemar in the name of Raba, who has said,* "R. Simeon concedes that if living creatures die, they may not be handled on the Sabbath [even cut up as food for dogs]." [Freedman: If they were in good health at twilight, so that one gave no thought to them, they cannot be used for the stated purpose on the Sabbath; but if the animal was dying at twilight and died after nightfall, on the Sabbath, Simeon would concur that it can be chopped up and fed to dogs, because the owner can have given thought to using the carcass for that purpose.] *But from the perspective of Mar b. R. Joseph in the name of Raba, who said,* "R. Simeon differed even in the case of living creatures that die, holding that they may be handled on the Sabbath [even cut up as food for dogs]," *what is there to say?*

E. *Here with what situation do we deal? It is a hen coop that contains an egg [laid that day; even Simeon admits that what is newly created on the Sabbath may not be handled].*

F. *But didn't R. Nahman say, "Anyone who permits [for use on the festival day] that which has not been set aside [for use on that day] also permits [for use on the festival] an object that [physically] comes into being [on that day], and anyone who prohibits [for use on the festival day] that which has not been set aside [for use on that day] also prohibits [for use on the festival] an object that [physically] comes into being [on that day]"?*

G. *It is a case in which there is the egg of a fledgling* [on which the chicken is sitting; that is entirely unfit; no one thinks the nest may be handled (Freedman)].

I.10 A. *When R. Isaac bar Joseph came, he said*, "R. Yohanan said, 'The decided law is in accord with R. Judah.' And R. Joshua b. Levi said, 'The decided law is in accord with R. Simeon.'"

B. Said R. Joseph, "That is in line with what Rabbah bar bar Hannah said R. Yohanan said, 'They have said, "The decided law is in accord with R. Simeon."'"

C. *"They have said..." – but didn't R. Yohanan take that position for himself?*

D. *Said Abbayye to R. Joseph, "And don't you think that R. Yohanan concurs with R. Judah's position? Isn't it the fact that R. Abba and R. Assi visited the household of R. Abba of Haifa, and a candelabrum fell on R. Assi's robe, but he didn't take it off? How come? Surely it is because R. Assi was R. Yohanan's disciple, and R. Yohanan took the position of R. Judah, who affirmed the principle that what cannot be used on the Sabbath also cannot be handled on that day!"*

E. *He said to him, "Do you speak of a candelabrum? The case of a candelabrum is exceptional, for* said R. Aha bar Hanina said R. Assi, 'R. Simeon b. Laqish gave instructions in Sidon: "A candelabrum that can be lifted with a single hand may be moved, but one that needs two hands may not."' And R. Yohanan said, 'So far as a lamp is concerned, we have in hand only the position of R. Simeon; as to a candelabrum, whether it can be lifted by one hand or by two, it may not be moved.' *How come? Rabbah and R. Joseph both say,* 'Since a person assigns a place for it [on the Sabbath], it is designated for that place in particular and is not to be moved elsewhere.'"

F. *Said Abbayye to R. Joseph, "But what about a bridal couch, for which one designates a particular place, and yet* said Samuel in the name of R. Hiyya, 'On the Sabbath a bridal couch [46A] may one set up and dismantle.'"

G. Rather, said Abbayye, "It refers to a candelabrum that can be dismantled, having movable joints." [Freedman: It may not be handled lest it fall to pieces and be put together again, which is tantamount to making a utensil.]

H. *If so, how come R. Simeon b. Laqish permits moving it?*

I. *What is the meaning of "removable joints"? It means, similar to joints, in that it has grooves.* [Freedman: It is all fastened in one place, but because it has grooves, it looks as though it were jointed for dismantling.]

J. Therefore, if it had real joints, whether it was large or small, it may not be handled; *if it was large and had grooves, it also may not be handled because of a large one made of joints. Where there is a difference of opinion it concerns a little one that had grooves. The one authority maintains that we make a precautionary decree against handling it, and the other maintains we do not make a precautionary decree.*

K. *Well, did R. Yohanan make any such statement?* But didn't R. Yohanan say, "The decided law accords with the unattributed Mishnah rule"? *And we have learned in the Mishnah:* Its [a chest's] device [trundle] – when it may be slipped off, it is not connected to it, and is not measured with it, and is not afforded protection with it in the tent of the corpse, and they do not drag [the trundle] on the Sabbath when there are coins in it [the chest] [M. Kel. 18:2A-B]. *Lo, if there is no money on it, it is permitted to be handled, and that is the case even though money may have been on it on the eve of the Sabbath [and that imposes the prohibition of touching what may not be used on the Sabbath].*

L. Said R. Zira, "Let our Mishnah paragraph pertain to one that had no money on it during all of twilight, so as not to contradict R. Yohanan's position."

I.11 A. Said R. Joshua b. Levi, "Once Rabbi went to Diospera and he gave instruction in the matter of the candelabrum in accord with the position of R. Simeon on a lamp" [the former: a branched candlestick, the latter, a single lamp].

B. *They asked him,* "Is the sense, in the matter of the candelabrum in accord with the position of R. Simeon on a lamp *that he gave a lenient ruling, or perhaps the sense is, he gave instruction in respect to a candelabrum so as to prohibit handling it, and in accord with R.*

           Simeon in regard to a lamp so as to permit handling it?"

   C.   *The question stands.*

I.12   A.   *R. Malkio visited the household of R. Simlai and moved the lamp* [that had gone out (Freedman)]. *R. Simlai objected.*

   B.   *R. Yosé the Galilean visited the locale of R. Yosé b. R. Hanina. He moved a lamp that had gone out, and R. Yosé bar Hanina objected.*

   C.   *When R. Abbahu came to the locale of R. Joshua b. Levi, he would carry a candle [on the Sabbath, since Joshua thought it was all right to do so under certain circumstances], and when he came to the locale of R. Yohanan, he didn't carry a candle.*

   D.   *Well, what's what? If he concurs with R. Judah, then let him act in accord with R. Judah! If he concurs with R. Simeon, then let him act in accord with R. Simeon!*

   E.   *In point of fact he concurs with R. Simeon, but it was because of the respect owing to R. Yohanan that he did not act in such a way.*

I.13   A.   *Said R. Judah, "As to an oil lamp, it is permitted to handle it; as to a naphtha lamp, it is forbidden to handle it."*

   B.   *Both Rabbah and R. Joseph say, "As to one of naphtha, it is also permitted to handle it."*

I.14   A.   *R. Avayya visited the household of Raba. His boots were muddy with clay, but he sat down on a bed before Raba. Raba took offense. Raba wanted to irritate him. He said to him, "How come both Rabbah and R. Joseph say, 'As to one of naphtha, it is also permitted to handle it'?"*

   B.   *He said to him, "It is because it is suitable for covering a utensil."*

   C.   *"Then all the chips in the courtyard should be permitted to be handled, since they are suitable for covering a utensil."*

   D.   *He said to him, "But the former is classified as a utensil, but the latter in no way are classified as a utensil!*

		Hasn't it been taught on Tannaite authority: [46B] Chains, earrings and nose rings are all articles of clothing, which may be worn on the Sabbath in a courtyard? *And said Ulla, "How come? Because they are classified as utensils. Here, too, since it is classified as a utensil, it may be handled."*

E. Said R. Nahman bar Isaac, "Blessed is the All-Merciful, that Raba did not humiliate R. Avayya."

I.15 A. To Rabbah, Abbayye contrasted *[Tannaite rules, as follows:]* "It has been taught on Tannaite authority: The leftovers of the oil in the lamp are forbidden. R. Simeon permits it. *Therefore R. Simeon rejects the principle that what is not suitable for use on the Sabbath also may not be touched. But it also has been taught on Tannaite authority:* R. Simeon says, 'Any [firstling] the blemish of which has not been discerned while it is still day [before the festival] – this is not [deemed to be] in the category of that which is ready [for festival use]' [M. Bes. 3:4C]. [Therefore he accepts the principle that what is not available for use prior to the holy day, for example, by sunset, may not be handled on the holy day itself.]"

B. *But how are the cases parallel? In the one case,* someone sits there and looks forward to when the lamp will go out [to save the oil]. *But here* does someone sit there and look forward to when the beast will be blemished? [He does want that to happen, but he doesn't expect it, but he does have reason to expect the lamp to go out (Freedman).] *Rather, he says, who can tell me that it ever will receive a blemish? And even if you say that it will, who can tell me that it will be a permanent blemish [such as that which will release the animal for slaughter]? And even if you say it will be permanent, who can say that a disciple of a sage will take up the case? [So it is hardly parallel.]*

C.   *Objected R. Ammi bar Hama,* "They abrogate vows on the Sabbath. And on the Sabbath they receive applications for the nullification of vows concerning matters which are required for the Sabbath [M. Shab. 24:5A-B]. *But why should this be the case? Rather, why not say, 'who can say that her husband will take up her case?'"* [Freedman: When a woman forswears benefit from anything, she rejects it for herself, and it falls into the category of what cannot be used; even if her husband annuls her vow, she could not have anticipated his doing so; so it should remain prohibited for handling on the Sabbath by reason of its having been prohibited for use.]

D.   *The answer there accords with what R. Phineas said in the name of Raba, for* said R. Phineas in the name of Raba, "Whoever takes a vow does so with the stipulation of her husband's concurrence."

E.   *Come and take note:* And on the Sabbath they receive applications for the nullification of vows concerning matters which are required for the Sabbath [M. Shab. 24:5A-B]. *But why should this be the case? Rather, why not say,* "Who can say that a sage will take up the case?"

F.   *In that case, if a sage won't take up the case, a court of three common persons will do; but here, who can say that a sage will take up the case?*

I.16   A.   *Abbayye raised the following question to R. Joseph,* "Did R. Simeon say, 'if the lamp went out, it may be handled'? Then, only if it went out may it be handled, but not if it went out. *Why not? Because we take the precaution, lest, through his handling it, it might go out [and the Torah forbids putting out a fire]. But, by contrast, we have heard as a tradition for R. Simeon, who has said, 'If it is something that one does not wish to have happen, it is permitted.' For it has been taught on Tannaite authority:* R. Simeon says, 'On the Sabbath, one may drag a bed, chair, or bench, so long as he does not intend thereby to make a groove in the dirt.'"

B. *[He said to him,] "In any case in which one intends for that to happen, there is a prohibition deriving from the Torah, but in any case in which one does not intend that to happen, R. Simeon makes a decree prohibiting such a thing by reason of the authority of rabbis. But if there is only a rabbinical prohibition, then even if it is intentional, R. Simeon to begin with permits the action."*

C. *Objected Rabbah,* "Clothes dealers sell [garments of diverse kinds] in their usual manner provided that they do not intend, in a hot sun, [for the garments to protect them] from the hot sun, or in the rain, [for the garments to protect them] from the rain. And the more scrupulous ones tie [the garments of diverse kinds] on a stick [M. Kil. 9:5]. *Now here is a case in which the prohibition of an intentional action is based on the law of the Torah – and yet if the action is not intended, to begin with R. Simeon permits that action!"*

D. *Rather, said Raba,* [47A] *"Set aside the lamp, oil, and wicks, since they are turned into the foundation for an act that is forbidden."* [The flame is forbidden; while the lamp is lit, everything is subsidiary to the flame; under such conditions, Simeon concurs that what cannot be used cannot be handled (Freedman).]

I.17 A. Said R. Zira said R. Assi said R. Yohanan said R. Hanina said R. Romanus, "Rabbi permitted me to handle a pan with the ashes in it." [Freedman: Ashes cannot be used so shouldn't be handled, but it is assumed that he was permitted to move the ashes on account of the pan, a utensil.]

B. *Said R. Zira to R. Assi, "Did R. Yohanan make such a statement? And have we not learned in the Mishnah:* A man takes up [handles] his child, with a stone in [the child's] hand, or a basket with a stone in it [M. Shab. 21:1A-B]? *And said Rabbah bar bar Hannah said R. Yohanan, 'We deal here with a basket full of produce.' So the operative consideration is that there is produce, but if there were no produce, it would not have been permitted to do so."*

C. *"He was astounded for a moment"* (Dan. 4:16). *Then he said, "Here, too, it is a case in which the pan has some grains of spice."*

D. *Said Abbayye, "So did the household of Rabbi value grains of spice? And should you propose, well, they're fit for the poor, hasn't it been taught on Tannaite authority:* The garments of the poor are judged by what is relative to the situation of a poor person, [who will value a very small piece of cloth], and the garments of the rich are judged by what is relative to the situation of a rich person [who will value only a larger piece of cloth but regard a small piece as worthless]. *But we do not assess the garments of the poor by appeal to the value placed on them by the rich."*

E. *Rather, said Abbayye, "It is comparable to a chamber pot. [One may empty a chamber pot, and so, too, a pan and ashes.]"*

F. *Said Raba, "There are two pertinent answers to this: first of all, a chamber pot is nauseating, but this isn't* nauseating; *furthermore, a chamber pot is out in the open, but this is covered. [The analogy fails.]"*

G. *Rather, said Raba, "When we were at the household of R. Nahman, we would handle a brazier on account of the ashes in it* [if the ashes were needed to cover something; these were relied upon for that purpose from prior to the Sabbath (Freedman)], *even if broken pieces of wood were lying on it."*

H. *An objection was raised:* But [Judah and Simeon] concur that if the lamp had fragments of a wick, it may not be handled. [The same would pertain to pieces of wood on a brazier; the lamp contains oil, as the brazier contains ashes (Freedman).]

I. *Said Abbayye, "We have learned this rule for Galilee"* [where oil is abundant and the residue would not be valued; so the lamp with the fragments of wick may not be handled on account of its oil (Freedman)].

I.18 A. *Levi bar Samuel came across R. Abba and R. Huna bar Hiyya, who were standing at the doorway of the household of R. Huna. He said to them, "What is the law as to reassembling a weaver's frame on the Sabbath?"*

B. *They said to him, "It's quite o.k."*

C. *He came before R. Judah. He said, "Both Rab and Samuel say, 'He who reassembles a weaver's frame on the Sabbath is liable to a sin-offering.'"*

D. *An objection was raised:* **He who puts back the branch of a candelabrum on the Sabbath is liable to a sin-offering. As to the joint of a whitewasher's pole, one may not reinsert it, but if he did so, he is exempt from a sin-offering, although the act is forbidden [cf. T. Shab. 13:5]. R. Simai says, "For a circular horn he is liable, for a straight one, he**

is exempt." [Freedman: The
difficulty is presented by the
branch of the candelabrum,
which is on the same principle as
the weaver's frame.]

E. *They made their ruling in line with
the Tannaite authority of that which
has been taught on Tannaite
authority:* The sockets of a bed,
legs of a bed, archer's tablets may
not be reinserted; if one did so, he
is exempt from penalty, [47B]
though it is forbidden to do so.
And they are not to be tightly
fixed, but if one did tightly fix
them, he is liable to a sin-offering.
Rabban Simeon b. Gamaliel says,
"If it is loose, it is permitted."
[Freedman: If it is so constructed
that it need be only loosely joined,
it is permitted even to begin with;
Abba and Huna likewise refer to
branches that set lightly in their
sockets.]

I.19 A. *At the household of R. Hama was a
folding bed, which they would set up
on festivals. Said one of the rabbis to
Raba, "What's your view? Do you
think this is an offhand construction
[not done in a professional way, and
therefore, because it is loosely fitted,
it is not classified as building and
that is why it is permitted to do
this]? Then even though it is not
prohibited by the Torah under such
circumstances, surely it is forbidden
by rabbis!"*

B. *He said to him, "I concur with
Rabban Simeon b. Gamaliel, who has
said, If it is loose, it is permitted."*

I.1, with a talmud at Nos. 2-4 inserts a Tannaite complement to the
Mishnah rule. Nos. 5-19 go on to a further amplification on the theme of
the Mishnah rule and the several possible positions in regard to the
principle behind that rule. This excellent composite has been organized
around its own interest in the fundamentals of the law, but then inserted
here because it fills out what in the Mishnah is a rather one-dimensional
statement.

3:6H-I

H. They put a utensil under a lamp to catch the sparks.

I. But [on the Sabbath] one may not put water into it, because he thereby puts out [the sparks].

There are abstract issues that generate no discussion beyond the case to which they pertain, for example, questions of the tangibility of what is scarcely to be touched, such as the status of sparks. These questions of physics lurk in the background at many points but rarely if ever generate sustained discussion in the way in which, in the preceding item, the issue of intentionality, the status of objects in the context of one's intentions for their use for instance, holds together a broad selection of cases and rules.

I.1　　A.　*But by doing so, one nullifies the utensil's status as a useful object ready for work [by putting it under the lamp in this way]!*

　　　　B.　Said R. Huna. R. Joshua, "Sparks are not tangible."

II.1　　A.　But [on the Sabbath] one may not put water into it, because he thereby puts out [the sparks]:

　　　　B.　*May we say that what we have here taught without attribution accords with the view of R. Yosé, who has said, "What indirectly brings about extinguishing fire is forbidden"?*

　　　　C.　*But do you really think so? While I may well say that R. Yosé made that ruling with respect to the Sabbath, does he hold that view also for the eve of the Sabbath? And should you say, well, here, too, it refers to the eve of the Sabbath, hasn't it been taught on Tannaite authority:* They put a utensil to catch the sparks on the Sabbath, and it goes without saying, on the eve of the Sabbath, but on the eve of the Sabbath one may not put in water because it puts out the sparks, and it goes without saying, on the Sabbath?

　　　　D.　*Rather, said R. Ashi, "You may even say that this represents the position of rabbis. The present case is exceptional, since by one's action he brings near what extinguishes the flame."* [Freedman: By

> pouring water into the utensil,
> and therefore as a preventing
> measure, it is forbidden even on
> the eve of the Sabbath.]

The paramount status of the premise of discourse – the assessment of indirect action and secondary effects – is shown at the end, when that criterion is explicitly invoked.

3

Bavli Shabbat
Chapter Seven

Folios 67B-76B

My survey is now abbreviated. I give the larger part of any discussion in which I find the imposition of one set of relationships upon another set of relationships, which I call my "mixed grid." I also identify any other general principles brought to bear upon the exegesis of specific Mishnah passages. For my right-hand column, by contrast, I give only the opening line or two of a given composition, and the briefest possible access to the consequent composites; what I mean to show is the proportion of the one kind of discussion to the other, and what we shall see here is that the quest for generalization, or exegesis of the Mishnah yielding analysis of principles capable of generalization ("generalizability"), forms an inconsequential part of the Talmud's reading of a Mishnah chapter or even most Mishnah passages (sentences or sets of sentences forming a completed propositional or syllogistic discourse). I realize that for the reader, wading through these truncated passages yields little that is of interest. But I have no other way of demonstrating beyond all shadow of a doubt that when we do decode the Bavli's exegetical program, uncovering sources of generalization, on the one side, and principles of philosophical reading of the Mishnah's mass of details, on the other, we in no way account for most of what is in the Bavli. And as we shall now see, that is itself a massive understatement. In fact, what I want readers to observe through direct encounter with the character of entire chapters is simple. The Bavli has no code to decode, so far as we should want to find a key in a set of coherent, encompassing principles, for example, of physics, theology, or philosophy, to its exegesis of the Mishnah. There are codes, but no code; all formulations of interstitial analysis such as I have identified in the prior monographs of this series prove topical and episodic. The shank of this book – the tedious review of chapters, with the repeated demonstration that the bulk of each chapter is devoted to topical and episodic exegesis of words and phrases of the Mishnah, the sources in Scripture of the Mishnah's rulings, the identities of the authority behind unassigned statements of the Mishnah, the harmony of the Mishnah rulings that appear to conflict with one another – all of this forms the Talmud – that, and not a code hidden within the whole and awaiting the cryptography of philosophical, theological, or physical exegesis.

7:1

A. A governing principle did they state concerning the Sabbath:
B. Whoever forgets the basic principle of the Sabbath and performed many acts of labor on many different Sabbath days is liable only for a single sin-offering.
C. He who knows the principle of the Sabbath and performed many acts of labor on many different Sabbaths is liable for the violation of each and every Sabbath.
D. He who knows that it is the Sabbath and performed many acts of labor on many different Sabbaths is liable for the violation of each and every [68A] generative category of labor.
E. He who performs many acts of labor of a single type is liable only for a single sin-offering.

> I.1   A.   *How come the Tannaite framer of the passage has used the phrase,* A governing principle [did they state concerning the Sabbath]? *Should I say that, since he wishes to use the language for his Tannaite statement,* And a further governing rule did they state, *he has used the language here,* A governing principle? *And so too, in the context of the rules of the Seventh Year, since he wanted to use the language,* And a further governing rule did they state, *he used the formulation also,* A governing principle [did they state concerning the Sabbath] [M. Sheb. 5:5, 7:1]? *Then what about the matter of tithing, in which tractate we find the language,* This is the governing principle [M. Ma. 2:7L], *but the language,* "governing principle" *is not used!*

At issue in what follows is how and whether we differentiate a variety of actions by reference to whether one knew what one was doing. The deeper concern of course is intentionality, and the governing principle is, one is guilty for an act done in full awareness that the act is wrong and in entire intentionality to violate the law. So within that principle we generate a variety of secondary questions on the interplay of knowledge and intentionality, on the one side, and prohibited actions, on the other.

II.1   A.   [Supply: Whoever forgets the basic principle of the Sabbath and performed many acts of labor on many different Sabbath days is liable only for a single sin-offering. He who knows the principle of the Sabbath and performed many acts of labor on many different Sabbaths is liable for the violation of each and every Sabbath:] *Both Rab and Samuel say, "Our Mishnah paragraph speaks of* a child who was kidnapped by gentiles or a proselyte who converted while living among gentiles, but if one originally knew about the Sabbath but in the end forgot about him, one is liable for violation of each and every Sabbath."

     B.   *We have learned in the Mishnah:* Whoever forgets the basic principle of the Sabbath and performed many acts of labor on many different Sabbath days is liable only for a single sin-offering. *Doesn't this bear the inference that, to begin with, he knew that principle?*

     C.   *Not at all. What is the sense of* Whoever forgets the basic principle of the Sabbath and performed many acts of labor on many different Sabbath days is liable only for a single sin-offering? *That the very existence of the Sabbath was forgotten by him. But if he knew and then forgot, what is the consequence? He would be liable for every Sabbath.*

D. *In that case, instead of formulating
    the Tannaite rule in the language,*
    He who knows the principle of
    the Sabbath and performed
    many acts of labor on many
    different Sabbaths is liable for
    the violation of each and every
    Sabbath, *it would have been more
    sensible to state matters as if* he
    knew...but in the end forgot... –
    and all the more so here!
E. *What is the meaning of* He who
    knows the principle of the
    Sabbath? *It means,* one who did
    know the principle of the Sabbath
    and forgot it. [68B] But if he never
    knew it, *what is the law?* He is
    liable for the violation of each
    and every Sabbath.
F. *Well, then, instead of formulating the
    Tannaite rule in the language,* H e
    who knows the principle of the
    Sabbath and performed many
    acts of labor on many different
    Sabbaths is liable for the
    violation of each and every
    Sabbath, *it would make more sense
    to formulate the Tannaite rule in this
    language:* He who knows the
    principle of the Sabbath – *and all
    the more so in this case.*
G. *Rather, our Mishnah paragraph deals
    with a case of one who knew but later
    on forgot, and Rab and Samuel's
    statement runs along these same
    lines: it involves someone who knew
    and then forgot, and this is how it
    was stated: both Rab and Samuel say,*
    "Even a child who was
    kidnapped by gentiles or a
    proselyte who converted while
    living among gentiles are in the
    status of one who knew the
    principle of the Sabbath but
    ultimately forgot, so he is liable."
H. *But R. Yohanan and R. Simeon b.
    Laqish both say,* "It is particularly
    in the case of one who knew and
    ultimately forgot [who would be
    liable], but in the case of a child
    who was kidnapped by gentiles

or a proselyte who converted while living among gentiles, he would be exempt."

I. *An objection was raised:* A governing principle did they state concerning the Sabbath: Whoever forgets the basic principle of the Sabbath and performed many acts of labor on many different Sabbath days is liable only for a single sin-offering. How so?

J. A child who was kidnapped by gentiles or a proselyte who converted while living among gentiles who did many acts of labor on many Sabbaths is liable for only a single sin-offering; such a person would be liable for eating forbidden blood, forbidden fat, or idolatry, also on one count alone. But Munbaz declares such a one entirely exempt.

K. And so did Munbaz argue before R. Aqiba, "Since one who sins deliberately is called a sinner, and one who sins inadvertently also is classified as a sinner, just as in the case of one who acted deliberately, the implication is that he had knowledge of the fact that what he was doing was forbidden, so in the case of one who acted inadvertently, he must at some point have had knowledge of the prohibited character of what he was doing [thus exempting the one in hand, who never had such knowledge to begin with]."

L. Said to him R. Aqiba, "So let me add to what you've said. Just as one who has acted deliberately, who knew what he was doing at the moment he was doing it, so is it the case that the one who acted inadvertently should be one who knew what he was doing while he was doing it?"

M. He said to him, "Yessiree! and all the more so have you added to the argument!"

N. He said to him, "But by your definition, such a person cannot be classified as inadvertent but as a deliberate violation of the law" [T. Shab. 8:5-6].

O. *Anyhow, the Tannaite formulation uses the language,* How so? A child who was kidnapped by gentiles or a proselyte who converted! *Now, from the perspective of Rab and Samuel, there is then no problem. But from the viewpoint of R. Yohanan and R. Simeon b. Laqish, isn't this a problem?*

P. *R. Yohanan and R. Simeon b. Laqish can say to you, "But isn't Munbaz around, who declares him exempt from culpability? So we rule in line with Munbaz."*

II.2 A. *So what's the scriptural basis for the ruling of Munbaz?*

B. "You shall have one torah for him who acts unwittingly" (Num. 15:29) and alongside, "And the soul that does something deliberately" (Num. 15:29). The deed that is done inadvertently is treated as comparable to one that is done deliberately; just as a deliberate action is one in which he knew what he was doing, so an inadvertent action must be one in which he knew what he was doing. [Only then is one obligated to a sin-offering.]

C. *And rabbis – how do they interpret this reference to "one torah"?*

D. *They interpret it in the way in which R. Joshua b. Levi interpreted Scripture to his son:* "'You shall have one torah for him who does anything in error, but the soul that does anything deliberately...'" (Num. 15:29-30); and it is written, [69A] "And when you shall err and not observe all these commandments" (Num. 15:22),

and further, "and the soul that
does anything deliberately – that
soul shall be cut off." So the
entirety of the Torah in this way
is treated as analogous to the
prohibition of idolatry. Just as, in
respect to idolatry, [they are] not
[liable] in the case of idolatry,
except in the case in which they
gave instruction in a matter the
deliberate commission of which is
punishable by extirpation, and
the inadvertent commission of
which is punishable by a sin-
offering, so in the case of all other
transgressions, the same rule
applies, namely, it must be a
matter the deliberate commission
of which is punishable by
extirpation, and the inadvertent
commission of which is
punishable by a sin-offering."

E. *Well, then, from Munbaz's
perspective, what can "inadvertence"
possibly be?*

F. For instance, if someone didn't
know the obligation to bring an
offering.

G. *And rabbis?*

H. *Forgetting the obligation to bring an
offering for a certain deed is not
classified as inadvertence.*

I. *And from rabbis' perspective, what
can "inadvertence" possibly be?*

J. R. Yohanan said, "So long as
one's error concerns extirpation,
even though he deliberately
sinned in respect to a negative
commandment [that would
constitute inadvertence]."
[Freedman: He knows that the
deed is forbidden by a negative
commandment, but he doesn't
know that the penalty is
extirpation; this constitutes
sinning in ignorance and involves
a sin-offering.]

K. And R. Simeon b. Laqish said,
"To be subject to the category of
inadvertence, one has to err both
in respect to the negative

commandment and in regard to the penalty of extirpation."

L. *Said Raba, "What is the scriptural basis behind the position of R. Simeon b. Laqish?* Said Scripture, 'And if any one of the common people sins unwittingly, in doing any of the things that the Lord has commanded not to be done, and be guilty' (Lev. 4:27) – the error must involve both the negative commandment and the penalty of extirpation that accompanies it."

M. *And as to R. Yohanan, how does he interpret this verse that is presented by R. Simeon b. Laqish?*

N. *He requires it in line with that which has been taught on Tannaite authority:* "[And if any one] of the common people [sin unwittingly, in doing any of the things that the Lord has commanded not to be done, and be guilty" (Lev. 4:27)] – excluding an apostate.

II.3 A. R. Simeon b. Eleazar says in the name of R. Simeon, "'[And if any one of the common people sin unwittingly, in doing any of the things that the Lord has commanded] not to be done, and be guilty' (Lev. 4:27) – he who would retract if he knew [and would not deliberately violate the law] presents an offering for his unintentional transgression; he who would not retract if he knew does not bring an offering for his unintentional transgression."

II.4 A. *We have learned in the Mishnah:* The generative categories of acts of labor [prohibited on the Sabbath] are forty less one [M. 7:2A]. *And we reflected on that statement: What need do I have for the enumeration?* And said R. Yohanan, "If someone did all of them in a single spell of inadvertence, he is liable on each and every count." *Now how are we going to find such a case? Well, if it involves a deliberate violation of the Sabbath, but inadvertence as to the various classifications of labor, then, from the perspective of R. Yohanan, who has said,* "So long as one's error concerns extirpation, even though he deliberately sinned in respect to a negative commandment [that would constitute inadvertence]," *you would find such a case, for instance, if he knew that it was Sabbath, which is subject to a negative commandment. But from the perspective of R. Simeon b. Laqish, who has said,* "To be subject to the category of inadvertence, one has to err both in respect to the negative commandment and in regard to the penalty of extirpation," *how did he know that it was the Sabbath?*

B. *He knew about the rule of not carrying things across the boundaries of private and public domain, in accord with the position of R. Aqiba [who maintains that that rule derives from the Torah].*

II.5 A. *Who is the Tannaite authority behind what our rabbis have taught on Tannaite authority:* If one was unaware of both this and that [that there is such a thing as the Sabbath and that this act of labor is forbidden on the Sabbath], that is a definition of an inadvertent sin of which the Torah speaks. If one was fully aware of this and of that, that is the definition of a deliberate action of which the Torah speaks. If one was unaware of the principle of the Sabbath but was fully informed as to the classifications of forbidden labor, or if he was uninformed of the classifications of forbidden labor but was fully informed about the Sabbath, or if he said, "I know that this act of labor is forbidden, but I don't know that on its account one is liable to an offering," or, "not liable" – he is liable?

B.   *In accord with whom? It is in accord with Munbaz.*

II.6 A.   Said Abbayye, "All concur in regard to an oath of utterance that one is not liable for an offering unless he is unaware that such an oath is forbidden." [Freedman: The offender must have forgotten his oath at the time of breaking it, so he is unaware that his action is forbidden by an oath.]

B.   All concur? *Who could that be?*

C.   It's R. Yohanan.

D.   *But that's self-evident! For when did R. Yohanan say otherwise? It is in a case in which the penalty of extirpation is invoked. But in the case of an oath of utterance, the penalty of extirpation doesn't pertain, so he did not take that view!*

E.   *Not at all, not at all! For it might have entered your mind that, since liability to an offering is an innovation here, for we don't find in the entire Torah that for violating a negative commandment one has to bring an offering, but here one does, then, even if he is unaware of the liability to an offering, he would have to bring an offering nonetheless.* [69B] *So we are informed that that is not the case.*

F.   *An objection was raised:* [With reference to the formulation, "Whatever a man may utter in an oath": this excludes one who is subject to constraint and not one who is forced to take the oath. He is not liable if he violates the imposed oath,] for what sort of inadvertent transgression of a rash oath framed concerning the past would someone be liable? [If the man knew at the time of taking the oath that he was swearing falsely, it is deliberate violation of the oath; if he did not, then, concerning the past, this is an inadvertent violation of the law of taking oaths!] It would involve one who says, "I know that this oath is binding, but I do not know whether or not one is liable to present an offering on that account." [Silverstone: Although it is a willful transgression, it is counted as unwitting, because he did not know about liability to the offering.]

G. *In accord with what authority is that formulation of matters?*

H. *It is in accord with Munbaz [Monobases],* [who has said, "Action taken in inadvertent ignorance of liability to an offering is classified as inadvertence."]

II.7 A. And said Abbayye, "All agree in the matter of heave-offering, that one is liable to the penalty of the added fifth in making restoration only if he is aware of the prohibition [that a nonpriest may not eat food in that category; he must be unaware that it is heave-offering but must suppose it is common food]."

B. All concur? *Who could that be?*

C. It's R. Yohanan.

D. *But that's self-evident! For when did R. Yohanan say otherwise? It is in a case in which the penalty of extirpation is invoked. But in the case of an oath of utterance, the penalty of extirpation doesn't pertain, so he did not take that view!*

E. *Not at all, not at all! For it might have entered your mind that death stands in stead of extirpation, so if one is ignorant of the death penalty, he is culpable; so we are informed to the contrary.*

F. Raba said, "The death penalty stands in the place of extirpation, and the added fifth stands in the place of an offering."

II.8 A. Said R. Huna, "If someone was going along the way or in the wilderness and doesn't know

which day is the Sabbath, he
counts six days and then observes
one day."

B.   Hiyya bar Rab says "He observes
one day and then counts six
days."

C.   *So what can possibly be at issue
between them?*

D.   *One authority enumerates in accord*
with the creation of the world, *the
other counts in accord* with the
creation of the first man [his first
complete day was the Sabbath
(Freedman)].

E.   *An objection was raised:* If someone
was going along the road and
doesn't know when is the
Sabbath, he keeps one day for six.
Now doesn't this mean, he counts
six days and observes one?

F.   No, he observes one day and
counts six.

G.   *If so, rather than framing matters as,*
he keeps one day for six, *the
passage should say,* he keeps one
day and counts six.   *And
furthermore, it has been taught on
Tannaite authority:* If someone was
going along the way or in the
wilderness and doesn't know
which day is the Sabbath, he
counts six days and then observes
one day.   *That refutes Hiyya bar
Rab.*

H.   *Sure does.*

II.9   A.   Said Raba, "Every day he
prepares enough food for that
day, *except on that day [which is the
Sabbath by his reckoning]."*

B.   *So on that day is he supposed to drop
dead?*

C.   *He prepares double the prior day.*

D.   *But maybe the preceding day was the
Sabbath!*

E.   Rather: "Every day he prepares
enough food for that day, *even on
that day [which is the Sabbath by his
reckoning]."*

F.   *Then as to that day that is the
Sabbath by his reckoning, how does
he accord it recognition?*

G. *By reciting the Sanctification of the Day and the Prayer of Separation [of that day from the rest of the week].*

II.10 A. Said Raba, "If [on the day that he discovered he has forgotten when it is the Sabbath, he nonetheless remembers how many days it is since he set out (Freedman)] he recognizes the temporal relationship to the day he departed, he may work the whole of that day [Freedman: on the seventh day after he set out, without any restrictions, since he certainly didn't commence his journey on the Sabbath]."

B. *Big deal!*

C. *What might you have imagined? Since he didn't depart on the Sabbath, he also didn't leave on a Friday either, so even if this man started out on Thursday, he should be permitted to work on two whole days. So we are informed that sometimes someone may have a chance to travel in a caravan and so happen to start out even on a Friday.*

III.1 A. Whoever forgets the basic principle of the Sabbath and performed many acts of labor on many different Sabbath days is liable only for a single sin-offering:

B. *How on the basis of Scripture do we know this fact?*

IV.1 A. He who knows that it is the Sabbath and performed many acts of labor on many different Sabbaths...:

B. *[70A] How does the first clause differ from the second?*

V.1 A. ...is liable for the violation of each and every generative category of labor:

B. *How on the basis of Scripture do we know that various types of labor are treated as distinct categories for the present purpose?*

The issue announced earlier recurs now in a different setting; the concern is the same, that is, differentiating among classifications of forgetfulness, a refinement of the fundamental question announced above.

V.4   A.   Asked Raba of R. Nahman, "If one is responsible for forgetting the principle of both [the Sabbath as a day on which labor is prohibited, and also that the given act of labor is prohibited on the Sabbath], what is the law?"

       B.   He said to him, "Lo, he is subject to a spell of inadvertence with respect to the Sabbath, so he is liable on only a single count."

       C.   "To the contrary! Lo, he is subject to inadvertence in respect to diverse generative acts of labor, so he is responsible on each count!"

       D.   *Rather, said R. Ashi, "We examine the case to see:* If he stops the work because of the Sabbath, he was unaware of the fact of the Sabbath and is liable on only one count; if he stops work on account of the various acts of labor, he was inadvertent as to the acts of labor and is liable on each count."

       E.   Said Rabina to R. Ashi, "Well, would he desist from labor on the Sabbath for any reason other than the prohibition pertaining to the acts of labor that he is performing, but would he desist from the prohibited acts of labor for any reason other than the Sabbath? So it really makes no difference."

V.5   A.   *We have learned in the Mishnah:* The generative categories of acts of labor [prohibited on the Sabbath] are forty less one [M. 7:2A].

       B.   *And we reflected on that statement: What need do I have for the enumeration?*

       C.   And said R. Yohanan, "If someone did all of them in a single spell of inadvertence, he is liable on each and every count."

D. *Now that poses no problem if you hold that one who is unaware of both is liable for each count on its own; then there is no problem.* [Freedman: If he is ignorant of all the forbidden labors of the Sabbath, the Sabbath is exactly the same as any other day to him, and he may be regarded as unaware of both.] *But if you hold that* one who is subject to unawareness of the principle of the Sabbath is liable on only a single count, *then how are you going to find such a case at all? If it involves a deliberate violation of the Sabbath, but inadvertence as to the various classifications of labor, then, from the perspective of R. Yohanan, who has said,* "So long as one's error concerns extirpation, even though he deliberately sinned in respect to a negative commandment [that would constitute inadvertence]," *you would find such a case, for instance, if he knew that it was Sabbath, which is subject to a negative commandment. But from the perspective of R. Simeon b. Laqish, who has said,* "To be subject to the category of inadvertence, one has to err both in respect to the negative commandment and in regard to the penalty of extirpation," *how did he know that it was the Sabbath?*

E. *He knew about the rule of not carrying things across the boundaries of private and public domain, in accord with the position of R. Aqiba [who maintains that that rule derives from the Torah].*

V.6 A. Said Raba, "If one reaped and ground grain to the volume of a dried fig, in a spell of unawareness of the Sabbath but of awareness as to the forbidden acts of labor [and is liable on a single count], and he again reaped and ground grain to the volume of a dried fig knowing that it was the Sabbath but unaware of the prohibition as to the various acts of labor [Freedman: he was told it was the Sabbath but forgot these acts are forbidden thereon; in this case he is culpable on two counts], and then he was informed about the matter of the reaping and grinding in unawareness of the Sabbath but was aware of the acts of labor [Freedman: so he set aside a sin-offering on account of both acts of labor, before having learned of his second series of offenses], and then he was informed of the reaping and grinding performed when aware of the Sabbath but unaware in regard to the labors, the atonement for [71A] the first act of reaping involves atonement for the second, and atonement for the first act of grinding involves atonement for the second. [Freedman: This is in respect to expiation; the sacrifice for his first two acts of reaping and grinding is an atonement for his second two acts, since all were performed in one state of unawareness, without any information in the interval, notwithstanding that his first unawareness differed in kind from his second unawareness.] But if he was first informed about the reaping performed when he was aware of the Sabbath but unaware of the forbidden labor, then atonement for this second reaping involves atonement for the first reaping and its accompanying grinding. [Freedman: When he makes atonement for his second reaping, he automatically makes atonement for the first as well, and since his first reaping and grinding only necessitate one sacrifice, his first grinding, too, is atoned for thereby.] But the corresponding grinding [the second one] stands as before. [Freedman: It is unatoned for until another sacrifice is brought.]"

B. Abbayye said, "Atonement for the first act of grinding involves atonement for the second as well; the classification, grinding, remains one and the same." [Freedman: All acts of grinding made in one state of unawareness are covered by this sacrifice, though it is not primarily offered on account of grinding at all.]

C. *But does Raba concur in the theory that atonement for one thing involves atonement for another as well? And lo, it has been stated:*

D. If one ate two olive's bulks of forbidden fat in a single spell of inadvertence and he was informed concerning one of them, and then he went and ate an olive's bulk of forbidden fat during the spell of inadvertence covering the second –

E. Said Raba, "If he brought an offering covering the first action, both the first and the second acts are atoned for, but the third is not atoned for. If he brought an offering for the third, the third and second are atoned for, but the first is not atoned for. If he brought an offering for the second act, all of them are atoned for." [Freedman: Since both the first and the third were eaten in the state of unawareness of the second, all are covered; but the first two rulings show he rejects the theory that atonement for one thing involves atonement for another as well.]

F. Abbayye said, "Even if he brought one offering for all of them, all of them are atoned for."

G. *After he heard what Abbayye said, it struck him as reasonable.*

H. *If so, then in the case of grinding as
    well, the same should apply to the
    grinding.*
I. *While he accepts the theory of direct
    involvement of atonement of one
    thing for something else, he doesn't
    accept the theory of indirect
    involvement.* [Freedman: Thus the
    first act of grinding is atoned for
    only because it is involved in the
    atonement for reaping; hence this
    in turn cannot involve the second
    act of grinding.]

V.7 A. *A matter that was self-evident to
         Abbayye and Raba was found a
         problem by R. Zira. For R. Zira
         raised this question of R. Assi, and
         some say, R. Jeremiah asked R. Zira,*
         "If one reaped or ground grain of
         the quantity of half a dried fig in
         unawareness of the Sabbath but
         full awareness of the prohibition
         of labor, and again reaped and
         ground grain of the same volume
         in awareness of the prohibition of
         the Sabbath but unaware of the
         prohibition of these particular
         acts of labor, can they be
         combined?"   [The requisite
         volume is made up only if we
         combine the two quite distinct
         classes of action.]
     B. He said to him, "So far as sin-
         offerings are concerned, they
         form distinct categories and do
         not combine." [Freedman: Had
         each reaping been sufficient to
         entail a sin-offering, a sacrifice for
         one would not make atonement
         for the other; he differs from
         Abbayye and Raba.]
     C. *Well, then, is it the fact that in any
         case in which actions are distinct as
         to sin-offerings to be presented in
         atonement, do these actions not
         combine so as to form the requisite
         volume to impose liability? And
         have we not learned in the Mishnah:*
         [If] he ate [forbidden] fat and
         [again ate] fat in a single spell of
         inadvertence, he is liable only

for a single sin-offering. [If] he ate forbidden fat and blood and remnant and refuse [of an offering] in a single spell of inadvertence, he is liable for each and every one of them. This rule is more strict in the case of many kinds [of forbidden food] than of one kind. And more strict is the rule in [the case of] one kind than in many kinds: For if he ate a half-olive's bulk and went and ate a half-olive's bulk of a single kind, he is liable. [But if he ate two half-olive's bulks] of two [different] kinds, he is exempt [M. Ker. 3:2A-F]? *And we reflected on this matter: Was it necessary to specify the detail of ...of a single kind, he is liable? And said R. Simeon b. Laqish in the name of Bar Teutani, "Here with what sort of case do we deal? With a case in which one ate two portions of forbidden fat out of two distinct dishes, and the rule accords with R. Joshua, who maintains that if we deal with separate dishes, then there is a* distinction to be drawn with regard to the offerings involved therein. *What might you have said here? The statement of R. Joshua does not distinguish between a result that is lenient and one that is strict? So here we are informed that one is liable, and it follows, he has made his statement when it yields a more strict ruling, but he has not made his statement when it yields a more lenient ruling." Now here is a case in which they are distinct as to the requirement of bringing sin-offerings, and yet they do join together!*

D. *He said to him, "The master repeats that conception with respect to the opening clause, so it is difficult for you [since it has to be explained as dealing with two distinct tureens]. But we repeat it in the context of the* *second clause, and to us it poses no problem. Thus: Was it necessary to specify the detail of ...*of a single kind, he is liable? *And said R. Simeon b. Laqish in the name of Bar Teutani, "Here with what sort of case do we deal? With a case in which one ate two portions of forbidden fat out of two distinct dishes, and the rule accords with R. Joshua, who maintains that* if we deal with separate dishes, then there is a distinction to be drawn with regard to the offerings involved therein. *What might you have said here? The statement of R. Joshua does not distinguish between a result that is lenient and one that is strict? Now, since the second clause speaks of one kind of commodity and two dishes,* [71B] *it follows that the first clause speaks of one kind of food and one dish. But if the first clause addresses one kind of food and one dish, then why bother to specify the rule, which is self-evident!"*

E. *Said R. Huna, "Here with what situation do we deal? A case in which there was awareness between the two acts of eating, and it represents the position of* Rabban Gamaliel, who said, 'If one is aware of half of the requisite measure only, that is null.'" [Freedman: It does not separate two acts of eating, when in each case only half the standard quantity to create liability is consumed.]

V.8   A. *It has been stated:* If one ate two olive's bulks of forbidden fat in a single spell of inadvertence, and he became aware of the first and then again he became aware of the second –

B. R. Yohanan said, "He is liable on two counts."

C. R. Simeon b. Laqish said, "He is liable on only one count."

D. R. Yohanan said, "He is liable for the second, on the basis of the phrase, 'for his sin he shall bring a sacrifice' (Lev. 4:35)."

E. R. Simeon b. Laqish said, "He is not liable for the second: 'of his sin...and he shall be forgiven.'" [Freedman: Even if he offers a sacrifice for part of his sin only, he is forgiven for the whole].

F. *But from R. Simeon b. Laqish's perspective, isn't it written, "for his sin he shall bring a sacrifice"?*

G. *That pertains after atonement.* [Freedman: If he offends a second time after having atoned for the first, he must make atonement again.]

H. *But from R. Yohanan's perspective, isn't it written, "of his sin...and he shall be forgiven"?*

I. *Here with what situation do we deal? A case in which he ate an olive and a half's bulk of forbidden fat, was informed about having eaten an olive's bulk of the same, then ate a half olive's bulk in the spell of inadvertence concerning the second half of the first volume. You might say that these two halves combine. So the verse cited by R. Simeon b. Laqish shows that that is not the case.*

V.9 A. *Said Rabina to R. Ashi, "[Here are two possibilities of what is at issue. The first is,] they disagree in a case in which the eating of the second piece became known to the sinner before he had designated an animal for a sin-offering for the first. In that case, this is what is at issue: The one authority maintains, spells of inadvertence may be subdivided* [Freedman: the knowledge first obtained concerning one piece divides this piece from the second, necessitating an offering for each], *and the other holds, only the distinctions between the designations for particular purposes of animals for sin-offerings themselves are made* [Freedman: and since a sacrifice was not designated until he learned of the

second piece, it atones for both].
*But as to the situation prevailing
after the designation of an animal as
a sin-offering for the first of the two
actions in inadvertence, R. Simeon b.
Laqish would concede to R. Yohanan
that he is liable for two animal-
offerings. Or perhaps, this is what is
at issue: They differ where the facts of
the matter became known to the
sinner after the act of designating a
beast as a sin-offering had taken
place. This is then what is at issue
between them: The one master holds,
the designation of beasts for offerings
is subject to division, while the other
maintains, only the acts of atonement
are subject to division. But if the
sinner had learned about eating the
second piece in what had been a spell
of inadvertence before he had set
apart an animal as a sacrifice on
account of the first piece, R. Yohanan
would concede to R. Simeon b. Laqish
that he is liable for only a single
animal-offering. Or perhaps they
differ in both cases?"*

B.   *He said to him, "It stands to reason
that they differ in both cases. For if it
should enter your mind that they
differ concerning the rule governing
the designation of the offering, but as
to the situation that prevails after the
designation of the offering, R. Simeon
b. Laqish concedes to R. Yohanan
that the man under the specified
conditions now would be liable for
two animal-offerings, then, instead of
reading the cited verse to refer to the
period after atonement has been
attained through the offering itself,
let him interpret it to refer to the rule
that pertains merely after the
designation of the animal for the
offering but prior to the actual
offering up of the beast itself. And if
they differ concerning the situation
after the designation of the beast,
though before the designation of the
beast R. Yohanan agrees with R.
Simeon b. Laqish, that he is liable for*

*only one animal-offering, then,
instead of reading the cited verse to
refer to one who ate as much as an
olive and a half's bulk of forbidden
fat, let him relate it to the situation
that would prevail if the man had
become aware of eating the second bit
of forbidden fat prior to designating
the beast. And if you should want to
propose that that itself is subject to
doubt and is set forth merely as a
hypothetical possibility, then how can
R. Yohanan interpret the verse? He
could read it as referring to one who
ate the bulk of an olive and a half.
And if you assume that they differ on
the situation prevailing after the
designation of the beast for the
offering, how can R. Simeon b.
Laqish interpret the verse? It would
refer to the situation prevailing after
atonement [the initial verse having
been offered up]."*

V.10 A. *Said Ulla, "From the perspective of
him who has said, 'The obligation to
present a guilt-offering for certainly
having incurred guilt does not
require that one have known about
the sin that he has committed at the
outset of the action [but only at the
end of the process of sinning],'* [72A]
it would follow that, if one had
sexual relations five times with a
betrothed handmaid, doing so
unwittingly [not knowing her
status] [in violation of Lev. 19:21,
which imposes the requirement of
a guilt-offering in such a
situation, the woman being
betrothed to someone else], [and
between each action, he was
informed of his prior offense, but
he forgot and went and did it
again], he would be obligated to
present only a single guilt-
offering." [Freedman: Since
knowledge of guilt is not
required, the knowledge that he
does possess is insufficient to
separate his actions and
necessitate a sacrifice for each.

But on the view that previous knowledge is essential for a guilt-offering, the matter will be disputed by Yohanan and Simeon b. Laqish, as before.]

B. *Objected R. Hamnuna: "Then what about the following case:* If he had sexual relations and then again went and had sexual relations, and designated an animal for an offering, and then said, 'Wait for me while I have sexual relations yet again,' [Freedman: so that the offering may atone for both actions?] *in such a case would he still be liable for only a single offering, too? [Surely not!]"*

C. *He said to him "But do you speak of a deed that is done after the designation of an animal for an offering? For such a situation I did not present my ruling."* [Freedman: This certainly marks off the prior offenses from the later one and a sacrifice is required to cover each.]

D. *When R. Dimi came, he said, "From the perspective of him who has said, 'The obligation to present a guilt-offering for certainly having incurred guilt does require that one have known about the sin that he has committed at the outset of the action [and not only at the end of the process of sinning],' it would follow that,* if one had sexual relations five times with a betrothed handmaid, doing so unwittingly [not knowing her status] [in violation of Lev. 19:21, which imposes the requirement of a guilt-offering in such a situation, the woman being betrothed to someone else], [and between each action, he was informed of his prior offense, but he forgot and went and did it again], he would be obligated to present an offering for each such action."

E. *Said to him Abbayye, "But lo, with reference to the sacrifice of a sin-*

offering, in which we require that the sinner have had knowledge of the prohibited character of the act prior to the sin [but have done the act itself in inadvertence], R. Yohanan and R. Simeon b. Laqish differed on that very matter" [and the same principle applies here, so how make such a statement (Freedman)].

F. *He shut up.*

G. *He said to him, "But perhaps you have made your statement with reference to a deed that took place after the designation of the animal for the sin-offering, and in line with the position of R. Hamnuna?"* [Freedman: But Yohanan and Simeon b. Laqish differ about a case in which all the actions took place prior to the designation of the animal.]

H. *He said to him, "Yup."*

V.11 A. *When Rabin came,* he said, "All parties concur in the case of the betrothed bondmaid [in one matter], and all parties concur in the case of the betrothed bondmaid [in yet another matter]. But there is a dispute concerning the betrothed bondmaid [in yet a third matter].

B. "All parties concur in the case of the betrothed bondmaid [in one matter]: *one is liable on only one count, in accord with the position of Ulla.*

C. "And all parties concur in the case of the betrothed bondmaid [in yet another matter]: *that one is liable on each count, in accord with R. Hamnuna.*

D. "But there is a dispute concerning the betrothed bondmaid [in yet a third matter]: *within the premise of him who says that the obligation to present a guilt-offering for certainly having incurred guilt does require that one have known about the sin that he has committed at the outset of the action [and not only at the end of*

the process of sinning], there is the
dispute between R. Yohanan and R.
Simeon b. Laqish."

V.12   A.   It has been stated:

B.   [72B] If one intended to raise up
what was plucked from the
ground but instead cut what was
attached to the ground, he is
exempt. [*What is the operative
consideration? It is because lo, he
did not have the intention of cutting
anything at all.*]

C.   If, however, he intended to cut
what was detached from the
ground but instead cut what was
attached to the ground,

D.   Abbayye said, "He is liable."

E.   Raba said, "He is exempt, *for lo, he
had no intention of cutting that
which was forbidden to be cut.*"

F.   Abbayye said, "He is liable, *for lo,
he had the intention in any event to
cut something.*"

G.   *Said Raba, "On what basis do I make
that statement? For it has been
stated on Tannaite authority:* There
is a more strict rule that applies to
the Sabbath than applies to other
religious duties, and there is a
more strict rule that applies to
other religious duties that does
not apply to the Sabbath. For in
the case of the Sabbath, if one has
done two forbidden actions in a
single spell of inadvertence, he is
liable for each one separately, a
rule that does not apply to other
religious duties. The more strict
rule applying to other religious
duties is that if one has performed
a forbidden action inadvertently,
without prior intention, he is
liable, which is not the rule for the
Sabbath."

V.13   A.   A master has said, "There is a
more strict rule that applies to the
Sabbath than applies to other
religious duties, and there is a
more strict rule that applies to
other religious duties that does
not apply to the Sabbath. For in

the case of the Sabbath, if one has done two forbidden actions in a single spell of inadvertence, he is liable for each one separately, a rule that does not apply to other religious duties" –

B. *How shall we illustrate that statement? If one should propose that a person did an act of reaping and one of grinding, then, in respect to other religious duties, it would be similar to eating both forbidden fat and blood. In such a case, one is liable on two counts, just as here he is liable on two counts.*

C. *Then with respect to other religious duties, what sort of case would yield the result that one is liable on only a single count?*

D. *If one ate forbidden fat and then more forbidden fat. In a parallel case involving the Sabbath it would be if one performed an act of reaping and then another act of reaping. In that case, however, in the one context [eating forbidden fat] he is liable on only one count, and in the other context, he also is liable on only one count.*

E. *The reference [to "other religious duties"] is specifically to idolatry, and it accords with what R. Ammi said. For* R. Ammi said, "If one has sacrificed, offered incense, and poured out a libation, all in a single spell of inadvertence, he is liable on only a single count," [while in the case of the Sabbath, as we see, one is liable on more than a single count].

F. *Then how have you interpreted the case? With respect only to idolatry? But you cannot assign the statement only to idolatry, for the end of the same sentence reads:* "The more strict rule applying to other religious duties is that, if one has performed a forbidden action inadvertently, without prior intention, he is liable, which is not the rule for the Sabbath." *Now what, in reference to idolatry, can possibly fall into the category of an action that has been performed inadvertently, without intention? If one supposed that a temple of an idol was a synagogue and prostrated himself to it, lo, his heart was directed to heaven. Rather, he saw a statue of a man and bowed to it. If, then, he accepted it as a god, what he did was done deliberately. If he did not accept it as a god, then what he did was null. Rather, what he did was out of love and awe.*

G. *That poses no problems to Abbayye, who has said that, in such a case, he is liable. But as to the view of Raba, who has said that he is exempt, what is there to be said?*

H. Rather, it is one who has the view that such an action is permitted. [Freedman, *Sanhedrin*, p. 425, n. 3: And since he has never known of any prohibition, it is not regarded as unwitting, but as unintentional too.]

I. *Then this is what is not the case for the Sabbath, for, in a similar circumstance, one would not be liable at all.*

J. *[But surely that conclusion is not possible], for when Raba poses his question to R. Nahman as to the rule governing a single spell of inadvertence in each of the two contexts, it is only whether one is liable on one count or on two counts. But it never entered his mind that one would be entirely exempt from all liability.*

K. *[73A] What difficulty is at hand? Perhaps one may say to you indeed that the first clause speaks of idolatry and the remainder of other religious duties.*

L. *The case of inadvertence, without intention — what would be such a case? It would be one in which one had the view that [when he found there was forbidden fat in his mouth], he thought that it was permitted fat and swallowed it [rather than spitting it out], a rule which, in a parallel case on the Sabbath, would produce the ruling of non-liability. [How so?] If one had the intention of lifting up something that was already harvested but turned out to cut something yet attached to the ground, he is exempt.*

M. *And from Abbayye's viewpoint, what would be an unwitting and unintentional sin? If he thinks that the forbidden fat is spit and swallows it. The meaning of "which is not the case for the Sabbath," in which instance, he would be exempt, would involve, by analogy,* one who intended to lift something detached but cut something attached to the soil; he is not liable. But if he intended to cut something detached and cut something attached to the soil, he is liable. [Freedman, *Sanhedrin*, p. 426, n. 2: Cutting or tearing out anything growing in the earth is a forbidden labor on the Sabbath. His offense was both unwitting and unintentional for (i) he had no intention of tearing out anything and (ii) he did not know that this was growing in the soil. Now, had he known that it was growing in the soil and deliberately uprooted it in ignorance of the forbidden nature of that action, his offense would have been unwitting but intentional. By analogy, had he intended to eat the melted fat, thinking that it was permitted, his offense would be regarded as unwitting but intentional. Since, however, he did not intend eating it at all, but accidently swallowed it, thinking at the same time that it was spittle, his offense was both unwitting and unintentional.]

V.14 A. *It has been stated:*

B. If the man intended to throw the stone two cubits and it fell four cubits away –

C. Raba said, "He is exempt."

D. Abbayye said, "He is liable."

E. Raba said, "He is exempt, *for lo, he didn't intend to toss the object the four cubits [that would incur liability].*"

F. Abbayye said, "He is liable, *for lo, he had every intention of throwing the object in general.*"

V.15 A. If he thought it was private domain but it turned out to be public domain,

B. Raba said, "He is exempt."

C. Abbayye said, "He is liable."

D. Raba said, "He is exempt, *for lo, he didn't intend to toss the object in a forbidden manner.*"

E. Abbayye said, "He is liable, *for lo, he had every intention of throwing the object in general.*"

V.16 A. *And it was necessary to give us the three disputes [these two plus the one we have just analyzed]. For had we been informed only of the initial one, we might have supposed that it was in that case in particular that Raba took the position that he did, since, after all, the man never intended to eat a piece of fat that was forbidden, but here, he did intend to throw the object for two cubits and he threw it for four, and it would not have been possible to throw it for four if he first didn't throw it for the two, so I might have supposed that he concurs with Abbayye. And had we been informed of the present instance, I might have supposed that here alone Raba takes the position that he does, since the man didn't intend to throw the object for four cubits, but if he thought it was private domain but it turned out to be public domain, since the man at any rate intended to throw it for four cubits, I might have supposed that he concurs with Abbayye. So the several examples of the dispute are required.*

V.17   A.   *We have learned in the Mishnah:*
The generative categories of acts of labor [prohibited on the Sabbath] are forty less one [M. 7:2A]. *And we reflected on that statement: What need do I have for the enumeration?* And said R. Yohanan, "If someone did all of them in a single spell of inadvertence, he is liable on each and every count."

   B.   *Now there is no problem for Abbayye, who has held that in a case such as this, one is liable. You would find such a case, for instance, if the man knew about the prohibition of the Sabbath and he knew about the prohibition of such actions, but did not know the rules governing the requisite volume that would incur liability. But from Raba's perspective, who maintains that he would be exempt, how can you find such a case?*

   C.   *It would involve a case in which he knew about the Sabbath but didn't know about the fact that the acts of labor were forbidden.*

   D.   *Well, that would pose no problem if he concurred with R. Yohanan, who said, "Since one has made an action inadvertently in a deed the penalty of which is extirpation, even though he deliberately violated a negative commandment, he is liable. Then you would find such a case when he knew that the labors were forbidden on the Sabbath by reason of a negative commandment. But if he concurred with R. Simeon b. Laqish, who maintains that one is liable only if he is in error as to the negative commandment and also as to the penalty of extirpation, then how in the stated case did he know about the Sabbath at all?*

   E.   *What he knew concerned the law of boundaries not to be transgressed, in accord with the position of R. Aqiba.*

7:2

A. The generative categories of acts of labor [prohibited on the Sabbath] are forty less one:

B. (1) he who sows, (2) ploughs, (3) reaps, (4) binds sheaves, (5) threshes, (6) winnows, (7) selects [fit from unfit produce or crops], (8) grinds, (9) sifts, (10) kneads, (11) bakes;

C. (12) he who shears wool, (13) washes it, (14) beats it, (15) dyes it;

D. (16) spins, (17) weaves,

E. (18) makes two loops, (19) weaves two threads, (20) separates two threads;

F   (21) ties, (22) unties,

G. (23) sews two stitches, (24) tears in order to sew two stitches;

H. (25) he who traps a deer, (26) slaughters it, (27) flays it, (28) salts it, (29) cures its hide, (30) scrapes it, and (31) cuts it up;

I. (32) he who writes two letters, (33) erases two letters in order to write two letters;

J. (34) he who builds, (35) tears down;

K. (36) he who puts out a fire, (37) kindles a fire;

L. (38) he who hits with a hammer; (39) he who transports an object from one domain to another –

M. lo, these are the forty generative acts of labor less one.

I.1 A. [73 B] *What's the point of the enumeration?*

     B. Said R. Yohanan, "To teach that if someone does them all in a single spell of inadvertence, he still is liable on each count separately."

II.1 A. He who sows and ploughs:

      B. *So let's examine the matter: Since ploughing is done before sowing, why shouldn't the Tannaite framer of the passage first make reference to ploughing, then to sowing?*

      C. *The Tannaite authority addresses the case of the Land of Israel, where they first sow and then plough.*

II.2 A. *A Tannaite statement:* Sowing, pruning, planting, bending a shoot, and drafting all form a single classification of labor.

      B. *So of what does the statement inform us?*

      C. *Thus he informs us that* one who does many acts of labor within a single classification of labor is liable on only a single count.

II.3 A. Said R. Abba said R. Hiyya bar Ashi said R. Ammi, "He who prunes is liable on the count of planting, and he who plants, bends the vine, or grafts is liable on the count of sowing."

B. *On account of sowing but not planting?*

C. *Say:* Also on the count of planting.

II.4 A. **Said R. Kahana, "If one pruned his** tree but requires the wood for fuel, he is liable on two counts, one on the count of planting, the other on the count of harvesting."

II.5 A. *Said R. Joseph, "One who cuts hay is liable on two counts, one for reaping, the other for planting."*

II.6 A. *Said Abbayye, "One who trims beets in the earth is liable on two counts: reaping and planting."*

III.1 A. Ploughs:

B. *A Tannaite statement:* Ploughing, digging, and trench making form a single classification of work.

III.2 A. Said R. Sheshet, "If someone had a mound of dirt and removes it, if he does this in the house, he is liable on the count of building; if he does this in the field, he is liable on the count of ploughing."

IV.1 A. Reaps:

B. *A Tannaite statement:* Reaping, vintaging, date gathering, olive collecting, fig gathering all form a single classification of labor.

IV.2 A. *Said R. Pappa, "One who throws a piece of dirt at a palm tree to bring down dates is liable on two counts: detaching and stripping."*

B. R. Ashi said, "This is not an ordinary manner of detaching nor is it an ordinary manner of stripping" [so he is not liable on either count].

V.1 A. Binds sheaves:

B. *Said Raba, "One who collects salt from a salt pan is liable on the count of binding sheaves."*

C. Abbayye said, "Binding sheaves is a classification of labor that applies only to what grows from the ground."

VI.1 A. Threshes:

B.   *A Tannaite statement:* Threshing,
     beating flax in the stalks, beating
     cotton   all   form   a   single
     classification of labor.

What follows asks about the differentiation of like things and
introduces an extrinsic principle of differentiation. This represents an
example of the notion that taxonomic classification rests not only on the
traits of things, as generally is the theory of the Mishnah, but also, or
only, on the taxic indicators supplied by Scripture itself. But it seems to
me difficult to find many sustained exegetical exercises that are
provoked by that principle.

VII.1   A.   **Winnows, selects [fit from unfit
             produce or crops], grinds, sifts:**
        B.   *But the acts of winnowing, selecting,
             and sifting are all the same thing
             anyhow! [How can one be liable on
             each count?]*
        C.   *Both Abbayye and Raba said, "Any
             type of labor that was performed in
             connection with setting up the
             tabernacle in the wilderness [74A],
             even though there may be acts of
             labor that bear likeness to one
             another, is regarded as a single
             classification of labor [and one would
             be liable on each count for several
             such otherwise comparable acts of
             labor]."*
        D.   *Well, then, why not enumerate
             pounding wheat as well [in a mortar,
             since pounding materials in a mortar
             was done to make dyes in the
             tabernacle's construction]?*
        E.   Said Abbayye, "It is because a
             poor man will eat his bread
             without pounding" [Freedman:
             hence it is omitted, for the
             Tannaite authority follows the
             general order of making bread,
             and bread for the poor is
             prepared with the husk of the
             wheat, but it is a primary labor
             forbidden on the Sabbath].
        F.   *Raba said, "Lo, who is the authority
             behind this passage? It is Rabbi, who
             has   said,* **The   generative
             categories of acts of labor
             [prohibited on the Sabbath] are**

       forty less one." [The actual number of classifications of labor derives from Scripture itself.]

    G. *Well, then, take away one of those and put in pounding?*

    H. *Rather, the answer of Abbayye clearly is correct.*

VII.2 A. *Our rabbis have taught on Tannaite authority:*

    B. [With reference to the forms of labor, **winnows, selects fit from unfit produce or crops**]: If before a person were various kinds of foods, he selects and eats what he wants, selects and leaves what he wants, but he must not make a selection and if he does, he is liable to present a sin-offering.

VII.3 A. *What in the world can that possibly mean?*

    B. *Said Ulla, "This is the sense of the statement:* He selects and eats what he wants for that day in particular, selects and leaves what he wants for that day in particular, but as to what is for the next day, he must not make a selection and if he does, he is liable to present a sin-offering."

    C. *Objected R. Hisda,* "So is it permitted to bake for use on that same day, is it permitted to cook for use on that same day?" [Freedman: Since you say that selecting for use on the next day entails a sin-offering, it is a forbidden labor in the full sense of the term and hence prohibited even if required for the same day.]

    D. Rather, said R. Hisda, "[*This is the sense of the statement:*]...he selects and eats less than the requisite quantity to involve liability, selects and leaves what he wants less than the requisite quantity to involve liability. But he should not select so much as the requisite quantity to involve liability, and if he selected the requisite volume, he then would be liable to a sin-offering."

E.   *Objected R. Joseph,* "So is it permitted to bake for use on that same day less than the requisite volume, [or is it permitted to cook for use on that same day less than the requisite volume]?"

F.   Rather, said R. Joseph, "[*This is the sense of the statement:*]...he selects and eats by hand, or selects and puts aside by hand; but he may not select with a basket or a dish, and if he does, he is not liable, though it is forbidden. He may not use a sieve or a basket sieve in making his selection, and, if he does so, he is liable to a sin-offering [being the usual mode of sifting and a primary form of labor]."

G.   *Objected R. Hamnuna,* "But then does the Tannaite formulation even mention a basket or a dish!?"

H.   Rather, said R. Hamnuna, "[*This is the sense of the statement:*]...he selects and eats: he eats what is edible from what is nonedible, selects and puts aside, taking the edible from the nonedible. But he may not select from the nonedible out of the edible, and if he does, he is liable to a sin-offering." [Freedman: The form is not the ordinary mode of sifting, the latter is.]

I.   *Objected Abbayye,* "But then does the Tannaite formulation even mention he eats what is edible from what is nonedible?"

J.   Rather, said Abbayye, "[*This is the sense of the statement:*]...he selects and eats right on the spot, he selects and leaves right on the spot, but on the same day he may not select for later eating, and if he does, he is regarded as though he selected to store away food and is liable to a sin-offering."

K.   *Rabbis stated this before Raba. He said to them, "Well said, Nahmani!"*

VII.4 A. If before a person were two kinds of food, and he selects and eats or selects and leaves over –

      B. *R. Ashi repeated,* "He is exempt."

      C. *R. Jeremiah of Difti repeated,* "He is liable."

      D. *R. Ashi repeated,* "He is exempt." *But lo, a Tannaite formulation has,* he is liable!

      E. *No problem, the one involves using a basket or a plate, the other, a sieve or a basket sieve.*

VII.5 A. *When R. Dimi came, he said,* "*It was the Sabbath for an address by R. Bibi, and R. Ammi and R. Assi came by. He tossed a basket of fruit before them [by the force of his gesture causing the leaves to fall from the fruit], but I don't know whether he did that because he maintained that* it is forbidden to pick out edible from nonedible food *or whether he wanted to give a generous portion.*"

VII.6 A. Hezekiah said, "He who picks lupines out of their husks is liable."

      B. *May one propose that Hezekiah takes the view,* it is forbidden to pick out edible from nonedible food?

VIII.1 A. Grinds:

      B. *Said R. Pappa,* "*One who cuts up beets very fine* is liable on the count of grinding."

      C. *Said R. Manasseh,* "*He who chops up chips for fuel* is liable on the count of grinding."

IX.1 A. Kneads and bakes:

      B. *Said R. Pappa,* "*The Tannaite before us has neglected the boiling of ingredients for dyeing [for example, for hangings and curtains], even though this took place in building the tabernacle, but treats nonetheless of baking [which didn't]!*"

IX.2 A. *Said R. Aha bar R. Avira,* "*Someone who throws a tent peg into a stove [for drying] is liable on the count of cooking.*"

      B. *Obviously!*

      C. *What might you have supposed? His intention was to harden the wood, so*

we are informed that the wood at first
softens and only then hardens.

IX.3   A.   Said Rabbah bar R. Huna, "One who
             boils pitch is liable on the count of
             cooking."
        B.   Obviously!
        C.   What might you have supposed?
             Since it hardens again, I might have
             imagined he isn't liable, so we are
             informed to the contrary.

IX.4   A.   Said Raba, "One who makes an
             earthenware barrel is liable on seven
             counts [to bring seven sin-offerings].
             He who makes an oven is liable on
             eight counts." [Freedman: The
             seven counts: the clods are
             crushed and powdered, which is
             grinding; the thick balls that don't
             powder well are removed, thus
             selecting; then it's sifted; the
             powder is mixed with water, thus
             kneading; the clay is smoothed,
             thus smoothing; the fire is lit in
             the kiln; the vessel is hardened,
             thus boiling. The eighth is that
             after the pot is hardened, a layer
             of loam is daubed on the inside to
             preserve the heat; this completes
             it and every special act needed to
             complete an article falls within
             "striking with a hammer." But a
             barrel doesn't need a special act
             of labor to complete it.]

X.1   A.   He who shears wool and washes
             [bleaches] it:
        B.   Said Rabbah bar bar Hannah said
             R. Yohanan, "He who on the
             Sabbath spins wool from an
             animal's back is liable on three
             counts: one because of shearing,
             the second because of hackling,
             and the third because of
             spinning." [Freedman: Spinning
             directly from the animal covers
             these three types of labor.]

X.2   A.   Our rabbis have taught on Tannaite
             authority:
        B.   He who pulls a wing from a
             bird, trims it, and plucks the
             down, is liable for sin-offerings
             on three counts [T. Shab. 9:20A].

C. And said R. Simeon b. Laqish, "The liability as to pulling the wing is on the count of shearing; the liability for cutting is on the count of severing; and the liability for smoothing is on the count of scraping" [so plucking or tearing are the same as shearing].

XI.1 A. **Ties, unties:**

B. *So where was there the need for tying in the building of the tabernacle?*

C. Said Raba, "They tied the tent pegs."

D. But that was tying with the intent of untying later on!

XII.1 A. **Sews two stitches:**

B. *But these wouldn't last [two stitches by themselves will come out of the cloth, and work that does not produce a permanent result isn't punished].*

XIII.1 A. **Tears in order to sew two stitches:**

B. *So where was there the need for tearing in the building of the tabernacle?*

C. *Both Rabbah and R. Zira say,* [75A] "A curtain that suffered a moth hole was torn around the hole and resewn."

XIII.2 A. Said R. Zutra bar Tobiah said Rab, "He who pulls the thread of a seam on the Sabbath is liable to a sin-offering, and he who learns anything at all from a Magus is liable to the death penalty, and he who knows how to calculated the seasons and planets but doesn't do so – it is forbidden to talk to him."

XIII.3 A. *As to the Magi –*

B. *Rab and Samuel –*

C. *One said, "It is pure sorcery."*

D. *The other said, "It is blasphemy."*

XIII.4 A. Said R. Simeon b. Pazzi said R. Joshua b. Levi in the name of Bar Qappara, "Whoever knows how to calculate the seasons and planets but doesn't do so – concerning him Scripture says, 'But they regard not the work of the Lord, neither have they considered the works of his hands' (Isa. 5:12)."

XIV.1 A. **He who traps a deer:**

B. *Our rabbis have taught on Tannaite authority:*

C. **He who hunts purple fish and splits it open is liable on only a single count.**

D. **R. Judah says, "He is liable on two counts" [cf. T. Shab. 8:2C].**

E. For R. Judah says, "Crushing is classified in the category of threshing."

F. They said to him, "Crushing is not classified in the category of threshing."

XIV.2 A. *Said Raba, "What is the theory behind rabbis' ruling? They take the view that threshing applies only to what grows from the earth."*

XIV.3 A. *Well, anyhow, let him be held liable on the count of taking a life?*

B. Said R. Yohanan, "This refers to a case in which he crushes it when it is dead."

C. *Raba said, You may even say that it is crushed alive; as to the taking of life, it is merely incidental to his primary engagement."*

XV.1 A. **Slaughters it:**

B. *On what count is one who slaughters liable in respect to the Sabbath?*

C. Rab said, "On the count of dyeing" [for the blood of the cut throat dyes the flesh (Freedman)].

D. And Samuel said, "Because of the taking of life."

XVI.1 A. **Salts it, cures its hide:**

B. *Yeah, but salting and curing the hide are one and the same thing!*

C. *Both R. Yohanan and R. Simeon b. Laqish say, "Take out one of these and put in instead 'drawing a line' [before cutting]."*

XVI.2 A. *Said Rabbah bar R. Huna, "One who salts meat is liable on the count of tanning."*

B. Raba said, "The considering of tanning doesn't apply to what is eaten."

XVII.1 A. **Scrapes it, and cuts it up:**

B. Said R. Aha bar Hanina, "He who on the Sabbath smooths the ground between columns is liable on the count of scraping."

XVII.2 A. Said R. Hiyya bar Abba, "Three things did R. Assi tell me in the name of R. Joshua b. Levi: 'He who on the Sabbath planes the tops of beams is liable on the count of cutting [to measure]. He who puts a poultice evenly over a sore is liable on the count of scraping. He who chisels around a stone on the Sabbath is liable on the count of striking with a hammer.'"

XVIII.1 A. He who writes two letters:

B. *Our rabbis have taught on Tannaite authority:*

C. If one wrote a very large letter and the space of the letter is sufficient to write two ordinary letters, he is exempt from penalty on this count. If he erased one large letter and there is room on the spot for writing two ordinary letters, he is liable.

D. Said R. Menahem b. R. Yosé, "The rule covering erasing is more strict than the rule covering writing" [T. Shab. 11:9-11].

XIX.1 A. He who builds, tears down; he who puts out a fire, kindles a fire; he who hits with a hammer:

B. *Rabbah and R. Zira both say, "Any action that involves completing the process of manufacturing an object is liable on the count of hitting with a hammer."*

XX.1 A. Lo, these are the forty generative acts of labor less one:

B. These... *serve to exclude the position of R. Eleazar, who imposes liability for derivative classes of forbidden action when performed along with a generative class of action.*

XXI.1 A. Less one:

B. Less one... *serves to exclude the position of R. Judah, as has been taught on Tannaite authority: R. Judah adds [to the list of* generative classes of action] one who closes up a web and beats on the woof [to even it out].

C. They said to him, "Closing up the web is covered in the classification of stretching the threads; and beating on the woof is covered in the classification of weaving."

7:3

A. And a further governing rule did they state:

B. Whatever is suitable for storage, which people generally store in such quantity as one has taken out on the Sabbath –

C. he is liable to a sin-offering on its account.

D. And whatever is not suitable for storage, which people generally do not store in such quantity as one has taken out on the Sabbath –

E. only he is liable on its account who stores it away [and who then takes it out].

I.1 A. Whatever is suitable for storage, which people generally store in such quantity as one has taken out on the Sabbath:

B. *What class of things is excluded by the language,* Whatever is suitable for storage?

C. *R. Pappa said, "It excludes menstrual blood."*

D. Mar Uqba *said, "It excludes lumber from an asherah tree."*

The following raises a very interesting question, which is certainly subject to application to a variety of cases and problems. Do laws apply without regard to circumstance, or do we accommodate the rule to the situation? That issue may be expressed in the case of taking account of personal preference or attitude when we deal with a general rule, for example, on how much of a volume of a substance will be taken into account by a person, so that that volume involves liability in the present context. One person may take account of more, another of less, for example, a poor person may regard as useful a much smaller volume of a substance than a rich person.

I.2 A. *Said R. Yosé bar Hanina, "This rule is not in accord with R. Simeon. For were it in accord with R. Simeon, hasn't he said, 'All of these rules have been stated only relative to the condition of those who are* storing things'" [so that there is no fixed rule deriving from general practice, but we assess each situation in terms of the intent of him who is doing the storing; a rich person would store more, a poor person, less, each valuing things in his own terms (Freedman).]

II.1 A. And whatever is not suitable for storage, which people generally do not store in such quantity as one has taken out on the Sabbath – only he is liable on its account who stores it away [and who then takes it out]:

B. [76A] *Said R. Eleazar, "This does not accord with R. Simeon b. Eleazar, for it has been taught on Tannaite authority:* A governing principle did R. Simeon b. Eleazar state, 'In the case of anything that is not regarded as suitable for storage, the like of which in general people do not store away, but which a given individual has deemed fit for storage and has stored away, and which another party has come along and removed from storage and taken from one domain to another on the Sabbath – the party who moved the object across the line that separated the two domains has become liable by reason of the intentionality of the party who stored away this thing that is not ordinarily stored.'"

7:4A-D

A. He who takes out a quantity of (1) straw sufficient for a cow's mouthful; (2) pea stalks sufficient for a camel's mouthful; (3) ears of grain sufficient for a lamb's mouthful; (4) grass sufficient for a kid's mouthful; (5) garlic or onion leaves, ([if] fresh, a dried fig's bulk), [and if] dry, sufficient for a kid's mouthful –

B. [Supply: he is liable,]

C. and they do not join together with one another [to form a quantity sufficient for culpability],

D. because they are not subject to equivalent measures.

I.1   A. Pea stalks sufficient for a camel's mouthful:

      B. *What is the definition of pea stalks?*

      C. Said R. Judah, "The stalks of various kinds of legumes."

I.2   A. *When R. Dimi came,* he said, "He who carries out a cow's mouthful of straw for a camel –

      B. "R. Yohanan said, 'He is liable.'

      C. "R. Simeon b. Laqish said, 'He is exempt.'

II.1 A. Ears of grain sufficient for a lamb's mouthful:

      B. *But hasn't it been taught on Tannaite authority:* as much as a dried fig?

      C. *Both represent exactly the same volume.*

III.1 A. Garlic or onion leaves, ([if] fresh, a dried fig's bulk), [and if] dry, sufficient for a kid's mouthful – [Supply: he is liable,] and they do not join together with one another [to form a quantity sufficient for culpability], because they are not subject to equivalent measures:

      B. Said R. Yosé bar Hanina, "and they do not join together with one another [to form a quantity sufficient for culpability] in the case of a strict result, but they do do so in the case of a lenient result." [Freedman: The commodity whose standard is greater does not combine with that whose standard is lesser to make up that lesser quantity, but the latter does combine with the former to make up the greater quantity; that which requires a lesser quantity is naturally more stringent.]

7:4E-I

E. He who takes out foodstuffs [for a human being] in the volume of a dried fig is liable.

F. And they do join together with one another [to form a quantity sufficient for culpability],

G. because they are subject to equivalent measures,

H. except for their (1) husks, (2) kernels, (3) stalks, (4) coarse bran, and (5) fine bran.

I. R. Judah says, "Except for the husks of lentils, which are cooked with them."

I.1 A. [Except for their (1) husks, (2) kernels, (3) stalks, (4) coarse bran, and (5) fine bran:] *But don't the husks and coarse bran join together with grain or flour? Haven't we learned in the Mishnah:* Five-fourths [qab] of flour is subject to dough-offering [once made into dough]. [If] it [i.e., the flour] and its leaven, fine bran, and coarse bran [together comprise] five-fourths [qab, the whole] is subject [to dough-offering once made into dough] [M. Hal. 2:6A-B]?

B. Said Abbayye, "The reason is that a poor person eats bread baked out of unsifted dough" [Freedman: But with respect to the Sabbath, bread of better quality is required for liability to be incurred].

II.1 A. R. Judah says, "Except for the husks of lentils, which are cooked with them":

B. *Lentils, not beans?! And hasn't it been taught on Tannaite authority:* R. Judah says, "Excluding the shells of beans and of lentils"?

4

Bavli Shabbat
Chapter Eight

Folios 76B-82A

The remarks at the beginning of Chapter Three explain the work of this chapter as well. Readers not interested in a detailed survey are advised to turn directly to the concluding chapter.

8:1

A. He who takes out (1) wine – enough to mix a cup; (2) milk – enough for a gulp; (3) honey – enough to put on a sore; (4) oil – enough to anoint a small limb; (5) water – enough to rub off an eye salve; and (6) of all other liquids, a quarter-log; (7) and of all slops [refuse], a quarter-log.

B. R. Simeon says, "All of them are [subject to the measure of] a quarter-log. And they have stated all these measures only with reference to those who store them away."

    I.1 A. [He who takes out wine – enough to mix a cup:] *A Tannaite statement:* Enough to mix a generous cup.

          B. *So how much is* enough to mix a generous cup?

    I.2 A. Said R. Nahman said Rabbah bar Abbuha, "The cup used for the blessing [Grace after Meals] has to have a quarter of a quarter-log of raw wine, so that it may be mixed and add up to a quarter-log in all [full to the brim]."

          B. *Said Raba, "So, too, we* [77A] *have learned as a Mishnah statement:* He

who takes out wine – enough to
mix a cup. *And in that connection
it was taught as a Tannaite
statement:* Enough to mix a
generous cup. *At the end of the
same passage, by contrast, it is
taught as the Tannaite formulation:*
And of all other liquids, a
quarter-log."

I.3   A.   *A Tannaite statement:*

      B.   "As to congealed wine, the
requisite volume is an olive's
bulk," the words of R. Nathan
[T. Shab. 8:10C].

I.4   A.   Said R. Joseph, "R. Nathan and R.
Yosé b. R. Judah have said the
same thing.

      B.   *"R. Nathan – as we have just said.*

      C.   *"R. Yosé b. R. Judah: As has been
taught on Tannaite authority:* R.
Judah says, 'Six opinions of the
House of Shammai's more
lenient, and the House of
Hillel's more stringent, rulings:
The blood of carrion – the House
of Shammai declare it clean.
And the House of Hillel declare
it unclean' [M. Ed. 5:1A-D]. Said
R. Yosé b. R. Judah, 'Even when
they declared it to be unclean,
they declared unclean only that
volume of congealed blood that is
of the volume of a quarter-log,
since it can congeal to the volume
of an olive's bulk.'"

II.1   A.   Milk – enough for a gulp:

      B.   *The question was raised:* Is the
correct spelling of the word
"gulp" with an alef or an ayin?

II.2   A.   *The question was raised:* [77B] Is the
correct spelling of the word
kernel [at M. 7:4H: except for
their husks, kernels, stalks,
coarse bran, and fine bran] with
an alef or an ayin?

II.3   A.   Is the word 'omemot [alef] or
omemot ['ayin]?

II.4   A.   *The question was raised:* Is the
correct spelling of the word for
close [They do not close the eyes

of a corpse on the Sabbath (M. 23:5K)] with an alef or an ayin?

II.5　A. *Our rabbis have taught on Tannaite authority:*

　　　B. He who carries out cow's milk – the minimum volume to incur liability is enough for a gulp.

II.6　A. *Asked R. Ashi, "Is that as much as is needed for dissolving, or for holding and dissolving [part remaining on the fingers]?"*

III.1　A. **Honey – enough to put on a sore:**

　　　B. *A Tannaite statement:* Enough to put on the opening of a sore.

III.2　A. *Asked R. Ashi, "...enough to put on the opening of a sore – Is that the whole opening of the sore, or just on the top of the sore, excluding enough to go around the whole sore, which isn't necessary as part of the requisite volume?"*

III.3　A. Said R. Judah said Rab, "Of whatever the Holy One, blessed be He, has created in his world, he has created nothing for nothing. He created the snail as a remedy for a scab, the fly as antidote to the hornet, the mosquito as antidote for a serpent's bite, a serpent as the antidote for an eruption, a crushed spider as the antidote to a scorpion's bite."

III.4　A. A serpent as the antidote for an eruption – *what do you do?*

　　　B. *You bring a black and a white snake, boil them to a pulp, and rub in the mush.*

III.5　A. *Our rabbis have taught on Tannaite authority:*

　　　B. There are five cases in which the weak frighten the strong: the fear cast by the Ethiopian gnat [Freedman] over the lion, the fear cast by the mosquito over the elephant, the fear cast by the spider over the scorpion, the fear cast by the swallow over the eagle, the fear cast by the stickleback fish over the leviathan.

III.6   A.   *R. Zira happened by R. Judah,*
              standing at the door of his father-in-
              law's household, and observed that he
              was in a rollicking frame of mind, so
              that, if he asked him any of the
              secrets of the universe, he would
              reveal them to him. He said to him,
              "How come the goats go at the head
              of the flock, then the sheep?"

III.7   A.   *As to the word for door, dasha, it*
              means, "Here is a way there."

III.8   A.   *Our rabbis have taught on Tannaite*
              authority:

         B.   There are three who get stronger
              as they get older, a fish, a snake,
              and a pig.

IV.1   A.   Oil – enough to anoint a small
              limb:

         B.   *Said the household of R. Yannai, "oil*
              – enough to anoint a small limb
              of a day-old baby."

IV.2   A.   *May we say that this follows along*
              the lines of a Tannaite dispute?

         B.   "Oil – enough to anoint a small
              limb and a limb of a day-old
              baby," the words of R. Simeon b.
              Eleazar.

V.1   A.   Water – enough to rub off an eye
              salve:

         B.   *Said Abbayye, "Note that in any case*
              in which there is a commonplace use
              and an uncommon use, rabbis
              followed the standards required for
              the common use of that thing, even
              when it produces a lenient decision.
              Where something may be routinely
              used for two common purposes, the
              rabbis followed the standards
              required for the common use so that
              it would produce a strict decision. In
              the case of wine, for instance,
              drinking it is common, using it for a
              remedy is not common. So rabbis
              followed the measure of wine
              sufficient for drinking, the more
              common use, and that yielded a
              lenient decision. In the case of milk,
              which it is common to eat and not
              common to use for a remedy, rabbis
              followed the measure that would be
              required for an act of eating, which

also produced a lenient ruling. When it comes to honey, which it is common to eat and also common to use for healing, rabbis followed the measure that would be required for use for healing, [which is smaller than the other and which therefore produces] a strict decision. As to water, in which case it is common to drink it but uncommon to use it for healing, how come rabbis followed the measure sufficient to use water for healing, so producing a strict ruling?" This, too, would be a common use (Freedman).]

VI.1   A.   And of all other liquids, a quarter-log:

B.   *Our rabbis have taught on Tannaite authority:*

C.   As to blood and all other liquids, the requisite measure for incurring liability by transporting such liquids on the Sabbath is a quarter-log.

D.   R. Simeon b. Eleazar says, "As to blood, it must be sufficient for painting one eye, for that is how a cataract of the eye is painted" [T. Shab. 8:10H-J].

E.   *And what kind of blood is that? It is the blood of a wild bird.*

VI.2   A.   The master has said: "Under what circumstances? That would concern carrying such a volume out from private to public domain. But as to storing it away, one who stores away on the Sabbath any volume whatsoever is liable" – *but isn't putting something away into storage not comparable to carrying something out? [How differentiate?]*

VI.3   A.   The master has said: "And sages concur with R. Simeon in the case of one who carries out slops to the public domain that liability is incurred for doing so with all slops [refuse], at the measure of a quarter-log" – *so what good are slops [that one should be liable, since*

           there is no penalty for carrying out
           something that is useless]!

8:2

A. He who takes out (1) rope – enough to make a handle for a basket; (2) reed cord – enough to make a hanger for a sifter or a sieve –

B. R. Judah says, "Enough to use it to take the measure of a shoe for a child" –

C. (3) paper – enough to write on it a receipt for a tax collector.

D. And he who takes out (1) a receipt for a tax collector is liable;

E. [78B] (2) used paper – enough to wrap around a small perfume bottle.

8:3

A. (3) Leather – enough to make an amulet; (4) parchment – enough to write on it a small pericope of the tefillin, which is "Hear O Israel";

B. (5) ink – enough to write two letters; (6) eye shadow – enough to shadow one eye.

8:4

A. (7) Lime – enough to put on the head of a lime twig; (8) pitch or sulphur – enough for making a small hole; (9) wax – enough to put over a small hole; (10) clay – enough to make the [bellow's] hole of the crucible of a goldsmith.

B. R. Judah says, "enough to make a prop."

C. (11) Bran – enough to put on the mouth of the crucible of a goldsmith;

D. (12) quicklime – enough to smear the little finger of a girl.

E. R. Judah says, "Enough to take off the hair [on the temples]."

F. R. Nehemiah says, "Enough to take off the hair on the forehead."

I.1 A. [He who takes out rope – enough to make a handle for a basket:] *for a cord, too, one should be liable if he carries out so much as is needed to make a hanger for a sieve or a basket sieve?*

I.2 A. *Our rabbis have taught on Tannaite authority:*

  B. As for palm leaves, the requisite volume is enough to make a handle for a basket made of twigs.

  C. As for bast – others say, "Enough to put on the opening of a small funnel for straining wine."

II.1 A. Paper – enough to write on it a receipt for a tax collector.

  B. *A Tannaite statement:*

C. How big is a tax collector's receipt? Enough paper for writing two letters.

II.2 A. *Our rabbis have taught on Tannaite authority:*

B. He who takes out a receipt of a tax collector, before he has shown it to the tax collector, is liable; after he has shown it to the tax collector, he is exempt.

II.3 A. *So what's at issue between these two positions?*

B. *Said Abbayye, "At issue is the agents of the collector [who holds that someone would have to show the receipt to such persons, and rabbis hold he doesn't need to have the receipt, being able to refer the man to the collector himself]."*

C. *Raba said, "At issue between them is the more important and less important tax collectors."*

II.4 A. *Our rabbis have taught on Tannaite authority:*

B. He who takes out a bond – if this is before it has been collected, he is liable. If it is after it has been collected, he is exempt.

C. R. Judah says, "Also one who takes out an already-collected bond is liable, since he needs the document" [T. Shab. 8:12A-C].

II.5 A. *So what's at issue between these two positions?*

B. *Said R. Joseph, "At issue between them is* the prohibition concerning the holding of an already-collected bond. *Rabbis maintain that* it is forbidden to keep an already collected bond, *and R. Judah maintains that* it is permitted to keep an already collected bond."

III.1 A. Leather – enough to make an amulet:

B. *Raba raised this question of R. Nahman:* "He who carries out from private to public domain a piece of hide – for how small a piece would liability be incurred?"

C. *He said to him, "It is in accord with what we have learned in the Mishnah:* Leather – enough to make an amulet."

IV.1   A. [79B] parchment – enough to write on it a small pericope of the tefillin, which is "Hear O Israel":

B. *By contrast:* parchment and inferior parchment – enough to write a mezuzah thereon [T. Shab. 8:13B].

IV.2   A. *What is the definition of mezuzah in this context?*

B. It is the parchment that is inserted into the phylacteries.

IV.3   A. *Now since the concluding clause states,* parchment – enough to write on it a small pericope of the tefillin, which is "Hear O Israel," *it must follow that in the first clause we are dealing with the mezuzah itself!*

B. *This is the sense of the Tannaite statement:* Parchment and inferior parchment – what is the requisite measure? As to inferior parchment, the requisite measure is sufficient to write thereon a mezuzah; as to parchment, it is sufficient to write thereon the smallest pericope of the tefillin, which is "Hear O Israel."

IV.4   A. Said Rab, "Inferior parchment – lo, it is classified as parchment. Just as on parchment the phylacteries may be written, so on inferior parchment, the phylacteries may be written."

B. *We have learned in the Mishnah:* parchment – enough to write on it a small pericope of the tefillin, which is "Hear O Israel," *from which it follows that parchment but not inferior parchment may be used!*

IV.5   A. *R. Pappa said, "Rab made his statement in accord with the position of the Tannaite authority of the household of Manasseh. For the Tannaite authority of the household of Manasseh [stated]:* If one wrote it on paper or a rag, it is unfit; on parchment, parchment treated with gallnut, or inferior parchment, it is fit."

IV.6 A. *May we then say that the following supports his view:*

B. Along these same lines, a scroll of the Torah that was worn out, or prayerbox [tefillin] that was worn out – people may not make of them doorpost markers containing verses of the Torah, for things are not brought down from a more weighty level of sanctification to a less weighty level of sanctification.

C. *It then follows that, if it were permitted to bring things down from a more weighty level of sanctification to a less weighty level of sanctification, it would be allowed to make a scroll of the Torah that was worn out, or prayerbox [tefillin] that was worn out into mezuzot [doorpost markers containing verses of the Torah]. Surely that means that it may be written on inferior parchment, as Rab maintains?*

V.1 A. Ink – enough to write two letters:

B. [80A] *A Tannaite statement:* Two letters – written in ink, t w o letters – written by pen, or t w o letters – in an inkstand.

V.2 A. *Raba raised this question:* "What is the law if it was sufficient ink for One letter – written in ink, o n e letter – written by pen, or o n e letter – in an inkstand?"

B. *The question stands.*

V.3 A. Said Raba, "If one took out enough ink to write two letters and wrote them while he was walking along, he is liable, because the act of writing is equivalent to the act of putting the thing down."

B. And said Raba, "If one carried out enough ink to write one letter and wrote it, and then he went back and brought out enough ink to write another letter, and wrote it, he is exempt. *How come? At the moment that he brought out the second quantity of ink, the volume of ink that he brought out first is now lacking [the ink having dried]."*

V.4   A. *Our rabbis have taught on Tannaite authority:*

B. If one carried out from private to public domain a half-fig and then went and carried out another half-fig in a single spell of unawareness, he is liable. If it was in two spells of unawareness, he is exempt.

VI.1   A. Eye shadow – enough to shadow one eye:

B. *...One eye?! But lo, people don't shadow only one eye!*

C. Said R. Huna, "Well, modest women will paint only one eye" [Freedman: going veiled, leaving only one eye visible].

VII.1   A. Lime – enough to put on the head of a lime twig:

B. *A Tannaite statement:* Enough to put on the head of a lime twig of a hunter's rod.

VIII.1   A. Wax – enough to put over a small hole:

B. *A Tannaite statement:* Enough to put on the small hole for wine.

IX.1   A. Clay – enough to make the [bellow's] hole of the crucible of a goldsmith:

B. *Does that bear the implication that the requisite measure as defined by R. Judah is larger? But we know as fact that rabbis' requisite measure is larger, for we have learned in the Mishnah: R. Judah says, "Enough to use it to take the measure of a shoe for a child" [M. 8:2B]!*

IX.2   A. [80B] *Our rabbis have taught on Tannaite authority:*

B. He who carries out hair – the minimal volume for culpability is enough to knead clay with it.

C. Clay – enough to make the [bellow's] hole of the crucible of a goldsmith [T. Shab. 8:15, 8:16A].

X.1   A.   **Quicklime – enough to smear the little finger of a girl:**

       B.   *A Tannaite statement:* Enough to smear the little finger of girls.

X.2   A.   "Six months with oil of myrrh" (Est. 2:12):

       B.   *What is oil of myrrh?*

       C.   R. Huna bar Hiyya said, "It is stacte."

X.3   A.   *It has been taught on Tannaite authority:*

       B.   R. Judah says, "[Olives for olive oil] from a manured field refers to olives that are not a third grown. And why is it used for smearing? Because it serves as a depilatory and skin-softener."

X.4   A.   *R. Bibi had a* daughter with dark skin, on which he put that ointment limb by limb, and this produced for her a husband who had four hundred zuz.

XI.1   A.   R. Judah says, "Enough to take off the hair [on the temples]." R. Nehemiah says, "Enough to take off the hair on the forehead":

       B.   *What is the definition of* hair [on the temples], *and what is the definition of* hair on the forehead?

XI.2   A.   *Does that bear the implication that the requisite definition of R. Judah is larger than that of rabbis? But lo, we have it as an established fact that the requisite measure defined by rabbis is larger!*

XI.3   A.   *An objection was raised:* Said Rabbi, "The opinion of R. Judah appears preferable in the case of loosely dissolved lime, and the opinion of R. Nehemiah appears preferable in the case of chalky lime" [T. Shab. 8:20F]. *Now, if you hold that they refer to the upper temple and lower temple respectively, surely both require loose lime!*

       B.   *Rather, said R. Isaac, "The household of R. Ammi state [that the Mishnah sentence refers to]* an earthen vessel with two spouts, one above, one below." [Freedman/Rashi: When one wishes to fill it with wine, he closes the lower spout with lime, and it is to that that Nehemiah refers.]

8:5

A.   (1) "Earth for clay – enough to make a seal for a large sack," the words of R. Aqiba.

B.   And sages say, "A seal for a letter."

C.   "(2) Manure or (3) fine sand – enough to manure a cabbage stalk," the words of R. Aqiba.

D.   And sages say, "Enough to manure a leek."

E.   (4) Coarse sand – enough to cover a plasterer's trowel;

F.   (5) reed – enough to make a pen.

G.   And if it was thick or broken – enough to [make a fire to] cook the smallest sort of egg, mixed [with oil] and put in a pan.

I.1   A.   Coarse sand – enough to cover a plasterer's trowel:

       B.   *A Tannaite statement:* Enough to put on the top of a plasterer's trowel.

I.2   A.   *Who is the Tannaite authority who maintains that sand improves plaster?*

       B.   *Said R. Hisda, "It is R. Judah, for it has been taught on Tannaite authority:* A person should not stucco the front of his house with cement, but if he mixed dirt or straw in it, it is permitted."

II.1   A.   Reed – enough to make a pen:

       B.   *A Tannaite statement:* A pen that reaches the finger joints [T. Shab. 8:21A-B].

II.2   A.   *R. Ashi raised this question: "Does that mean the upper or the lower joint?"*

       B.   *So you'll have to live with that one.*

III.1 A.   And if it was thick or broken – enough to [make a fire to] cook the smallest sort of egg, mixed [with oil] and put in a pan:

       B.   *A Tannaite statement:* Beaten up with oil and put in a stew pot.

III.2 A.   *Said Mar b. Rabina to his son, "Have you heard what 'the smallest sort of egg' is?"*

       B.   *He said to him, "It's the egg of a turtle dove. How come? Because it's small."*

8:6

A.   (1) Bone – enough to make a spoon.

B.   R. Judah says, "Enough to make a tooth [of a key] with it."

C.   (2) Glass – enough to scrape the end of a shuttle;

D.   (3) pebble or stone – enough to throw at a bird.

E.   R. Eliezer b. R. Jacob says, "Enough to throw at a beast."

I.1   A.   Bone – enough to make a spoon. R. Judah says, "Enough to make a tooth [of a key] with it":

    B.   *Does that bear the implication that the requisite definition of R. Judah is larger than that of rabbis? But lo, we have it as an established fact that the requisite measure defined by rabbis is larger!*

I.2   A.   *Our rabbis have taught on Tannaite authority:*

    B.   The wards of a lock are insusceptible to uncleanness. If one fixed them into the lock, they are susceptible to uncleanness. But if the lock serves a revolving door, even when fixed to the door and nailed on with nails, the wards are insusceptible, because whatever is attached to the soil is classified as is the soil [insusceptible to uncleanness].

II.1   A.   Glass – enough to scrape the end of a shuttle:

    B.   *A Tannaite statement:* glass – enough to break across two threads at once.

III.1   A.   Pebble or stone – enough to throw at a bird. R. Eliezer b. R. Jacob says, "Enough to throw at a beast":

    B.   Said R. Jacob said R. Yohanan, "But that is the case only if [the stone is big enough for] the animal to feel it."

III.2   A.   *Zonin [Zeno] went into the house of study. He said to them,* "My lords, what is the requisite size of stones used in the toilet [for removing shit]?"

    B.   They said to him, "The size of an olive, a nut, and an egg."

III.3   A.   *It has been taught on Tannaite authority:*

B. R. Yosé says, "The size of an olive, a nut, and an egg."

III.4 A. *It has been taught on Tannaite authority:*

B. On the Sabbath it is permitted to take along three rounded pebbles into the privy. [Such a privy has no walls, and ordinarily one could not carry an object into it.]

III.5 A. Said Rafram bar Papa said R. Hisda, "Parallel to the dispute in the present passage is the dispute concerning the etrog."

B. *But there the dispute concerns a Mishnah rule* [namely: **The measure of the smallest acceptable citron (M. Suk. 3:7A)**], *while here the dispute concerns a Tannaite statement that is external to that document! Rather,* as is the dispute with reference to the etrog so is the dispute here.

III.6 A. Said R. Judah, "But not with a brittle stone."

B. *What is the definition of* a brittle stone?

III.7 A. Said Raba, "On the Sabbath it is forbidden to utilize a chip as a suppository in the way in which one does so on weekdays."

B. *Objected Mar Zutra, "So is he supposed to endanger himself?"*

III.8 A. Said R. Yannai, "If the privy has a fixed location, one may bring in a handful of stones; if not, only a stone the size of the leg of a small spice mortar may be brought in."

III.9 A. Said Abbayye to R. Joseph, "If rain fell on it and the stain was washed away, what's the law?"

B. He said to him, "If the mark thereof is perceptible, it is permitted."

III.10 A. Rabbah bar R. Shila asked R. Hisda, [81B] "What is the law as to bringing up stones after himself to the roof?"

B. He said to him, "The honor owing to human beings is so considerable that it overrides the

negatives of the Torah." [One
may do so.]

III.11 A. Said R. Huna, "It is forbidden on
the Sabbath to take a shit in a
ploughed field."

B. *How come? Should I say that it
would be on the count of treading?
Then even on a weekday it should
also be forbidden to do so [in someone
else's ploughed field]! And should I
say it is on account of the grass
[which one may pick up in
connection with taking some dirt for
toilet paper]? Then didn't R.
Simeon b.* Laqish say, "As to a
pebble on which grass has
sprouted, it is permitted to use
that for toilet paper on the
Sabbath, but if one takes the grass
off on the Sabbath, he is liable to a
sin-offering"? *Rather, it is lest he
take a clod from somewhere high and
toss it down to somewhere low, in
which case he would be liable on the
count that was described by what
Rabbah said, for* said Rabbah, "If
someone had a hole and filled it
up, if it is in the house, he is liable
on the count of building, and if it
is in the field, he is liable on the
count of ploughing."

III.12 A. *Reverting to the body of the
foregoing:* Said R. Simeon b.
Laqish, "As to a pebble on which
grass has sprouted, it is permitted
to use that for toilet paper on the
Sabbath, but if one takes the grass
off on the Sabbath, he is liable to a
sin-offering" –

III.13 A. *Said Abbayye, "Since the subject of
the perforated pot has come to hand,
let's talk about it:* If it was lying on
the ground and one put it on
pegs, he is liable on the count of
detaching; if it is lying on pegs
and one put it on the ground, he
is liable on the count of planting."

III.14 A. Said R. Yohanan, "On the Sabbath
it is forbidden to wipe oneself
with a sherd."

III.15 A. *Raba repeated the rule and explained that it was on account of tearing the hair, and so he found a contradiction between two statements of R. Yohanan. For has* R. Yohanan said, "It is forbidden to wipe oneself with a sherd on the Sabbath"? *Then he takes the view that* it is forbidden to do something even if he doesn't intend to do it. But hasn't R. Yohanan said, "The decided law is in accord with the unattributed Mishnah rule"? *And have we not learned in the Mishnah:* **A Nazir shampoos and parts his hair [with his fingers], but he does not comb his hair [M. Naz. 6:3D]?** *So it's better to represent matters in line with the presentation of R. Nathan bar Oshayya.*

III.16 A. *What's the point of the reference to witchcraft?*

        B. *It is in accord with the following: R. Hisda and Rabbah bar R. Huna were traveling in a boat. A noble lady said to them, "Sit me with you," but they didn't sit her with them.*

III.17 A. *Said R. Huna to his son, Rabbah, "How come you don't frequent R. Hisda's teaching, since his traditions are very sharp?"*

        B. *He said to him, "Why should I go to him? When I go to him, he goes into session for rather secular teachings. He said to me, 'One who goes into the toilet shouldn't sit down too fast or push too much, because the rectum sets on three teeth-like glands, and the teeth-like glands of the rectum might become dislocated, so threatening good health.'"*

        C. *He said to him, "He's engaged in matters of good health, and you call these secular matters?! All the reason for you to go to him."*

III.18 A. If before someone were a pebble and a sherd –

        B. R. Huna said, "He wipes himself with the pebble and he doesn't dry himself with the sherd."

III.19 A. If before someone were a pebble and grass –

           B. R. Hisda and R. Hamnuna –

           C. One said, "One wipes himself with a pebble and doesn't wipe himself with grass."

           D. The other said, "He wipes himself with grass and doesn't wipe himself with a pebble."

III.20 A. He who has to take a shit but doesn't do it –

           B. R. Hisda and Rabina –

           C. One said, "He smells like a fart."

           D. The other said, "He smells like shit."

III.21 A. He who has to take a shit but can't –

           B. Said R. Hisda, "Let him stand up and sit down again, stand up and sit down again."

III.22 A. *Our rabbis have taught on Tannaite authority:*

           B. He who comes into a house to take a regular meal should first walk ten lengths of four cubits – others say, four of ten – and take a shit and then go in and sit in his regular place.

8:7

A. "Potsherd – enough to put between one board and another," the words of R. Judah.

B. R. Meir says, "Enough to scoop up fire."

C. R. Yosé says, "Enough to hold a quarter-log [of liquid]."

D. Said R. Meir, "Even though there is no proof for the proposition, there is at least a hint for it: 'And there shall not be found among the pieces of it a sherd to take fire from the earth' (Isa. 30:14)."

E. Said to him R. Yosé, "From that same verse there is proof [for my proposition]: 'Or to scoop up water withal out of the cistern.'"

       I.1 A. *The question was raised: Is the requisite measure defined by R. Meir greater, or is the requisite measure defined by R. Yosé greater?*

           B. *It stands to reason that the measure of R. Yosé is greater, while the cited verse suggests that R. Meir's requisite measure is greater. For if you should imagine that R. Yosé's requisite is greater, then will the*

> prophet first curse a small utensil
> and then a big one?

II.1   A.   Said to him R. Yosé, "From that
              same verse there is proof [for my
              proposition]: 'Or to scoop up
              water withal out of the cistern'":

        B.   *Didn't R. Yosé give a good answer to*
              R. Meir?

The upshot of this chapter and the next are outlined at the conclusion
of Chapter Five.

5

Bavli Shabbat
Chapter Nine

Folios 82A-90B

The remarks at the beginning of Chapter Three explain the work of this chapter as well. Readers not interested in a detailed survey are advised to turn directly to the concluding chapter.

9:1

A. Said R. Aqiba, "How do we know of an idol that it imparts uncleanness when it is carried in the same way that a menstruating woman [when she is carried, imparts uncleanness to the one who carries her]?

B. "Since it is said, 'You shall cast them away like a menstrual thing, you shall say to it, Get thee hence' (Isa. 30:22) –

C. "Just as the menstruating woman imparts uncleanness when she is carried so an idol imparts uncleanness when it is carried."

I.1   A. *There we have learned in the Mishnah:* He [the wall of] whose house was adjacent to [and also served as the wall of the temple of] an idol, and [whose house] fell down – it is forbidden to rebuild it. What should he then do? He pulls back within four cubits inside his own property and then rebuilds his house. [82B] [If there was a wall belonging] both to him and to [the temple of an] idol, it is judged to be divided half and half. The stones, wood, and mortar deriving from it impart uncleanness in the status of a dead creeping thing, for it is said, "You will utterly detest it" (Deut. 7:26).

B. R. Aqiba says, "In the status of a menstruant['s uncleanness], as it is said, 'You shall cast them away as a menstrual thing; you shall say unto it, Get you hence' (Isa. 30:22). Just as a menstruating woman imparts uncleanness to one who carries her [or objects that she carries], so also an idol imparts uncleanness to one who carries it" [M. A.Z. 3:6].

I.2 A. *And said Rabbah, "As to carrying the unclean thing, all concur that the object imparts uncleanness when it is carried, since it is treated as comparable to menstrual uncleanness. Where there is a disagreement, it concerns an immovable stone [so heavy that when someone sits on it, her added weight makes no difference to utensils on which it is resting]. [The issue is, are utensils beneath such a heavy stone made unclean when an idol is put on top of it?] R. Aqiba holds that* it is comparable to menstrual uncleanness: just as menstrual uncleanness effects contamination even through an exceptionally heavy stone, so an idol does the same; *rabbis compare the idol to a dead creeping thing:* just as a dead creeping thing doesn't effect contamination through a very heavy stone [on top of which it is placed, to things that bear the weight underneath], so an idol doesn't effect contamination through its weight transferred through an exceptionally heavy stone."

I.3 A. *And R. Eleazar said, "With respect to an exceptionally heavy stone, all parties concur that uncleanness is not transferred from the top to objects that bear the weight underneath under the present circumstances. Where they differ, it concerns the issue of whether or not the idol conveys uncleanness to one who carries it. R. Aqiba takes the view that it is comparable to a menstruating woman:* just as the menstruating woman conveys uncleanness to the one that carries her, so an idol conveys uncleanness to the one who carries it. *And sages maintain that it is comparable to a dead creeping thing:* Just as a dead creeping thing does not convey uncleanness to one who carries it, so an idol doesn't convey uncleanness to one who carries it."

B. *Now, from R. Aqiba's perspective, what purpose is then served by the comparison of an idol to a dead creeping thing [as at Deut. 8:26]?*

C. *The comparison to the dead creeping thing serves to cover the utensils that are necessary to make use of the idol.*

I.4   A. *An objection was raised:* An idol is comparable to a dead creeping thing, and the utensils that are necessary to utilize it are likewise unclean like a dead creeping thing. R. Aqiba says, "An idol is unclean like a menstruating woman, but the utensils that are necessary to use the idol are unclean like a dead creeping thing." *Now from R. Eleazar's perspective, that poses no problem. But from the viewpoint of Rabbah, it is a problem.*

B. *Rabbah may say to you, "Is this of greater weight than the Mishnah, which says in so many words,* **the stones, wood, and mortar deriving from it impart uncleanness in the status of a dead creeping thing,** *which we explained to mean, What is the sense of* dead creeping thing? *It means* an idol doesn't effect contamination through its weight transferred through an exceptionally heavy stone. *Here, too,* it doesn't effect contamination through its weight transferred through an exceptionally heavy stone."

I.5   A. *An objection was raised:* A gentile male or female, an idol and utensils that are used with it are unclean, but shifting them does not convey uncleanness. R. Aqiba says, "Both they and also shifting them convey uncleanness." *Now from R. Eleazar's perspective, that poses no problem. But from the viewpoint of Rabbah, it is a problem.*

        B. *Rabbah may say to you, "And from our perspective, can you maintain of a gentile male or female,* they are unclean, but shifting them does not convey uncleanness? *But hasn't it been taught on Tannaite authority:* 'Speak to the children of Israel and say to them, When any man has a flux' (Lev. 15:2) – the children of Israel contract uncleanness through flux, and gentiles do not contract uncleanness through flux, but sages have made the decree concerning them that they should be regarded for all purposes as tantamount to those afflicted with flux?"

I.6   A. *As to an idol, there is no problem in finding a case in which others move it, but how in the world is it ever going to be in the situation of moving others?*

        B. *Said R. Ammi b. R. Yeba, "It is in line with that which has been taught on Tannaite authority:* [If] the Zab [unclean with flux uncleanness as described at Lev. 15] is on one side of the scale and food and drink are on the second, if the Zab outweighed them, they are unclean. [83B] If they outweighed him, they are clean."

I.7   A. *In accord with what authority is the following, which has been taught on Tannaite authority:* All unclean things that move clean things –

the clean things remain clean, except for the movement of a person afflicted with flux. For we don't find a parallel in the entire Torah to that rule? *May we say that it is not in accord with R. Aqiba, for were it in accord with R. Aqiba, then from his perspective there also is the case of an idol!*

B. *You may even say that it is in accord with R. Aqiba, for the intent of the Tannaite rule is, "the person afflicted with flux and anything in the same category."*

I.8 A. *R. Hama bar Guria asked:* "As to an idol, does that status affect its limbs or not? In a case in which an unskilled laborer can restore the limbs, that is no question, since in that case, these are treated as though they were still attached. *Where it is a question, it is a case in which an unskilled laborer can't put the limbs back. Now what is the rule? Since an unskilled laborer can't put the limbs back, it is as though it were broken, or maybe in such a case it's not lacking anything anyhow?"*

B. *There are those who phrase the question in the following manner: "In a case in which an unskilled laborer cannot restore the limbs, there is no problem; it is as though it were broken. Where it is a problem, it is a case in which an unskilled laborer can put the limbs back. What is the rule? Since an unskilled worker can put the limbs back, it is as though it were joined together? Or perhaps now, in any event, the parts are strung about and detached?"*

C. *The question stands.*

I.9 A. *R. Ahadeboy bar Ammi raised this question:* "What is the rule governing an idol of the volume of less than an olive?"

B. *Objected to this question R. Joseph, "What's the purpose of such a question? If it has to do with the prohibition of the idol, let it be no different from the fly of Baal Eqron, for it has been taught on Tannaite authority:* 'And they made Baal berit their god' (Judg. 8:33) – this refers to the fly god of Baal Eqron. It teaches that every one of them made a model of his god and put it in his pocket. When he thought of it, he would take it out of his pocket and caress it and kiss it. *Rather, the question is, What is the status of such a thing so far as uncleanness is concerned? Since it is treated as comparable to a dead creeping thing, just as a dead creeping thing conveys uncleanness only if it is of the bulk of a lentil, so a piece of an idol also conveys uncleanness only if it is of the bulk of a lentil? Or perhaps it is treated as comparable to a corpse: just as a corpse conveys uncleanness in the volume of an olive's bulk, so this would convey uncleanness in the volume of an olive's bulk?"*

I.10   A.   *And from the perspective of rabbis, what's the practical consequence of this ruling that it is comparable to a dead creeping thing? It is that it won't convey uncleanness if it is carried. And what's the practical consequence of comparing it to a menstruating woman? That it does not retain uncleanness in the limbs that have been cut off. And of the comparison to the corpse? That it doesn't impart uncleanness in so small a volume as that of a lentil.*

9:2A-B

A.   "How do we know of a boat that it is insusceptible to uncleanness?

B.   "Since it says, 'The way of a ship in the midst of the sea' (Prov. 30:19)."

I.1   A.   *Well, it's pretty obvious that the way of the ship is in the midst of the sea. Here we are informed of the comparison to the sea: Just as the sea is insusceptible to* uncleanness, so the ship is insusceptible to uncleanness.

B. *It has been taught on Tannaite authority:* Hananiah says, "We may draw the clarifying analogy from the case of sacking [only wooden utensils that are like sacking can be unclean, in line with Lev. 11:32] – just as sacking can be carried whether empty or filled, so anything that can be carried empty or filled is in its status, *excluding a boat, which can be carried empty but not filled.*

I.2 A. Said R. Judah said Rab, "A person should never refrain from going to the schoolhouse, even for a single moment, for lo, how many years has this Mishnah paragraph been repeated in the house of study, but the reason for it was never set forth, until R. Hanina b. Aqabayya came along and explained it."

I.3 A. Said R. Jonathan, "A person should never refrain from going to the schoolhouse or from Torah teachings, even at the hour of his death, for lo, it is said, 'This is the torah, when a man dies in a tent' (Num. 19:14) – even at the hour of death one should be occupied in the Torah."

B. Said R. Simeon b. Laqish, "The teachings of the Torah are fulfilled only in him who kills himself for the Torah, as it is said, 'This is the torah, when a man dies in a tent' (Num. 19:14)."

I.4 A. Said Raba, [84A] "And from the perspective of Hanania, carrying by means of oxen is classified as carrying [since only oxen can carry Jordan boats]. For we have learned in the Mishnah: **There are three classifications of wagons: One built like an arm chair is susceptible to uncleanness from pressure such as is exerted by a menstruating woman, one made as if a bed is susceptible to** uncleanness deriving from a corpse; one made of stone is susceptible to no form of uncleanness [M. Kel. 24:2]. And said R. Yohanan, 'But if it has a receptacle that can hold pomegranates, it is susceptible to corpse uncleanness.' There are three classifications of chest: A chest with an opening at the side is usable as a bench and so is susceptible to pressure uncleanness like a chair or a bed; one with a hole at the top is susceptible to corpse uncleanness, and a very large one is susceptible to no form of uncleanness [M. Kel. 24:3]."

I.5   A. *Our rabbis have taught on Tannaite authority:*

       B. Pressure uncleanness inflicted on an earthenware utensil is null. [Freedman: If a person afflicted with flux uncleanness or a menstruant sits on an earthenware utensil, but does not enter the contained air space of the utensil, he or she does not transfer pressure uncleanness to the utensil merely by exerting pressure through sitting on it.]

       C. R. Yosé says, "Also a ship."

I.6   A. *What's the sense of his statement?*

       B. *Said R. Zebid, "This is the sense of the statement:* Pressure uncleanness inflicted on an earthenware utensil is null – but if such a person touches the clay utensil on its contained inner space, it is unclean. Also a ship made of clay is susceptible to uncleanness, in accord with Hananiah. R. Yosé says, 'Also a ship': it is insusceptible to uncleanness. And that is in accord with our Tannaite authority."

I.7   A. *How on the basis of Scripture do we know the fact that* pressure uncleanness inflicted on an earthenware utensil is null?

B. Said Hezekiah, "Said Scripture, 'and whosoever touches his bed' (Lev. 15:5) – Scripture treats as comparable himself [the person afflicted with flux uncleanness] and the bed that belongs to him; just as he can be cleaned in an immersion pool, so his bed can be cleaned in an immersion pool – [supply: thus excluding clay utensils, which cannot be cleaned in an immersion pool]."

I.8 A. Raba said, "The fact that pressure uncleanness inflicted on an earthenware utensil is null derives from the following verse: 'and every open vessel, which has no covering tightly sealed upon it, is unclean' (Num. 19:15). Then if it has a seal tightly closing it, it is clean. [The uncleanness must affect the contained air space of the utensil.] *Aren't we dealing with a utensil that one had assigned to serve as a seat for his wife, who is menstruating, and the All-Merciful has said that it is nonetheless unaffected by use as a chair and so is insusceptible to pressure uncleanness."*

9:2C-E

C. "How do we know of a garden bed, six handbreadths square, that five different kinds of seed may be sown in it, four on the sides and one in the middle [M. Kil. 3:1]?

D. "Since it says, 'For as the earth brings forth her bud and as the garden causes seeds sown in it to spring forth' (Isa. 61:11) –

E. "'Its seed' is not said, but 'Its seeds.'"

I.1 A. *What is the implication of the cited verse that yields this result?*

B. Said R. Judah, "'For as the earth brings forth her bud' (Isa. 61:11) – 'brings forth' *is one,* 'her bud' *is one, thus two;* 'her seeds' *stands for two, thus four;* 'causes to spring forth' *stands for one, five species in all.* [85A] *And rabbis established the fact that five species sown in a space six handbreadths square will not draw nourishment from one another."*

I.2   A.   *What is the point of reference of the phrase,* which they have set of old?

      B.   Said R. Samuel bar Nahmani said R. Yohanan, "'These are the sons of Seir the Horite, the inhabitants of the earth' (Gen. 36:20) – *so is everybody else the inhabitants of the firmament?* Rather, these were the experts in how to cultivate the earth. For they would say, 'This entire measuring rod of land is for olives, that for vines, the other for figs." [Freedman: They knew how to divide land for cultivation and they must have known how much earth each species required for its sustenance; that is the source of rabbis' knowledge.]

II.1   A.   [Six handbreadths square:] Said R. Assi, "The internal area of the seed bed must be six handbreadths square, not counting the borders." [Freedman: The area stated in the Mishnah does not include the borders.]

      B.   *So, too, it has been taught on Tannaite authority:* The internal area of the seed bed must be six handbreadths square, not counting the borders.

II.2   A.   And how much must its borders be?

      B.   *It is in line with what we have learned in the Mishnah:* R. Judah says, "The width [of the row] must be as wide as the width of the sole of a foot" [M. Kil. 3:3G].

II.3   A.   Said Rab, "We have learned the rule of the Mishnah to pertain to a seed bed in a waste plot." [Freedman: But if the seed bed is surrounded by other beds sown with different varieties, only the two handbreadths of space occupied by the borders of the two contiguous beds will be between them, while three handbreadths are required between two rows of different plants.]

B. *But what about the corner space [left unsown? So there really can be a bed surrounded by other beds, contrary to Rab's observation].*

II.4 A. *Said Ulla, "In the West they raised this question:* What is the law if someone drew one furrow across the whole?" [Freedman/Rashi: From north to south, crossing the middle seeds; the furrow is either one of the five species of seeds or a sixth. Is this a distinguishing mark, permitting the situation to continue?]

II.5 A. Said R. Kahana said R. Yohanan, "He who wants to fill up his entire patch with vegetables makes it into beds six handbreadths square, describing in each a circle of a diameter of five handbreadths, filling the corner with whatever he wants" [which arrangement demonstrates for all to see that there is no planting of mixed seeds].

9:3

A. "How do we know of her who emits semen on the third day [after having had sexual relations] that she is unclean?

B. "Since it says, 'And be ready against the third day, [come not near a woman]' (Ex. 19:15).

C. "How do we know that they bathe a child on the third day after circumcision, even if this coincides with the Sabbath?

D. "Since it says, 'And it came to pass on the third day when they were sore' (Gen. 34:25).

E. "How do we know that they tie a red thread on the head of the scapegoat [which is sent forth]?

F. "Since it says, 'Though your sins be as scarlet, they shall be white as snow' (Isa. 1:18).

9:4

A. "How do we know that on the Day of Atonement anointing is tantamount to drinking?

B. "Even though there is no direct proof of the proposition, there is a hint at that proposition,

C. "since it says, 'And it came into his inward parts like water and like oil into his bones' (Ps. 109:18)."

I.1   A.   [As will be seen in materials set
forth presently, with reference to
the allegation that **How do we
know of her who emits semen
on the third day** [after having
had sexual relations] **that she is
unclean?**] *the first clause is not in
accord with the principle of R.
Eleazar b. Azariah [below, D], but
the second is in accord with R.
Eleazar b. Azariah, for in regards R.
Eleazar b. Azariah, we have heard the
tradition that she is clean.*

B.   *One who does not care to assign the
Mishnah rule to a conflict of
Tannaite authorities repeats the first
clause as* **clean,** *and assigns the
whole of the passage to accord with
R. Eleazar b. Azariah, but one who
does care to assign the passage to a
conflict of Tannaite opinion will
attribute the first clause to rabbis and
the second to R. Eleazar b. Azariah.*

I.2   A.   *When rabbis made this statement
before R. Pappa, and some say, R.
Pappa to Raba, [he replied],* "Well,
*there's no problem in respect to the
views of R. Eleazar b. Azariah. He
concurs with rabbis, who take the
view that on Thursday, there was an
abstention from sexual relations.*
[Freedman: On the occasion of the
giving of the Torah, for which
sexual relations had to be
suspended for a long enough
period to insure cleanness, took
place on the Sabbath, at the very
beginning of which they were
permitted to immerse and purify
themselves if there had been a
seminal discharge on Friday;
some may have had sexual
relations at the end of Thursday
and yet they were fit for
revelation on the Sabbath, which
shows that a discharge of semen
on the third day does not defile.]
*And R. Ishmael concurs with R.
Yosé, who said, 'It was on
Wednesday prior to the giving of the
law that they abstained from sexual*

relations.' But in accord with what position does R. Aqiba take the view that he does?" [Freedman: For the Torah speaks of days, meaning, whether sexual relations took place at the beginning or at the end of the day, she would be clean on the third or fourth day without regard to the numbers of periods that had elapsed.]

I.3　A.　[86B] *Lo, one way or the other, they were in the status of those who had immersed but had to await sunset for the completion of their rite of purification!*

　　　B.　*Abbayye bar Rabin and R. Hanina bar Abin both said, "The Torah was given even to those who were in the status of those who had immersed but had to await sunset for the completion of their rite of purification."*

I.4　A.　*Well, anyhow, why couldn't they have immersed at twilight and received the Torah at twilight?* [Freedman/Rashi: According to Aqiba, if God wanted exactly five periods to elapse, why did he postpone revelation until the morning, which suggests that six periods are necessary?]

　　　B.　Said R. Isaac, "'From the beginning I have not spoken in secret' (Isa. 48:16)."

I.5　A.　Said R. Hiyya b. R. Abba said R. Yohanan, "This represents the views of R. Ishmael and R. Aqiba, but sages say, 'Six complete periods' *are what we require [for the discharge to become null]."*

I.6　A.　Said R. Hisda, "The dispute concerns a case in which the semen derived from the woman, but if it derived from a man, it is unclean so long as it is wet."

　　　B.　Objected R. Sheshet, "'And every garment and every skin on which is the seed of copulation shall be washed with water and be unclean until the evening' (Lev. 15:17) – excluding semen that stinks. [It no longer can inseminate, so is no longer a source of uncleanness.] *Doesn't this refer to what comes from a man?"*

I.7   A.   R. Pappa raised this question: "What is the rule governing Israelite semen in a Samaritan belly? *Is it that, because Israelites are anxious about keeping the religious duties, their bodies heat up [and ruin the semen in three days] but that is not true of gentiles, who are not anxious about keeping the religious duties? Or do we say that, just as they eat dead creeping things, so their bodies, too, are overheated? And should you say, just as they eat dead creeping things, their bodies are overheated and ruin the semen in three days, what about Israelite semen in a beast's belly? Do we say, a woman, who has a fore-uterus, makes the semen stink, but an animal doesn't, having none? Or perhaps it makes no difference?"*

       B.   *So worry about it.*

I.8   A.   *Our rabbis have taught on Tannaite authority:*

       B.   On the sixth of the month [of Sivan] the Ten Commandments were given to Israel.

       C.   R. Yosé says, "On the seventh of that month."

I.9   A.   *Said Raba, "All parties concur that they reached the Wilderness of Sinai on the first of the month. For here it is written,* 'on this day they came into the wilderness of Sinai' (Ex. 19:1), *and further,* 'This month shall be unto you the beginning of months' (Ex. 12:2). Just as here, the intention is to refer to the first of the month, so there, too, the first of the month is what is meant. *Further, all parties concur that* the Torah was given to Israel on the Sabbath. *Here it is written,* 'Remember the Sabbath day to keep it holy' (Ex. 20:8) and elsewhere, 'And Moses said to the people, Remember this day' (Ex. 13:3). Just as there he spoke on that very day to which he referred, so here, too, he spoke on the very day to which he referred. *Where there is a dispute, it concerns the fixing of the New Moon for that month. R. Yosé takes the view that the New Moon was fixed on Sunday, and on that day, Moses said nothing to them, because they were tired from their trip. On Monday he said to* them, 'and you shall be to me a kingdom of priests' (Ex. 19:6). *On Tuesday he told them the religious duty of setting boundaries around the mountain; on Wednesday they separated themselves from sexual relations with their wives. Rabbis maintain that on Monday the New Moon was fixed, and on that day, Moses said nothing to them, because they were tired from their trip. On Tuesday he said to them,* 'and you shall be to me a kingdom of priests' (Ex. 19:6). *On Wednesday he told them the religious duty of setting borders around the mountain, on Thursday the abstinence from sexual relations was accomplished."*

I.10 A. "And adding one day [to the period of sanctification prior to revelation, Ex. 19:10, 19:15]":

B. *What was the exposition of Scripture that he set forth?*

C. *He thought along these lines:* It is written, "And sanctify themselves today and tomorrow" (Ex. 19:10) – today must be like tomorrow. Just as tomorrow means the prior night, so today must encompass the prior night. *But since the prior night applying to today has already gone by, it must follow that there are two days exclusive of today to be observed.*

I.11 A. "Going celibate [even without having had a daughter]":

B. *What was the exposition of Scripture that he set forth?*

C. *He thought along these lines:* If concerning the Israelites, with whom the Presence of God spoke for only a single moment, and that was at a specified time, the Torah has said, "do not come near a woman," then I, who am singled out for divine speech at any time, and no particular time has been set for me, all the more so should do so.

I.12 A. "Breaking the tables":

B. *What was the exposition of Scripture that he set forth?*

C. *He thought along these lines:* If concerning the Passover lamb, only one of six hundred and thirteen commandments, the Torah has said, "No outsider shall eat thereof," then how much the more so should this apply to the whole of the Torah, when all of the Israelites have betrayed it!

I.13 A. *Come and take note:* "And be ready against the third day" – *that's a challenge to the position of R. Yosé!*

B. *Lo, we've already said,* Moses had decided on his own volition about adding one day [to the period of sanctification prior to revelation, Ex. 19:10, 19:15]!

I.14 A. *Come and take note:* "The third, the third day of the month, the third day of the week" – *that's a challenge to the position of rabbis!*

B. *Rabbis will say to you,* "Lo, who is the authority behind the unattributed passage? It is none other than R. Yosé."

I.15 A. *As to that first reference to the third, what's the point?*

B. *It is in line with that which has been taught on Tannaite authority:*

C. "And Moses reported the words of the people to the Lord" (Ex. 19:8). "And Moses told the words of the people to the Lord" (Ex. 34:9):

I.16 A. *Come and take note:* "The sixth, the sixth day of the month, the sixth day of the week" – *that's a challenge to the position of rabbis!*

B. *Rabbis will say to you, "Lo, here, too, who is the authority behind the unattributed passage? It is none other than R. Yosé."*

I.17 A. *As to that first reference to the sixth, what's the point?*

B. Raba said, [87B] "It refers to their making camp."

C. R. Aha bar Jacob said, "It refers to their making journeys" [particularly from Rephidim, Ex. 19:2; he holds that they left Rephidim and came to the wilderness of Sinai on the same day (Freedman)].

I.18 A. *Come and take note:* As to the Nisan in which the Israelites left Egypt, on the fourteenth of the month, they slaughtered their Passover-offerings; on the fifteenth they went out; that evening the firstborn were smitten.

B. *Do you really imagine that it was that evening?!*

I.19 A. *Come and take note: They did not make it a full thirty days, but only twenty-nine days:* As to the Nisan in which the Israelites left Egypt, on the fourteenth they slaughtered their Passover-offerings; on the fifteenth they went forth; that evening the firstborn were smitten.

B. Do you really imagine that it *was* that evening?!

I.20 A. *Said R. Pappa, "Come and take note:* 'And they took their journey from Elim, and all the congregation of the children of Israel came into the wilderness of Sin on the fifteenth day of the second month' (Ex. 16:1) – now that day was a Sabbath, for it is written, 'and in the morning, then you shall see the glory of the Lord' (Ex. 16:7), and it is written, 'Six days you shall gather it' (Ex. 16:26). [The manna first fell on the day after they arrived at Sin, and since they could gather it for six days, that must have been a Sunday, the prior day, a Sabbath (Freedman)]. *But since the fifteenth of Iyyar coincided with the Sabbath, the first of Sivan had to have fallen on a Sunday. And that's a problem for rabbis."*

I.21   A. *Said R. Assi of Khuzistan to R. Ashi,* "Come and take note: 'And it came to pass in the first month of the second year, on the first day of the month, that the tabernacle was erected' (Ex. 40:17)." *And a Tannaite statement [thereon is as follows:]* That day received ten crowns [of distinction]: It was the first day of Creation, the first day of the princes' offerings for the dedication of the tabernacle, the first day for the priesthood, the first day for public offerings, the first day for the fall of fire from heaven, the first day for the priests' eating of Holy Things, the first day for the presence of God in Israel, the first day for the priestly blessing of Israel, the first day on which the high places were forbidden, the first day for the reckoning of months. *Now since the first of Nisan that year was on a Sunday, then the first of Nisan of the previous year has to have been on a Wednesday. For it has been taught on Tannaite authority:* Others say, "Between one Feast of Weeks and the next, or between one New Year and the next, there can be a difference of only four days of the week, or, in an intercalated year [bearing an extra month], five. [T. Ar. 1:11] [Jung, p. 52, n. 2.: Others hold that all months are full and defective in strict rotation, making a total of 354 days, which is four days over fifty weeks, leaving four days of the week as interval between one new year and the other in a normal year and five in a prolonged year.] *So the first of Iyyar had to have come on a Friday, and the first of Sivan on a Sabbath – a problem to both R. Yosé and rabbis!"*

I.22 A. *Come and take note: For it has been taught on Tannaite authority in the compilation, Seder Olam:* The Nisan in which the Israelites left Egypt, the Nisan in which the Israelites went forth from Egypt – on the fourteenth they slaughtered their Passover-offerings, on the fifteenth they went forth, and that day was a Friday. *Now, since the first of Nisan was on the Sabbath eve or Friday, the first of Iyyar was on a Sunday, the first of Sivan on a Monday – yielding a problem for R. Yosé!*

B. *R. Yosé may tell you, "Well, whose view is this? It's just rabbis'."*

I.23 A. *Come and take note:* R. Yosé says, "On Monday Moses went up the mountain and came down, on Tuesday Moses went up and came down, on Wednesday he went up but didn't come down again. Now, since he didn't come down on Wednesday, whence did he come down again? So it must be, on Wednesday he went up and came down, on Thursday he built the altar and made an offering, on Friday he had no more time." *Wasn't that because of the Torah?* [Freedman: This supports rabbis, that the Torah was given on the sixth of the month.]

B. *No, it was because of the trouble of preparing for the Sabbath.*

I.24 A. *A certain Galilean expounded before R. Hisda, "Blessed be the All-Merciful, who gave a Torah divided into three parts to a people divided into three parts through a third-born son [after Miriam and Aaron] on the third day of the third month."*

B. *In accord with whom did he present that exposition? In accord with R. Yosé.*

I.25 A. "And they stood under the mount" (Ex. 19:17):

B. Actually underneath the mountain.

C. Said R. Abdimi bar Hama bar Hasa, "This teaches that the Holy One, blessed be He, held the mountain over Israel like a cask and said to them, 'If you accept the Torah, well and good, and if not, then there is where your grave will be.'"

I.26 A. *Said Hezekiah, "What is the meaning of the verse, 'You caused sentence to be heard from heaven, the earth feared and was tranquil' (Ps. 76:9)? If it feared, why was it tranquil, and if it was tranquil, why did it fear? But to begin with, there was fear, but at the end, tranquillity."*

B. Why the fear?

C. *It is in line with what R. Simeon b. Laqish said, for said R. Simeon b. Laqish, "What is the meaning of the verse of Scripture, 'And there was evening, and there was morning, the sixth day' (Gen. 1:31)? This teaches that the Holy One, blessed be He, made a stipulation with all of the works of creation, saying to them, 'If Israel accepts my Torah, well and good, but if not, I shall return you to chaos and void.'"*

I.27 A. Expounded R. Simai, "At the moment that the Israelites first said, 'we shall do,' and then, 'we shall listen,' six hundred thousand ministering angels came to each Israelite and tied on to each of them two crowns, one for the 'we shall do' and the other for the 'we shall listen.' When the Israelites sinned, however, a million two hundred thousand angels of destruction came down and took them away: 'And the children of Israel stripped themselves of their ornaments from Mount Horeb' (Ex. 33:6)."

I.28   A.   Said R. Eliezer, "At the moment that the Israelites first said, 'we shall do,' and then, 'we shall listen,' an echo came forth and proclaimed to them, 'Who has told my children this secret, which the ministering angels take advantage of: 'Bless the Lord, you angels of his, you mighty in strength who fulfil his word, who hearken to the voice of his word' (Ps. 103:2) – *first they do, then they hear*."

I.29   A.   *Said R. Hama b. R. Hanina, "What is the meaning of the verse of Scripture,* 'As the apple tree among trees of the wood, so is my beloved among the sons' (Song 2:3)? Why are the Israelites compared to an apple? To tell you, just as an apple – its fruit appears before the leaves, so the Israelites gave precedence to 'we shall do' over 'we shall hearken.'"

I.30   A.   *There was a Sadducee who saw Raba reviewing his studies, sitting with his fingers under his heel, so that the fingers spurted blood as he ground them down. He said to him, "Rash folk, whose mouths talked before their ears heard! You still persist in your impetuosity. You first of all ought to have listened, and if you could do it, then you could accept, but if not, you should not have accepted [the Torah]."*

        B.   *He said to him, "We* [88B] *who walked in integrity – of us it is written,* 'The integrity of the upright shall guide them' (Prov. 11:3), *but of those people who walked in perversity it is written,* 'But the perversity of the treacherous shall destroy them' (Prov. 11:3)."

I.31   A.   *Said R. Samuel bar Nahmani said R. Jonathan, "What is the meaning of the verse of Scripture,* 'You have ravished my heart, my sister, my bride, you have ravished my heart with one of your eyes' (Song 4:9)? To begin with, with one of your eyes, but when you carry out [the Torah], with both of your eyes."

I.32 A. Said Ulla, "Shameless is the bride who fornicates in her own bridal canopy."

B. *Said R. Mari son of Samuel's daughter, "What is the pertinent verse of Scripture? 'While the king sat at his table, my spikenard gave up its fragrance' (Song 1:12)."*

C. *Said Raba, "Still his love is with us, what is written being 'gave,' and not, 'went rotten.'"*

I.33 A. *Our rabbis have taught on Tannaite authority:*

B. Of those who are humiliated but don't humiliate others, hear themselves reviled but don't answer, act out of love and accept suffering with joy Scripture says, 'But those who love him are as the sun when he goes forth in his might' (Judg. 5:30)."

I.34 A. *Said R. Yohanan, "What is the meaning of this verse of Scripture: 'The Lord gives the word, they who publish the good news are a great host' (Ps. 68:12)? Every act of speech that came forth from the mouth of the Almighty was divided into seventy languages."*

I.35 A. *A Tannaite statement of the household of R. Ishmael: "'And like a hammer that breaks the rock into pieces' (Jer. 23:29) – just as a hammer yields ever so many sparks, so every work that came forth from the mouth of the Holy One, blessed be He, was divided into seventy languages."*

I.36 A. *Said R. Hananel bar Pappa, "What is the meaning of the following verse of Scripture: 'Hear, for I will speak princely things' (Prov. 8:6)? Why are the teachings of Torah compared to a prince? To tell*

you: Just as a prince has the
power to kill or grant life, so
teachings of the Torah have the
power to kill or to grant life."

B. *That is in line with what Raba said,*
"For those that go to the right of it, it
is an elixir of life, and for those that
go to the left of it, it is a deadly
poison."

I.37 A. *Said R. Joshua b. Levi, "What is the*
meaning of that which is stated in
Scripture, 'My beloved is to me as
a bundle of myrrh, that lies
between my breasts' (Song 1:13)?
Said the community of Israel
before the Holy One, blessed be
He, 'Lord of the world, even
though my life is distressed and
embittered, yet my love lies
between my breasts.'

B. '"My beloved is to me as a cluster
of henna flowers in the vineyards
of En Gedi' (Song 1:14): he to
whom all things belong will atone
for me for the sin of the kid that I
stored up for myself.'"

I.38 A. *And said R. Joshua b. Levi, "What is*
the meaning of the following verse of
Scripture: 'His cheeks are as a bed
of spices' (Song 5:13)? From
every word that came forth from
the mouth of the Holy One,
blessed be He, the world was
filled with spices. But since, by
the first word, the world was
filled, where did the fragrance of
the second go? The Holy One,
blessed be He, brought forth
wind from his treasury and made
each pass on in sequence: 'his lips
are as lilies dripping myrrh that
passes on' (Song 5:13) – read the
word for lilies as though it
yielded the sense 'that lead step
by step.'"

I.39 A. And said R. Joshua b. Levi, "At
every word that came forth from
the mouth of the Holy One,
blessed be He, the souls of the
Israelites went forth, as it is said,
'My soul went forth when he

spoke' (Song 5:6). But since their souls departed at the first word, how could they receive the next? He brought down dew, with which he will resurrect the dead, and brought them back to life: 'your God sent a plentiful rain, you confirmed your inheritance when it was weary' (Ps. 68:10)."

I.40   A.   And said R. Joshua b. Levi, "At every word that came forth from the mouth of the Holy One, blessed be He, the Israelites retreated for twelve miles, but the ministering angels led them back: 'the hosts of angels march, they march' (Ps. 68:13) – read the word as though its consonants yielded 'they lead.'"

I.41   A.   And said R. Joshua b. Levi, "When Moses came up on high, the ministering angels said before the Holy One, blessed be He, 'Lord of the world, what is one born of woman doing among us?' He said to them, 'He has come to receive the Torah.'

      B.   "They said before him, 'This secret treasure, hidden by you for nine hundred and seventy-four generations before the world was created, are you now planning to give to a mortal? "What is man, that you are mindful of him, and the son of man, that you think of him, O Lord our God, how excellent is your name in all the earth! Who has set your glory upon the heavens" (Ps. 8:5, 2)!'

I.42   A.   And said R. Joshua b. Levi, "When Moses came down from before the Holy One, blessed be He, Satan came and said before him, 'Lord of the world, where is the Torah?'

      B.   "He said to him, 'I gave it to the earth.'

I.43   A.   And said R. Joshua b. Levi, "At the time that Moses went up on high, he found the Holy One in session, affixing crowns to the letters [of the words of the Torah]. He said to him, 'Moses, don't people greet each other with "peace" where you come from?'"

I.44   A.   And said R. Joshua b. Levi, "What is the meaning of the statement, 'And when the people saw that Moses delayed coming down from the mountain' (Ex. 32:1)? Read the word for delay as though its consonants yielded the word 'the sixth hour has come.'"

I.45   A.   *Said one of the rabbis to R. Kahana, "Have you heard the meaning of the words 'Mount Sinai'?"*

       B.   He said to him, "The mountain on which miracles [nissim] were done for Israel."

I.46   A.   *That is in line with what R. Yosé b.* R. Hanina said, "It has five names: the wilderness of Sin, for there the Israelites were given commandments; the wilderness of Kadesh, where the Israelites were sanctified; the wilderness of Kedemot, for there the Israelites were given priority; the wilderness of Paran, [89B] for there Israel was fruitful and multiplied; and the wilderness of Sinai, for there hatred descended for the gentiles. But what really is its name? Horeb is its name."

II.1   A.   **"How do we know that they tie a red thread on the head of the scapegoat [which is sent forth]? Since it says, 'Though your sins be as scarlet, they shall be white as snow' (Isa. 1:18)":**

       B.   *Rather than* "like scarlet threads," *what is needed is* "like a scarlet thread"!

II.2   A.   *Raba expounded, "What is the meaning of this verse of Scripture:* 'Go now and let us reason together, shall the Lord say' (Isa. 1:18)? *Instead of 'go' what is required is 'come.'*

       B.   "In the time to come the Holy One, blessed be He, will say to

II.3 A. *Said R. Samuel bar Nahmani said R. Jonathan, "What is the meaning of the verse of Scripture:* 'For you are our father, though Abraham doesn't know us, and Israel doesn't acknowledge us, you Lord are our father, our redeemer, from everlasting is your name' (Isa. 63:16)?

      B. "In the time to come the Holy One, blessed be He, will say to Abraham, 'Your children have sinned against me.' He will answer him, 'Lord of the world, let them be wiped out for the sake of the sanctification of your name.'

II.4 A. Said R. Hiyya bar Abba said R. Yohanan, "It was quite appropriate for our father Abraham to go down to Egypt in iron chains, but the accumulated heavenly favor saved him from such a fate: 'I drew them with the cords of a man, with bands of love, and I was to them as they that take off the yoke on their jaws and I laid meat before them' (Hos. 11:4)."

9:5

A. He who brings out wood – [is liable if he carries out] enough to cook a small egg;

B. spices – enough to spice a small egg;

C. and they join together with one another [to make up the requisite quantity to impose liability].

D. (1) Nutshells, (2) pomegranate shells, (3) woad, and (4) dyer's madder – enough to dye a garment as small as a hairnet;

E. (5) urine, (6) soda, (7) soap, (8) cimolian earth, or (9) lion's leaf – enough to launder a garment as small as a hairnet.

F. R. Judah says, "Enough to spread over a bloodstain."

I.1 A. *We've already learned the same as a Tannaite statement:* Reed – enough to make a pen. And if it was thick or broken – enough to [make a fire to] cook the smallest sort of egg, mixed [with oil] and put in a pan.

B. *What might you otherwise have supposed? In that case the reason is that it is really useful for no purpose, but as to wood, since it's fit to serve as the tooth of a key, no matter how small a volume of wood would be involved, one would be culpable; so we are informed that that is not the case.*

II.1 A. Spices – enough to spice a small egg:

B. *By way of contradiction:* [As regards] spices – If two or three different types of prohibitions pertain to one kind of spice, or to three distinct kinds of spices – it is forbidden, for the spices join together [to render forbidden that which they flavor. R. Simeon says, "Two or three different types of prohibitions which pertain] to one kind of spice, or two different kinds of spices subject to one type of prohibition do not join together to render forbidden the food which they flavor" [M. Orl. 2:10A-E]. [90A] *And said Hezekiah, "Here we deal with several types of sweeteners; since all of them are suitable for sweetening what is in the pot, [they join together as specified]." So the operative criterion is that they are fit for sweetening a dish, but otherwise not?*

C. *Here, too, it is what is fit for sweetening.*

III.1 A. Nutshells, pomegranate shells, woad, and dyer's madder – enough to dye a garment as small as a hairnet:

B. *By way of contradiction:* As to dyes that have been dissolved, the requisite measure is the amount needed to dye a sample of wool.

C. Said R. Nahman said Rabbah bar Abbuha, "The point is that someone won't go to the trouble to steep dyes to dye therewith merely a sample color for wool."

IV.1 A. Urine:

B.   For forty days.

V.1   A.   Soda:

     B.   *A Tannaite statement:* This refers to Alexandrian, not Antipatrian soda.

VI.1   A.   Soap:

     B.   Said R. Judah, "This is *ahala.*"

VII.1   A.   Cimolian earth:

     B.   Said R. Judah, "This is 'pull-out-stick-in.'"

VIII.1 A.   Lion's leaf:

     B.   *Said Samuel, "I asked those who go down to the sea, and they told me, [Slotki:] 'It is called ashlaga, and it is found between the cracks of pearls and is extracted with an iron nail.'"*

9:6

A.   (1) Pepper in any quantity at all; (2) tar in any quantity at all; (3) various sorts of spices and metal tools in any quantity at all;

B.   (1) stones of the altar, (2) dirt of the altar, (3) worn-out holy books, and (4) their worn-out covers – in any quantity at all.

C.   They store them away in order to hide them [for permanent storage].

D.   R. Judah says, "Also: He who takes out any of the appurtenances of an idol in any quantity at all [is liable],

E.   "since it says, 'And there shall cleave nought of the devoted thing to your hand' (Deut. 13:17)."

I.1   A.   Pepper in any quantity at all:

     B.   In any quantity at all? *What's it good for?*

     C.   Tic tacs.

II.1   A.   Tar in any quantity at all:

     B.   *What's it good for?*

     C.   For [Freedman:] megrim.

III.1   A.   Various sorts of spices...in any quantity at all:

     B.   *Our rabbis have taught on Tannaite authority:*

     C.   He who carries out a perfume with a bad smell – in any quantity at all; if it is good oil – in any quantity at all; if it is crimson – any quantity at all; if it is a closed rose – one will do it.

IV.1   A.   Various sorts of metal tools in any quantity at all:

     B.   *What's it good for?*

     C.   *It has been taught on Tannaite authority:*

		D.	R. Simeon b. Eleazar says "For out of it one can make a small goad."

IV.2 A. *Our rabbis have taught on Tannaite authority:*

        B. [He who says, "Lo, I pledge myself to bring] iron":

IV.3 A. [He who says, "Lo, I pledge myself to bring] copper" should not bring] less than [the value of] a silver ma'ah [M. Men. 13:4C]:

        B. It has been taught on Tannaite authority:

        C. R. Eliezer b. Jacob says, "He must present nothing less than a small copper hook."

V.1 A. **Worn-out holy books, and their worn-out covers – in any quantity at all:**

        B. *Said R. Judah, "The worm that eats scrolls, the worm that eats silk, the grape-mite, the fig-worm, and the pomegranate worm all represent a danger."*

V.2 A. *There was a disciple in session before R. Yohanan, who was eating figs. He said to him, "My lord, there are thorns in figs."*

        B. *He said to him, "The worm has killed that man."*

9:7

A. He who takes out a peddler's basket, even though there are many different sorts of things in it, is liable only for a single sin-offering.

B. Garden seeds – less than a dried fig's bulk.

C. R. Judah b. Beterah says, "Five."

D. [The standard measures for the following are:] [90B] (1) for cucumber seeds – two, (2) gourd seeds – two, (3) Egyptian bean seeds – two;

E. [the standard measure for] (1) a clean, live locust – in any quantity whatsoever;

F. [the standard measure for] (2) a dead one – the size of a dried fig;

G. [the standard measure for] (3) 'a vineyard bird' [a kind of locust] whether alive or dead – in any quantity at all,

H. for they store it away for [later use as] a remedy.

I. R. Judah says, "Also one who takes out a living unclean locust – in any quantity at all,

J. "for they store it away for a child to play with it."

I.1   A.   [Garden seeds – less than a dried fig's bulk:] *By way of contradiction [to the view that for seeds, the seed for at least two plants involves culpability]:* "Manure or fine sand enough to manure a cabbage stalk," the words of R. Aqiba. And sages say, "Enough to manure a leek" [M. Shab. 8:5C-D].

       B.   *Said R. Pappa, "In the one case, it speaks of what was sown, in the other, what was not sown, because someone doesn't take the trouble to carry out only a single seed for sowing."*

II.1   A.   Two cucumber seeds:

       B.   *Our rabbis have taught on Tannaite authority:*

       C.   He who carries out seeds, if it is for planting, two are the requisite number to incur liability, and if it is for eating, enough to fill the mouth of a pig.

       D.   And how much does it take for a pig's mouthful? One.

       E.   If it is for fuel, as much as is needed to boil a soft-boiled egg.

       F.   If it is for calculating, two; others say, five [T. Shab. 8:31J-N].

II.2   A.   *Our rabbis have taught on Tannaite authority:*

       B.   He who takes out two hairs of a horse's tail or a cow's tail, lo, this one is liable, because he makes them into hunting nets.

       C.   He who takes out two stiff bristles of a pig, lo, this one is liable; of palm bands, two; of palm fillets, one [T. Shab. 9:1-2A].

III.1 A.   A vineyard bird [a kind of locust] whether alive or dead – in any quantity at all:

       B.   *So what's a vineyard bird?*

IV.1   A.   R. Judah says, "Also one who takes out a living unclean locust – in any quantity at all, for they store it away for a child to play with it":

B. *But the initial Tannaite authority thinks that that is not so. How come? It is lest the child eat it.*

C. *If so, then it should be the same for a clean locust, for lo, R. Kahana was standing before Rab and passing a shoshiba locust [an edible one] in front of his mouth. The other said to him, "Take it away, so that people won't say you're eating it and violating the law, 'you shall not make yourselves abominable' (Lev. 11:43)."*

This chapter yields not a single principle that would generate a problem elsewhere. That does not mean we have no unstated but generative principle, to the contrary. At every line we work with the principle that Scripture forms the source of all rulings of the Mishnah, which is subordinate and dependent. But the various cases and problems pursue their own interests, and the rather general conception behind them all in no way links each to any other. Here is a fine example of how the Talmud works – and also how it does not work. And we see, for this chapter, that it does not work in the way in which I posited at the outset. Can I discern in this chapter the presence of a set of issues that alert the framers of the Bavli's exegesis of the Mishnah to potentialities for generalization and abstraction that inhere in a given rule? No. All I see is one problem, the scriptural origin of Mishnah rules, worked out in countless ways, but definitive of none of the details. But when I claim that two sets of intersecting principles are brought into juxtaposition – my mixed grid – I speak of details and more details. To demonstrate so omnipresent a generalization that Scripture is the source for everything in the Mishnah (so far as the exegetical program of the Bavli is concerned), I hardly need to pay attention to the details of a single discussion anywhere; all I need to do is point to the presence of the formula, "Whence is the source of this statement?" and its variations – no code there! The opposite of a code is paramount: what the Bavli wishes to say everywhere, it says openly and explicitly everywhere.

6

Bavli Shabbat
Chapter Eleven

Folios 96A-102A

The remarks at the beginning of Chapter Three explain the work of this chapter as well. The results set forth at the end of Chapter Five are replicated in the foregoing repertoire of the chapter. Readers not interested in a detailed survey are advised to turn directly to the concluding chapter.

11:1

A. He who throws [an object] from private domain to public domain, [or] from public domain to private domain, is liable.

B. [He who throws an object] from private domain to private domain, and public domain intervenes –

C. R. Aqiba declares [him] liable [to a sin-offering].

D. And sages exempt [him].

11:2

A. How so?

B. Two balconies opposite one another [extending] into the public domain –

C. he who stretches out or throws [an object] from this one to that one is exempt.

D. [If] both of them were [different private domains on the same side of the street and] at the same story,

E. he who stretches [an object over] is liable, and he who throws from one to the other is exempt.

F. For thus was the mode of labor of the Levites:

G. Two wagons, one after the other, in the public domain –

H. they stretch beams from this one to that one, but they do not throw [them from one to the other] –

173

I.1   A.   [96B] [He who throws:] *Note: Throwing is a derivative of the generative classification of labor of carrying out. But as to carrying from private to public domain, how on the basis of Scripture do we know that that act is forbidden on the Sabbath?*

I.2   A.   *Thus we have found that it is forbidden on the Sabbath to carry objects out from private domain to public domain. How do we know that carrying objects in from public domain to private domain also is forbidden?*

       B.   *It's a matter of reasoning. When it comes to taking something from one domain to another, what difference does it make if it is taking something out or bringing something in?*

I.3   A.   *And as to that which we have learned in the Mishnah:* He who throws [something from a distance of] four cubits toward a wall — [if he throws it] above ten handbreadths, it is as if he throws it into the air [which is public domain]. [If it is] less than ten handbreadths, it is as if he throws an object onto the ground [which is private domain]. He who throws [an object to a distance of] four cubits on the ground, is liable [M. Shab. 11:3] — *How do we know that he who throws an object for four cubits in public domain is liable?*

       B.   Said R. Josiah, "It is in the model of curtain weavers [for the hangings of the tabernacle], who toss their needles to one another across public domain."

I.4   A.   Said R. Judah said Samuel, "[The sin] of the wood gatherer [at Num. 15:32ff.] was that he carried the wood for four cubits in public domain."

       B.   *In a Tannaite formulation it is taught:* He was [guilty on the count of] cutting them off. [That is *equivalent to harvesting, detaching produce from the ground.]*

I.5 A. *Our rabbis have taught on Tannaite authority:*

B. "The gatherer of wood was Zelophahad. Here the word 'wilderness' occurs, 'and while the children of Israel were in the wilderness, they found a man gathering sticks' (Num. 15:32), and elsewhere the word 'wilderness' occurs, 'our father died in the wilderness' (Num. 27:3). Just as in the latter context reference is to Zelophahad, so here the same meaning pertains," the words of R. Aqiba.

C. Said to him R. Judah b. Beterah "[Aqiba!] One way or the other you are destined to stand in judgment. If you are right, the Torah protected him and you expose him, and if you are wrong, you slander that righteous man" [Sifré to Numbers CXIII:I.3].

I.6 A. Along these same lines:

B. "'And the anger of the Lord was kindled against them, and he departed' (Num. 12:9) – this teaches that Aaron, too, was smitten with the skin ailment," the words of R. Aqiba.

I.7 A. Said R. Simeon b. Laqish, "He who casts suspicion on genuinely upright people is smitten in his body, for it is written, 'And Moses said, but behold, they will not believe me' (Ex. 4:1). *But it was perfectly clear to the Holy One, blessed be He, that the Israelites were faithful.* He said to him, 'They are faithful, children of the faithful, but you are the one who in the end will prove unfaithful. They are faithful: 'And the people believed' (Ex. 4:31); they are the children of the faithful: 'And Abraham believed in the Lord' (Gen. 15:6). But you are the one who in the end will prove unfaithful: 'And the Lord said to Moses and Aaron, because you didn't believe in me' (Num. 20:12)."

I.8   A.   Said Raba, and some say, R. Yosé bar Hanina, "A good reward comes more quickly than punishment. With reference to punishment: 'And he took it out and behold it was afflicted with the skin ailment, as white as snow' (Ex. 4:6), while with reference to a good reward: 'And he took it out of his bosom and behold it was turned again as his other skin' (Ex. 4:7) – from his very bosom it had already turned as his other skin."

I.9   A.   "But Aaron's rod swallowed up their rods" (Ex. 7:12):

      B.   Said R. Eleazar, "It was a miracle inside of a miracle."

II.1 A.   [He who throws an object] from private domain to private domain, and public domain intervenes – R. Aqiba declares [him] liable [to a sin-offering]. And sages exempt [him]:

      B.   *Rabbah raised this question: "Do they differ concerning space within ten handbreadths of the ground? Then this is what is subject to dispute: The one authority maintains,* 'An object caught in the air is equivalent [in respect to the Sabbath] to one that has come to rest,' *and the other authority holds,* 'An object caught in the air is not equivalent [in respect to the Sabbath] to one that has come to rest.' But as to the passage of the object above ten handbreadths from the ground, all parties concur that one is exempt, *and we do not treat as analogous throwing an object and reaching an object across such a space. Or perhaps they differ as to the space above ten handbreadths from the ground. And this is what is subject to dispute: One authority holds that we do treat* as analogous throwing an object and reaching an object across such a space. And the other authority holds that we do not treat as analogous throwing an object and reaching an object across such a space. But as to the passage of an object within ten handbreadths of the ground, all parties concur that he is liable. How come? Because 'an object caught in the air is equivalent [in respect to the Sabbath] to one that has come to rest.'"

II.2   A. *And [Hamnuna] differs from R. Eleazar, for* said R. Eleazar, "R. Aqiba imposed liability even if the object traveled more than ten handbreadths above the ground," *and the reason that they made reference in particular to the public domain itself was to tell you how far rabbis were willing to go in taking the opposite view.*

       B. *And [Eleazar] differs from R. Hilqiah bar Tobi, for* said R. Hilqiah bar Tobi, "If the object passes within three handbreadths of the ground, all parties concur that he is liable; if it passes more than ten handbreadths above the ground, all parties concur that he is exempt. If it passes from three to ten handbreadths above the ground, then we come to the dispute between R. Aqiba and rabbis."

II.3   A. The master has said, "If the object passes within three handbreadths of the ground, the operative consideration is only the matter of Sabbath rest, so if both properties belong to him, to begin with it is permitted to carry" –

II.4   A. *Said R. Hisda to R. Hamnuna, and some say, R. Hamnuna to R. Hisda, "What is the basis of that which rabbis have stated: 'Any space that is within three handbreadths of the ground is equivalent to being joined to the ground'?"*

B. He said to him, "It is because it's not possible to trim the public domain with a plane and scissors." [Freedman: The ground cannot be perfectly leveled and it must contain bumps of that height; therefore everything within three handbreadths of the ground is regarded as joined to the ground.]

II.5 A. *Our rabbis have taught on Tannaite authority:*

B. If one tossed an object from public domain to public domain, with private domain intervening –

C. Rabbi declares the act liable.

D. And sages declare it exempt.

II.6 A. *It is obvious that* if he intended to toss the object eight cubits but threw it four, it is as though he wrote SIM as part of SIMEON [and he is liable, since that would form a word on its own]. But if one intended to throw an object four cubits and he threw it for eight, what is the law? *Do we maintain the view, well, anyhow, he did what he planned in transporting the object? Or do we say well, anyhow, it didn't land where he wanted?*

II.7 A. *Our rabbis have taught on Tannaite authority:*

B. **He who tosses an object from public domain to public domain with private domain intervening –**

C. **If it traveled four cubits over public domain [both segments of public domain being regarded as joined together] he is liable. [98A] If it traveled less than four cubits over public domain, he is exempt [cf. T. Shab. 10:1A-C].**

II.8 A. *So what's the point?*

B. *Here's the point:* Distinct portions of a given domain join together, *so that we don't invoke the rule,* An object caught in the air is equivalent [in respect to the

Sabbath] to one that has come to rest.

II.9　A.　Said R. Samuel bar Judah said R. Abba said R. Huna said Rab, "If someone transfers an object through four cubits of public domain that is roofed over, he is exempt from liability, since that area is not comparable to the case of the flags of the wilderness." [Freedman: The definition of what constitutes forbidden work on the Sabbath depends on the work that was done in connection with the tabernacle in the wilderness; carrying was necessary, so carrying an object four cubits is work. But there it was done under the open sky, hence Rab's statement; the same applies here. By "flags of the wilderness" is meant the whole disposition and encampment of the Israelites; they didn't have any cover in public ground.]

　　　B.　*But is that true?　Weren't the wagons covered?　And* said Rab in the name of R. Hiyya, "As for the wagons, the space that was underneath them, between them, and at their sides is classified as public domain." [Freedman: The width of the wagons was five cubits, five cubits of space was allowed between them in breadth, and the boards were ten cubits in length; when placed crosswise on top of the wagons they projected two and a half cubits on both sides; so the space between them was completely covered over, and yet he calls it public domain.]

II.10　A.　*Our rabbis have taught on Tannaite authority:*

　　　B.　"The boards were a cubit thick at the bottom and tapered to a fingerbreadth thick at the top: 'They shall be entire to the top thereof' (Ex. 26:24), and elsewhere, 'the waters were entire and were cut off' (Josh. 3:17)," the words of R. Judah.

C.   And R. Nehemiah says, "Just as at the bottom they were a cubit thick, so at the top they were a cubit thick: 'And in like manner they shall be entire.'"

II.11   A.   "And the middle bar in the midst of the boards shall pass through from end to end" (Ex. 26:28):

B.   *A Tannaite statement:* It stood there by a miracle [one long straight bar that passed along three walls, the necessary bending between the angles of the walls was miraculously done by itself (Freedman)].

II.12   A.   "Moreover you shall make the tabernacle with ten curtains; the length of each curtain shall be twenty-eight cubits" (Ex. 26:1-2):

B.   *Assign the length over the breadth of the tabernacle – how long was it? Twenty-eight cubits. Take off ten for the roof, thus leaving nine cubits on each side.*

II.13   A.   "And you shall make curtains of goats' hair for a tent over the tabernacle; eleven curtains you shall make them; the length of each curtain shall be thirty cubits and the breadth of each curtain four cubits" (Ex. 26:7-8);

II.14   A.   *So, too, it has been taught on Tannaite authority:*

B.   "'And the cubit on one side and the cubit of the other side, of that which remains in the length of the curtains of the tent' (Ex. 26:13) – this was to cover the cubit of the sockets," the words of R. Judah.

C.   R. Nehemiah says, "It was to cover the cubit of the boards."

II.15   A.   *A Tannaite statement of the household of R. Ishmael:*

B.   To what was the tabernacle comparable? To a woman who goes out into the street with her skirts trailing behind her on the ground.

II.16   A.   *Our rabbis have taught on Tannaite authority:*

       B.   The boards of the tabernacle were cut out and the sockets were grooved [99A], and the claps in the loops looked like stars set in the sky."

II.17   A.   *Our rabbis have taught on Tannaite authority:*

       B.   The lower curtains were made of blue wool, purple wool, crimson thread, and fine linen, and the upper ones were made of goats' hair. It took more skill to make the upper ones than the lower ones. For in respect to the lower ones it is written, "And all the women who were smart did spin with their hands" (Ex. 35:25), and in reference to the upper ones, "And all the women whose heart stirred them up in wisdom spun the goats' hair" (Ex. 35:26).

II.18   A.   *And it has been taught on Tannaite authority in the name of R. Nehemiah:* "It was washed directly on the goats and spun on the goats."

III.1   A.   **Two balconies opposite one another [extending] into the public domain – he who stretches out or throws [an object] from this one to that one is exempt. [If] both of them were [different private domains on the same side of the street and] at the same story, he who stretches [an object over] is liable, and he who throws from one to the other is exempt:**

       B.   Said Rab in the name of R. Hiyya, "As for the wagons, the space that was underneath them, between them, and at their sides is classified as public domain." [Freedman: The width of the wagons was five cubits, five cubits of space was allowed between them in breadth, and the boards were ten cubits in length; when placed crosswise on top of

the wagons they projected two
and a half cubits on both sides; so
the space between them was
completely covered over, and yet
he calls it public domain.]

C. Said Abbayye, "Between one
wagon and another at its side was
the space of a full wagon length.
And how much was that? Five
cubits. *Why was this required,
when four and a half would have
been enough?* [Freedman: Either
for three rows of boards lying on
their breadth, yielding four and a
half cubits, or four rows lying on
their thickness, leaving an
additional half cubit to cover the
extra space needed for the bars.]
*So that the boards wouldn't bump
into each other*" [Freedman/Rashi:
if laid on their breadth].

11:2I-K

I. The bank of a cistern and the rock ten handbreadths high and
    four broad –

J. he who takes [something] from that area or who puts something
    onto that area is liable.

K. [If they were] less than the stated measurements, he is exempt
    [from any penalty for such an action].

I.1   A. *Why employ for the Tannaite
            formulation,* The bank of a cistern
            and the rock, *rather than simply
            saying,* a cistern and the rock?
            *That odd formulation supports the
            position of R. Yohanan, for* R.
            Yohanan has said, "A cistern and
            its bank combine to reach the
            requisite height of ten
            handbreadths [such that the
            cistern forms private domain]."

        B. *So, too, it has been taught on
            Tannaite authority:*

I.2   A. *R. Mordecai addressed this question
            to Rabbah:* "A pillar in public
            domain, ten handbreadths high
            and four broad, and one tossed
            something which came to rest on
            it – what is the law? *Do we say, lo,
            removing the object violated a
            prohibition and bringing it to rest*

*violated a prohibition, or, perhaps,
since it comes from a place that is not
subject to liability, it is not a
culpable action?"*

I.3   A.   *Said R. Misha, "R. Yohanan raised
this question:* A wall in public
domain, ten handbreadths high
but not four broad, surrounding
neglected public domain and thus
turning it into private domain,
and one throws something and it
lands on top of the wall – what is
the law? *Do we say, since it is not
four handbreadths broad, it is a place
that is not subject to liability? Or
maybe, since it turns the area into
private domain, it is as though it
were filled up* [reaching the top of
the wall so that the wall and the
neglected public domain are one,
the whole now forming private
domain (Freedman)]?"

I.4   A.   *R. Yohanan raised this question:* "A
pit nine handbreadths deep, from
which one removed a piece [a
handbreadth in thickness,
bringing the pit to a depth of] ten
handbreadths deep – what is the
law? *Does the taking up of the piece
[thus deepening the pit] and the
making of the partition take place
simultaneously, in which case he is
culpable? Or is he not culpable?
And if you should propose that, since
there was no partition ten
handbreadths deep to begin with, he
is not liable, then,* if a pit was ten
handbreadths deep and one put
into it a piece of dirt and so
diminished the depth, what is the
law? *Might we say that putting
down the object and removing the
partition thereby took place at one
and the same time, in which case he
is liable, or is he not liable?"*

       B.   *You may solve the problem for him
by his own statement, for we have
learned in the Mishnah:* He who
throws [something from a
distance of] four cubits toward a
wall – [if he throws it] above ten

handbreadths, it is as if he throws it into the air [which is public domain]. [If it is] less than ten handbreadths, it is as if he throws an object onto the ground [which is private domain]. He who throws [an object to a distance of] four cubits on the ground, is liable [M. 11:3A-D]. *Surely it doesn't come to rest there [but bounces]!* And said R. Yohanan, "This rule was repeated in regard to a cake of juicy figs [which stick]." *Now why should this be the case? Surely it diminishes the four cubits!* [Freedman: for the thickness of the figs must be deducted; nonetheless, he is culpable, and the same reasoning applies to the second problem here].

I.5   A.   *Raba raised this question:* "If one threw a board and it landed on poles [ten handbreadths high but not four square, and the board is four square], what is the law [as to the construction's constituting private domain, since it is now ten handbreadths high and four square]?"

       B.   *So what's the point of his question? Is it the law governing a case in which an article comes to rest and also forms a partition at one and the same moment? But that is precisely the question R. Yohanan raised!*

I.6   A.   *Said Raba,* "It is clear to me: Water that is lying on water – lo, that is a situation in which it has come to rest. A nut that is lying upon water – lo, that is [100A] not a situation in which it has come to rest."

       B.   *Raba raised this question:* "A nut that is lying in a utensil, and a utensil is floating on water – do we invoke the criterion of the situation of the nut, in which case it has come to rest, or do we go by the criterion of the utensil, which, being unstable, has not come to rest?"

    C.   *The question stands.*

The issue here is subject to generalization: Do we invoke as our criterion the principal object or the subsidiary one?

I.7	A.	As to oil floating on wine there is a dispute between R. Yohanan b. Nuri and rabbis, *for we have learned in the Mishnah:* Oil which is floating on the surface of wine, and one who has immersed on that day and awaits sunset for the completion of his rite of purification [a tebul-yom] touched the oil – he has rendered unfit only the oil.
	B.	R. Yohanan b. Nuri says, "Both of them are deemed connected to one another" [M. T.Y. 2:5H-K].
I.8	A.	Said Abbayye, "In the case of a pit in public domain ten handbreadths deep and eight wide, into which one tossed a mat – he is liable; but if he divided it with a mat, [down the middle], he is not liable." [Freedman: The thickness of the mat leaves less than four square handbreadths on either side, so that neither is now private domain.]
I.9	A.	And said Abbayye, "A pit in public domain, ten handbreadths deep and four wide, filled with water, into which one tossed something – he is liable. If it is full of produce and one tossed something into it, he is not liable. *How come? The water does not have the effect of nullifying the partition, but the produce nullifies the partition.*"

11:3A-D

A.   He who throws [something from a distance of] four cubits toward a wall –

B.   [if he throws it] above ten handbreadths, it is as if he throws it into the air [which is public domain].

C.   [If it is] less than ten handbreadths, it is as if he throws an object onto the ground [which is private domain].

D.   He who throws [an object to a distance of] four cubits on the ground, is liable.

I.1   A.   [He who throws [something
              from a distance of] four cubits
              toward a wall:] *But lo, the object
              doesn't come to rest!*

        B.   Said R. Yohanan, "We learn the
              Mishnah rule with reference to
              throwing ripe figs [which will
              stick]."

I.2   A.   Said R. Judah said Rab said R.
              Hiyya, "If one threw an object
              above ten handbreadths and it
              went and came to rest in a hole of
              any size at all, that brings us to
              the dispute of R. Meir and rabbis,
              *for R. Meir takes the view that in our
              imagination we hollow the hole to
              complete it to the requisite
              dimensions, so liability is incurred,
              and rabbis take the view that we do
              not do so.*"

I.3   A.   Said R. Judah said Rab, "A
              mound   that   reaches   ten
              handbreadths within a space of
              four handbreadths [Freedman:
              which is too steep to be climbed
              in an ordinary stride, so the top is
              classified as private domain],
              onto the top of which one tossed
              an object, which came to rest – he
              is liable."

11:3E-F

E.   [If] he threw [an object] within the space of four cubits and it
      rolled beyond four cubits, he is exempt.

F.   [If he threw an object] beyond four cubits and it rolled back into
      four cubits, he is liable.

I.1   A.   [If he threw an object beyond
              four cubits and it rolled back
              into four cubits, he is liable:] *But
              lo, the object doesn't come to rest!*

        B.   Said R. Yohanan, "That is a case
              in which beyond the four cubits it
              comes to rest on something,
              whatever the dimensions thereof,
              [even for a moment]."

I.2   A.   *So, too, it has been taught on
              Tannaite authority:*

        B.   If someone threw an object
              beyond four cubits but the wind
              blew it and brought it back, and

even if it carried it out again, he is not liable; if the wind held it for a moment, even if it carries the object in again, he is liable."

I.3 A. Said Raba, "For an article that is carried within three hand-breadths of the ground to be regarded as having come to rest, in rabbis' opinion, it has to be put down on something of some small size at least."

B. *In session Maremar reported this tradition. Said Rabina to Maremar,* [100B] *"Isn't this what our Mishnah paragraph says, on which R. Yohanan commented, 'That is a case in which beyond the four cubits it comes to rest on something, whatever the dimensions thereof, [even for a moment]'?"*

11:4

A. He who throws [an object to a distance of] four cubits into the sea is exempt.

B. If it was shallow water and a public path passed through it, he who throws [an object for a distance of] four cubits is liable.

C. And what is the measure of shallow water?

D. Less than ten handbreadths in depth.

E. [If there was] shallow water, and a public path goes through it, he who throws into it to a distance of four cubits is liable.

I.1 A. *Said one of the rabbis to Raba, "There is no problem understanding why there are two references to 'passing through.' So we are informed that if it is possible to pass through, although with difficulty, that is classified as passing through; if it is possible to use with difficulty only, that is not classified as use.* [Freedman: A public road that passes through a pool counts as public domain; a pit in the street nine handbreadths deep can be used but only inconveniently, so it is not the same as a pillar of that height on which one can put a burden, which is classified as public domain.] *But how come there are two references to shallow water?"*

11:5

A. He who throws [an object] (1) from the sea to dry land or (2) from dry land to the sea,

B. or (3) from the sea to a boat, or (4) from a boat to the sea,

C. or (5) from one boat to another,

D. is exempt.

E. [If] boats are tied together, they move [objects] from one to the next.

F. If they are not tied together, even though they lie close together, they do not carry [objects] from one to the other.

I.1 A. *It has been stated:*

B. *A boat –*

C. R. Huna said, "They may stick a projection, of whatever size, over the side of the ship, and from it water may be drawn from the sea."

D. *R. Hisda and Rabbah b. R. Huna say,* "One makes an enclosure of four cubits and draws water that way." [Freedman: An enclosure above the water is made, which renders the water immediately below technically private domain, and through this, the water is drawn.]

I.2 A. *Said R. Huna, "As to the Mesenean canal boats [which are narrow and taper down at the bottom, being less than four handbreadths wide there and so not regarded as private domain],* they may not carry in them more than four cubits [just as one may not do so in public domain for more than four cubits]. And we have made that statement only if they have a breadth of four handbreadths at less than three handbreadths from the bottom; but if they have a breadth of four handbreadths at less than that distance from the bottom, *we have no objection; if they are filled with canes and bullrushes to the height at which they do have a breadth of four handbreadths, we also have no objection."*

II.1 A. [If] boats are tied together, they move [objects] from one to the next. If they are not tied together, even though they lie close together, they do not carry [objects] from one to the other:

B. *That's obvious!*

C. *Said Raba, "Not at all. The rule is necessary* to allow carrying by means of a small boat that is tethered between the ships, [which are fastened to the opposite sides of the tender]."

II.2 A. Said Samuel, "And that is the rule even if they are tied together by a cloak ribbon."

B. *So what's the point? If it can hold them together, that is obvious, and if it can't hold them together, why should that be so?*

C. *In point of fact, it can hold them together, but Samuel's intent is to exclude a point he himself has made, for we have learned in the Mishnah:* [If] one tied the ship with something which can hold it still, [or] held down a cloak with a stone, it brings the uncleanness; if it is with something that doesn't hold it still, it doesn't transmit to it uncleanness [M. Oh. 8:5I], on which Samuel made the statement, "and that is the case if it was fixed with an iron chain." That is so, in particular, when it pertains to uncleanness, in line with the verse "one that is slain with a sword" (Num. 19:16) – lo, metal that touches a corpse is unclean in the status of the corpse itself, [that is, as a generative source of uncleanness, so the chain will impart uncleanness to the ship], *but so far as the Sabbath is concerned, since it can hold the ship still, even if it is a cloak ribbon, that would suffice.*

11:6

A. [102A] He who throws [an object] and realizes [remembers what he has done] after it leaves his hand,

B. [if] another person caught it,

C. [if] a dog caught it,

D.   or [if] it burned up in a fire [intervening in its flight path] –
E.   he is exempt.
F.   [If] he threw it intending to inflict a wound,
G.   whether at a man or at a beast,
H.   and realizes [what he has done] before it inflicted the wound,
I.   he is exempt.
J.   This is the governing principle: All those who may be liable to sin-offerings in fact are not liable unless at the beginning and the end, their [sin] is done inadvertently.
K.   [But] if the beginning of their [sin] is inadvertent and the end is deliberate, [or] the beginning deliberate and the end inadvertent, they are exempt – unless at the beginning and at the end their [sin] is inadvertent.

I.1   A.   [He who throws an object and realizes what he has done after it leaves his hand, if another person caught it...he is exempt:] *Lo, if it should come to rest, he would be liable. But didn't he realize what happened? And we have learned in the Mishnah:* All those who may be liable to sin-offerings in fact are not liable unless at the beginning and the end, their [sin] is done inadvertently.

      B.   *Said R. Kahana, "The latter clause refers to a bolt and a cord* [that are tied together, that is, someone threw a bolt while holding the cord in his hand; if he realizes before it reaches the ground, he can pull it back, if he doesn't, then the fact that it comes to rest is deliberate; but if the article has entirely left his control and he can't prevent its falling, the result is regarded as inadvertent, whether or not he remembers the matter (Freedman)]."

The next item is a fabricated case that permits us to explore the principle that intentionality must govern at all phases of an action. Here the generalization is offered at the outset, and it clearly governs a wide variety of cases. Then we are given a concrete case, but it is framed to allow us to consider all of the intricacies of uniform intentionality.

II.1 A.   This is the governing principle: All those who may be liable to sin-offerings in fact are not liable unless at the beginning and the end, their [sin] is done inadvertently. [But] if the beginning of their [sin] is inadvertent and the end is deliberate, unless at the beginning and at the end their [sin] is inadvertent:

B. *It has been stated:*
C. If the object traveled for two cubits when the one who threw it did so inadvertently, but the next two cubits of the voyage were subject to his deliberate will, and then two more cubits unwittingly –
D. Rabbah said, "He is exempt."
E. Raba said, "He is liable."
F. Rabbah said, "He is exempt" – *even in the opinion of Rabban Gamaliel, who said,* "If one is aware of half of the requisite measure only, that is null." [Freedman: It does not separate two acts of eating, when in each case only half the standard quantity to create liability is consumed.] *That is the case in that situation, because, when he completes meeting the requisite standard for culpability, he completes it entirely inadvertently, but here, he completes the requisite standard deliberately, so that would not apply.*
G. *Then to what case would this refer? If it is to one who throws, well, he acts inadvertently throughout [once the object has left his hand]!*
H. *Rather, it refers to one who is carrying an object [and can stop in the middle of his progress through public domain].*
I. Raba said, "He is liable" – *and even from the perspective of rabbis, who maintain,* "If one is aware of half of the requisite measure only, that is effective," *in that case, he has the power to stop the action, but here he doesn't have the power to stop the action, so that is here not the case.*

J.   *Then to what case would this refer?*
     It can't be to one who is carrying an
     object in public domain, since he can
     stop the action.
K.   *Rather, it refers to one who throws*
     the object.

II.2   A.   Said Raba, "If one threw an object
                 and it fell into the mouth of a dog
                 or into a furnace, he is liable."
            B.   *But we have learned in the Mishnah:*
                 [If] a dog caught it, or [if] it
                 burned up in a fire [intervening
                 in its flight path] – he is exempt!

7

Bavli Shabbat
Chapter Sixteen

Folios 115A-122B

The remarks at the beginning of Chapter Three explain the work of this chapter as well. The results set forth at the end of Chapter Five are replicated in the foregoing repertoire of the chapter. Readers not interested in a detailed survey are advised to turn directly to the concluding chapter.

16:1A-F

A. All Holy Scriptures –
B. they save them from fire,
C. whether they read in them or do not read in them.
D. And even though they are written in any language [besides Hebrew], [if they become useless] they require storage [and are not to be burned].
E. And on what account do they not read in [some of] them?
F. Because of the neglect of the [proper study of the Torah in the] study house.

I.1   A. *It has been stated:*
       B. If they were written in an Aramaic translation of Scripture or in any other language –
       C. R. Huna said, "They do not save them from a fire."
       D. And R. Hisda said, "They do save them from a fire."

I.2   A. *Our rabbis have taught on Tannaite authority:*

B.   As to written out blessings and amulets, even though they contain letters or passages of the Torah in abundance, they do not save them on the Sabbath from a fire but are allowed to burn up where they are.

C.   In this connection they have said: those who write blessings are as though they burned the Torah.

I.3   A.   *The exilarch asked Rabbah bar R. Huna,* "If they were written in paint, red ink, gum ink, or calcanthum [cf. T. Shab. 13:4A], in Hebrew, do they save them from a fire or do they not save them from a fire?"

B.   *The question is raised from the perspective of him who said that they save Holy Writings written in other languages and it is also a question from the perspective of him who holds that we do not do so.*

I.4   A.   *R. Huna bar Halub raised this question of R. Nahman:* "A scroll of the Torah in which it is not possible to count eighty-five letters, such as the section, 'And it came to pass when the ark set forward' (Num. 10:35-36) – what is the law on saving it from a fire on the Sabbath?"

B.   *"Well, why not ask about the passage, 'and it came to pass...' itself?"*

I.5   A.   *The question was raised: As to the eighty-five characters,* do they have to be contiguous or may they even be scattered?

B.   R. Huna said, "They have to be contiguous."

C.   R. Hisda said, "They may even be scattered."

I.6   A.   *Our rabbis have taught on Tannaite authority:*

B.   "And it came to pass when the ark set forward that Moses said..." (Num. 10:35-6):

C.   For this passage, the Holy One, blessed be He, provided markers beginning and end [setting it off from its context], to say [116A] that this is not its correct location.

I.7 A. *In accord with whom is that which* R. Samuel bar Nahmani said R. Jonathan said, "'Wisdom has hewn out her seven pillars' (Prov. 9:1) – this refers to the seven scrolls of the Torah"*?*

B. *In accord with whom? In accord with Rabbi.*

I.8 A. *The question was raised:* Do they save the blank spaces of a scroll of the Torah from a fire or do they not save them from a fire?

B. *Come and take note:* A scroll of the Torah that wore out, if eighty-five letters can be collected therein, as in the section, "and it came to pass when the ark set forward," they save it, and if not, they don't. *Now why should this be the case? Conclude that it should be saved because of the blank space.*

I.9 A. *Reverting to the body of the foregoing:* **The blank spaces and other books of the heretics they do not save from a fire, but they are to be allowed to burn where they are, even with the mentions of the Divine Name that may be contained therein.**

B. **R. Yosé says, "On a weekday, one cuts out the Divine Names that they contain and hides them and burns the rest."**

I.10 A. *Joseph bar Hanina asked R. Abbahu,* "As to the scrolls that happen to belong to a temple of idolatry, do they save them from a fire or do they not save them from a fire?"

B. *"Well, uh, yes, but, well, uh, heah, hum, no" – and he didn't have in hand a solid reply!*

I.11 A. *Rab wouldn't walk into a temple of idolatry, all the more so a church; Samuel wouldn't go into a church, but he would go into a temple of idolatry.*

B.   *They said to Raba, "How come you didn't come to the temple of idolatry?"*

I.12   A.   *Imma Shalom, the wife of R. Eliezer, was sister of Rabban Gamaliel. There was a certain philosopher in her neighborhood [116B] who bore the good name of not taking bribes. They wanted to ridicule him. She brought him a gold lamp, went to him, and said to him, "I want to take a share in the estate of my father."*

II.1   A.   And on what account do they not read in [some of] them? Because of the neglect of the [proper study of the Torah in the] study house:

B.   Said Rab, "They made that statement only when the study house is in session, but when it is not the time of the study house, they may read them."

16:1G-K

G.   They save the case of the scroll with the scroll and the case of the phylacteries with the phylacteries,

H.   even though there is money in them.

I.   And where do they [take them to] save them?

J.   To a closed alley [which is not open as a thoroughfare and so is not public domain].

K.   Ben Beterah says, "Also: to one which is open [as a thoroughfare]."

I.1   A.   *Our rabbis have taught on Tannaite authority:*

B.   "If the fourteenth of Nisan coincided with a Sabbath, one may flay the Passover-offering only as far as the breast [to take the sacrificial portions out of the lamb; the rest of the flaying, to prepare the meat for eating, is left over until the evening]," the words of R. Ishmael b. R. Yohanan b. Beroqah.

C.   And sages say, "One may do so until he flays the whole of the beast."

I.2   A.   *Now there is no problem understanding the position of R. Ishmael b. R. Yohanan b. Beroqah.*

For the requirements of the Most High are being carried out in accord with the religious duty pertaining thereto. But what can possibly explain the position of rabbis?

B. Said Rabbah bar bar Hannah said R. Yohanan, "Said Scripture, 'The Lord has made everything for his own purpose' (Prov. 16:4)."

I.3 A. *And how does R. Ishmael b. R. Yohanan b. Beroqah deal with the verse,* "The Lord has made everything for his own purpose" (Prov. 16:4)?

I.4 A. *Said R. Hisda said R. Uqba, "How did the colleagues of R. Ishmael b. R. Yohanan b. Beroqah answer R. Ishmael b. R. Yohanan b. Beroqah?"*

B. *This is what they said to him:* "Since it is the fact that **they save the case of the scroll with the scroll and the case of the phylacteries with the phylacteries,** shouldn't we flay the Passover-offering from its hide?" [That is the principal labor (Freedman).]

II.1 A. And where do they [take them to] save them? To a closed alley [which is not open as a thoroughfare and so is not public domain]. Ben Beterah says, "Also: to one which is open [as a thoroughfare]":

B. *What is the definition of an* **open** alley *and what is the definition of a* closed alley?

16:2

A. They save food enough for three meals –

B. [calculated from] what is suitable for human beings for human beings, what is suitable for cattle for cattle.

C. How so?

D. [If] a fire broke out on the night of the Sabbath, they save food for three meals.

E. [If it broke out] in the morning, they save food for two meals.

F. [If it broke out] in the afternoon, [they save food for] one meal.

G. R. Yosé says, "Under all circumstances they save food for three meals."

I.1 A. [**They save food enough for three meals:**] *But since the man's*

> *trouble is subject to permission, why not let him save more than that?*

I.2   A. *Reverting to the body of the foregoing:* If a barrel of wine was broken on top of one's roof, he may bring a utensil and put it underneath, on condition that he not bring yet another utensil and catch the falling liquid [as it drops down] or another utensil and place it against the roof.

I.3   A. *Our rabbis have taught on Tannaite authority:*

       B. If one has saved bread made of fine flour, he may not save one made of coarse; if coarse, he may still save one of fine flour.

       C. One may save food on the Day of Atonement for use on the Sabbath, but not on the Sabbath for the Day of Atonement, and, it goes without saying, not on the Sabbath for a festival or on a **Sabbath for the next following Sabbath [T. Shab. 13:7B-C, 13:6N-R].**

I.4   A. *Our rabbis have taught on Tannaite authority:*

       B. **If one forgot a loaf of bread in the oven, and the day became sanctified through the advent of the Sabbath, they may save enough of it to serve as food for three meals.**

I.5   A. *Is that so? But lo, the Tannaite authority of the household of R. Ishmael [stated],* "'You shall not do any work' (Ex. 20:10) – excluding the sounding of the ram's horn and the removal of bread from the oven wall, which is an act of skill and not work.

I.6   A. Said R. Hisda, "A person should always get up early [on Friday] to provide for the requirements of the Sabbath: 'And it shall come to pass on the sixth day that they shall prepare that which they bring in' (Ex. 16:5) – on the spot."

I.7   A.   Said R. Abba, "And on the Sabbath one is liable to break bread using two loaves.

II.1   A.   How so? [If] a fire broke out on the night of the Sabbath, they save food for three meals. [If it broke out] in the morning, they save food for two meals. [If it broke out] in the afternoon, [they save food for] one meal. R. Yosé says, "Under all circumstances they save food for three meals":

       B.   *Our rabbis have taught on Tannaite authority:*

       C.   How many meals is a person required to eat on the Sabbath?

       D.   Three.

       E.   R. Hidqa says, "Four meals is a person obligated to eat on the Sabbath."

II.2   A.   Said R. Yohanan, "Both authorities interpret the same verse of Scripture: 'And Moses said, eat that today, for today is a Sabbath to the Lord, today you shall not find it in the field' (Ex. 16:25). *R. Hidqa takes the view that the three 'todays' are counted in addition to the meal of the prior evening, while rabbis maintain that they encompass the meal of the prior evening.*"

II.3   A.   *Now with reference to that which we have learned in the Mishnah:* Whoever has sufficient food for two meals may not take [food] from a soup kitchen. [Whoever has sufficient] food for fourteen meals may not take [money] from the [communal] fund [M. Pe. 8:7F-G], *in accord with which authority is that rule formulated? It can be neither rabbis nor R. Hidqa. It cannot be rabbis, for they would require fifteen meals, and it cannot be R. Hidqa, for there should be sixteen!*

II.4   A.   *And as to that which we have learned in the Mishnah:* They give to a poor man traveling from place to place no less than a loaf [of bread] worth a dupondion, [made from wheat which costs at least] one sela for four seahs. [If such a poor person] stayed overnight, they give him enough [to pay] for a night's lodging. [If such a poor person] spent the Sabbath, they give him food for three meals [M. Pe. 8:7A-D], *must we say that this represents the position of rabbis but not R. Hidqa?*

B. *In point of fact it represents the view of R. Hidqa, dealing with a case in which he already has one meal with him, so we say to him, "Eat what you have with you."*

II.5   A. *What is the definition of* enough [to pay] for a night's lodging?

B. *Said R. Pappa, "A bed and a cover."*

II.6   A. *Our rabbis have taught on Tannaite authority:*

B. As to the plates on which one ate in the evening, one may wash them to eat with them in the morning; in the morning, one may wash them to eat with them at noon; at noon, one may wash them to eat with them at dusk; at dusk and thereafter, one may not wash them again [until sunset].

II.7   A. Said R. Simeon b. Pazzi said R. Joshua b. Levi in the name of Bar Qappara, "Anyone who fulfills the duty of eating three meals on the Sabbath is saved from three punishments: the anguish of the Messiah, the judgment of Gehenna, and the war of Gog and Magog.

B. "The anguish of the Messiah: Here there is reference to 'day' and elsewhere, 'behold I will send you Elijah the prophet before the great and terrible day of the Lord comes' (Mal. 3:2).

II.8   A. Said R. Yohanan in the name of R. Yosé, "To anyone who makes the Sabbath a time of rejoicing they give an inheritance without limit: 'Then you shall delight yourself in the Lord and I will make you ride on the high places of the earth and I will feed you [118B] with the heritage of Jacob your father' (Isa. 58:14). That will not be like that of Abraham: 'Arise, walk through the land in the length of it' (Gen. 13:17), nor like that of Isaac: 'For to thee and your seed I will give all these lands' (Gen. 26:3), but like that of Jacob: 'And you shall spread abroad to the west, east, north, and south' (Gen. 28:14)."

II.9   A.   Said R. Judah said Rab, "To anyone who makes the Sabbath a time of rejoicing they give whatever his heart desires: 'Delight yourself also in the Lord and he will give you your heart's desires' (Ps. 37:4). Now I don't know what this 'delight' is, but when it says, 'and you shall call the Sabbath a delight' (Isa. 58:13), you must say, that refers to the pleasure of the Sabbath."

II.10   A.   In what way does one show his delight in the Sabbath?

B.   R. Judah b. R. Samuel bar Shilat in the name of Rab said, "With a beet dish, a large fish, and plenty of garlic."

II.11   A.   Said R. Hiyya bar Abba said R. Yohanan, "Whoever keeps the Sabbath in accord with its rule, even if he worships an idol like the generation of Enosh, do they forgive: 'Blessed is Enosh who does this...who keeps the Sabbath from profaning it' (Isa. 56:2) – read the letters that yield 'profaning it' as though they bore vowels to yield 'being forgiven.'"

II.12   A.   Said R. Judah said Rab, "If the Israelites had observed the first Sabbath, no nation or language could have ruled over them: 'And it came to pass on the seventh day that there went out some of the people to gather' (Ex. 16:27), followed by, 'Then came Amalek' (Ex. 17:8)."

II.13   A.   Said R. Yohanan in the name of R. Simeon b. Yohai, "If the Israelites keep two successive Sabbaths in a proper manner, they will be saved immediately: 'Thus says the Lord concerning the eunuchs that keep my Sabbaths' (Isa. 56:4), followed by, 'even them will I bring to my holy mountain' (Ex. 56:7)."

II.14   A.   Said R. Yosé, "May my portion be among those who eat three meals on the Sabbath."

        B.   And said R. Yosé, "May my portion be among those who complete the recitation of the Hallel-Psalms every day."

II.15   A.   Said R. Yosé, "I had sexual relations five times, and I planted five cedars in Israel."

        B.   *Who are they?*

        C.   R. Ishmael b. R. Yosé, R. Eleazar b. R. Yosé, R. Halafta b. R. Yosé, R. Abtilos b. R. Yosé, and R. Menahem b. R. Yosé.

II.16   A.   Said R. Yosé, "I never called my wife my wife, or my ox my ox, but my wife I call 'my home,' and my ox 'my field.'"

II.17   A.   *Said R. Nahman, "May I be rewarded for observing three meals on the Sabbath."*

II.18   A.   *Said R. Joseph to R. Joseph b. Rabbah, "As to your father, concerning what religious duty is he most zealous?"*

II.19   A.   *And said Abbayye, "May I be rewarded, for when I saw a neophyte rabbi who had completed his tractate, [119A] I made it a festival day for the rabbis."*

II.20   A.   *R. Hanina would stand in his cloak on the eve of the Sabbath at sunset and exclaim, "Come and let us go forth to greet the Sabbath, the Queen."*

II.21   A.   *Rabbah bar R. Huna visited the household of Rabbah bar R. Nahman. They served him three seahs of cakes made in oil. He said to them, "So did you know I was coming?"*

II.22   A.   *R. Abba bought meat for thirteen half-zuzes and handed the meat over to his servants at the door hinge, saying to them, "Rush, quick, rush, quick" [for the Sabbath]."*

II.23   A.   *R. Abbahu would sit on an ivory stool and fan the fire [to help with the cooking].*

II.24   A.   *Joseph the Sabbath Lover: There was a gentile in his neighborhood who had a lot of property. The Chaldaeans told him, "Joseph the Sabbath Lover is going to consume all your property." He went and old all his property and bought a jewel with the proceeds; this he put in his turban. As he was crossing a bridge, the wind blew off the turban and threw it into the water. A fish swallowed it.*

II.25   A.   *Rabbi raised this question to R. Ishmael b. R. Yosé:* "Through what deeds do the rich folk in the Land of Israel enjoy the merit [that brings them heavenly favor in the form of wealth]?"

II.26   A.   For said R. Hiyya bar Abba, "One time I was received as a guest in the home of a householder in Laodicea, and they brought before me a table of gold borne by sixteen men; there were sixteen silver chains fixed to it, with plates, goblets, pitchers, and flaxes set thereon, and on it there were all kinds of food, dainties and spices. When they set it down, they cited the verse, 'The earth is the Lord's and the fullness thereof' (Ps. 24:1), and when they took it away after the meal they recited, 'The heavens are the heavens of the Lord but the earth he has given to the children of men' (Ps. 115:16).

II.27   A.   Said Caesar to R. Joshua b. Hananiah, "How come the food cooked for the Sabbath has such a wonderful fragrance?"

II.28   A.   *Said the exilarch to R. Hamnuna, "What is the meaning of the verse of*

Scripture, 'and you shall call the
holy of the Lord honorable' (Isa.
58:13)?"

II.29   A.   "And you shall honor it" (Isa.
58:13) –

         B.   Rab said, "By bringing in the holy
day earlier than usual."

         C.   Samuel said, "By ending it later
than usual."

II.30   A.   *The sons of R. Pappa bar Abba said
to R. Pappa, "What about us, for
example, who eat meat and wine
every day – how are we supposed to
treat the Sabbath as a special day?"*

         B.   *He said to them, "If it is your custom
to eat early, eat later; if it is your
custom to eat late, eat earlier."*

II.31   A.   *R. Sheshet: In the summer he would
seat the rabbis in a place that the sun
reached, and in the winter, in a
shady place, so that they would leave
quickly.*

II.32   A.   *R. Zira* [119B] *would make the
rounds of pairs of rabbis, saying to
them, "By your leave, don't profane
it."*

II.33   A.   *Said Raba, and some say, R. Joshua
b. Levi, "Even an individual praying
by himself on the eve of the Sabbath
has to say the verses of the Sabbath,
'And the heaven and the earth
were finished' (Gen. 2:1)."*

II.34   A.   Said R. Eleazar, "How on the
basis of Scripture do we know
that speech is equivalent to
action? 'By the word of the Lord
were the heavens made' (Ps.
33:6)."

II.35   A.   Said R. Hisda said Mar Uqba,
"Whoever says the Prayer on the
eve of the Sabbath and includes
the Sabbath verses, 'And the
heaven and the earth were
finished...' (Gen. 2:1ff) – the two
angels who accompany a person
put their hands on his head and
say to him, 'and your iniquity is
taken away and your sin atoned
for' (Isa. 6:7)."

II.36   A.   *It has been taught on Tannaite
authority:*

B. R. Yosé bar Judah says, "Two
ministering angels accompany a
person on the eve of the Sabbath
from synagogue to home, one
good, the other bad. And when
he comes home and finds the
candle burning, the table set, the
bed laid out, the good angel says
to him, 'May it be God's will that
things should be this way on
other Sabbaths,' and the bad
angel willy-nilly says, 'Amen.'
But if it is not that way, then the
bad angel says, 'May it be God's
will that things should be this
way on other Sabbaths,' and the
good angel willy-nilly says,
'Amen.'"

II.37　A. Said R. Eleazar, "A person should
always set his table on the eve of
the Sabbath, even if he only needs
to put out food in the volume of
an olive."

II.38　A. *R. Abbahu would prepare for the end
of the Sabbath a calf three years old.
He would eat of it only a kidney.
When Abimi, his son, grew up, the
boy said to him, "So why waste so
much? Let's leave a kidney from
Friday."*

II.39　A. Said R. Joshua b. Levi, "Whoever
says the formula, 'Amen, may his
great name be blessed,' with all
his strength – they tear up for
him the decree that has been
issued against him: 'When
retribution was annulled in Israel,
for the people offered themselves
willingly, Bless you the Lord'
(Judg. 5:2). Why was 'retribution
annulled'? Because 'the people
offered themselves willingly.'"

II.40　A. Said R. Simeon b. Laqish,
"Whoever responds 'Amen' with
all his might – they open for him
the gates of the Garden of Eden:
'Open you the gates, that the
righteous nation, which keeps
truth, may enter in' (Isa. 26:2).
Don't read the letters that yield
'that keeps truth' in that way, but

as if they bore vowels to yield, 'that say amen.'"

II.41 A. Said R. Judah b. R. Samuel in the name of Rab, "Fire takes place only in a place in which there is a desecration of the Sabbath, as it is said, 'But if you will not hearken to me to hallow the Sabbath day and not to bear a burden...then will I kindle a fire in the gates thereof, and it shall devour the palaces of Jerusalem and it shall not be quenched' (Jer. 17:27)."

II.42 A. Said Abbayye, "Jerusalem was ruined only because they violated the Sabbath therein: 'And they have hidden their eyes from my Sabbaths, therefore I am profaned among them' (Ezek. 22:26)."

II.43 A. Said R. Judah said Rab, "*What is the meaning of the verse of Scripture,* 'Do not touch my anointed and do my prophets no harm' (1 Chr. 16:22)? 'Do not touch my anointed': This refers to the schoolchildren in the household of their teacher. '...And do my prophets no harm': This refers to disciples of sages."

II.44 A. Said R. Simeon b. Laqish in the name of R. Judah the Patriarch, "The world endures only for the breath of the children in the schoolhouse of their teacher."

II.45 A. And said Raba, "Jerusalem was destroyed only once faithful people had disappeared from among them, as it is said, 'Run you to and fro through the streets of Jerusalem and see now and know and look in the spacious piazzas there, see if you can find a man, if there be any who does justly, who seeks truth, and I will pardon him' (Jer. 5:1)."

16:3

A.   They save a basket full of loaves of bread,

B.   even if it contains enough food for a hundred meals,

C.   a wheel of pressed figs, and a jug of wine.

D.   And one says to others, "Come and save [what you can] for yourselves [as well]."

E.   Now if they were intelligent, they come to an agreement with him after the Sabbath.

F.   Where do they [take them to] save them?

G.   To a courtyard which is included within the Sabbath limit that fuses the area into a single domain [erub].

H.   Ben Beterah says, "Also: To one which is not included within the Sabbath limit that fuses the area into a single domain [erub]."

16:4

A.   And to that place [M. 16:3F-H] one takes out all his utensils.

B.   And he puts on all the clothing which he can put on, and he cloaks himself in all the cloaks he can put on.

C.   R. Yosé says, "Eighteen items of clothing."

D.   And he goes back, puts on clothing, and takes it out,

E.   and he says to others, "Come and save [the clothing] with me."

I.1   A.   [They save a basket full of loaves of bread, even if it contains enough food for a hundred meals:] *But lo, to begin with the Tannaite rule states explicitly:* They save food enough for three meals – *and no more!*

        B.   Said R. Huna, No problem, the one speaks of a case in which he comes to save the entire basket, in the other, he comes to collect food. If he comes to save, he can save it all, if he comes to collect, he can collect only enough for three meals."

I.2   A.   R. Huna b. R. Joshua raised this question: "If he took off his garment and collected and put things therein, collected and put things therein, *what is the rule? Is he comparable to one who comes to save [food] or to one who comes to collect?"*

II.1   A.   A wheel of pressed figs, and a jug of wine. And one says to others, "Come and save [what you can] for yourselves [as well]." Now if they were intelligent, they come to an agreement with him after the Sabbath:

B. An agreement? *Whatever for?*
    They have acquired title of what was
    in fact ownerless property?

III.1 A. Where do they [take them to]
           save them?   To a courtyard
           which is included within the
           Sabbath limit that fuses the area
           into a single domain [erub]. Ben
           Beterah says, "Also: To one
           which is not included within the
           Sabbath limit that fuses the area
           into a single domain [erub]":

       B. *How come the language here is,* for
           yourselves, *while in connection*
           with saving clothing, the language
           that is used is, [And he says to
           others, "Come and save the
           clothing] with me?

III.2 A. *Our rabbis have taught on Tannaite*
           authority:

       B. "One may put on clothing and
           carry it out and take it off and
           then go back and put on clothing
           and carry it out and take it off,
           even the entire day," the words of
           R. Meir.

16:5

A. R. Simeon b. Nannos says, "They spread out a lamb's hide over a
    chest, box, or cupboard, which has caught fire,

B. "for it will [only] singe."

C. And they make a partition with any sort of utensils, whether
    filled [with water] or empty, so that the fire will not pass.

D. R. Yosé prohibits doing so with new clay utensils filled with
    water,

E. for they cannot take the fire, so will split open, and [the water
    within them] will put out the fire.

I.1 A. Said R. Judah said Rab, "In the
         case of a cloak that has caught fire
         on one side, they put water on it
         on the other side, and if the fire
         happens to go out, it happens to
         go out."

     B. *An objection was raised:* In the case
         of a cloak that has caught fire on
         one side – one takes it off and
         covers himself with it, and if the
         fire goes out, it goes out. And
         so, too, if a scroll of the Torah
         catches fire, one may spread it

out and read in it, and if the fire
goes out, it goes out. [But it is
not permitted to put water on the
burning object.] [T. 13:6A-C, D-
F].

I.2   A.   *Our rabbis have taught on Tannaite
authority:*

       B.   A lamp that is on a board – one
may shake the board and the
lamp falls, and if it goes out, it
goes out.

I.3   A.   *A Tannaite statement:*

       B.   A lamp that is behind the door –
one may open and close the door
in a normal way, and if the lamp
goes out, it goes out.

I.4   A.   Said R. Judah, "On the Sabbath a
person may open a door that is
opposite a fire."

       B.   *Abbayye cursed this statement:
"With what situation do we deal? If
it is a case in which a wind is
blowing, then what would be the
reason behind the view of him who
might prohibit doing so? If there is
no wind blowing [except what is
created by the door], then what can
possibly explain the position of the
one who permits doing so?"*

The issue of indirect causation is articulated in the following, and
that differentiation between direct and indirect cause forms a
considerable source of differentiation in topical exegesis.

II.1   A.   And they make a partition with
any sort of utensils, whether
filled [with water] or empty, so
that the fire will not pass. R.
Yosé prohibits doing so with
new clay utensils filled with
water, for they cannot take the
fire, so will split open, and [the
water within them] will put out
the fire:

       B.   *Does that bear the implication that
rabbis hold,* indirectly causing a
flame to go out is permitted, *and
R. Yosé maintains,* indirectly
causing a flame to go out is
forbidden? *But lo, we have a
tradition that reverses the positions,*

for it has been taught on Tannaite authority:

C. People may make a partition of empty bottles and full ones not likely to burst; and what are full ones not likely to burst? Metal utensils.

D. R. Yosé says, "Also utensils made in Kefar Shihin and Kefar Hananiah are not likely to burst" [he, too, permits only utensils not likely to burst].

E. *And should you say, reverse our Mishnah formulation, well, while R. Yosé of the rule formulated external to the Mishnah argues within the position of the rabbis,* [Freedman: even if they are likely to burst, he will permit utensils, but even on the more stringent view of rabbis, utensils such as those of the specified villages should be permitted, too,] *well, now, can you really reverse these positions at all? And hasn't Rabbah bar Tahalipa said in the name of Rab, "Who is the Tannaite authority who holds,* indirectly causing a flame to go out is forbidden? *It is R. Yosé"?*

F. *In point of fact, do not reverse the positions, but the whole of the Tannaite formulation external to the Mishnah belongs to R. Yosé, but the version is flawed, and this is the proper Tannaite formulation of the matter:* People may make a partition of empty bottles and full ones not likely to burst; and what are full ones not likely to burst? Metal utensils. And also, utensils made in Kefar Shihin and Kefar Hananiah are not likely to burst. For R. Yosé says, "Also utensils made in Kefar Shihin and Kefar Hananiah are not likely to burst."

II.2   A. *Well, then, there is a striking conflict between statements of rabbis and between statements of R. Yosé, for it has been taught on Tannaite authority:*

B. Lo, if the Divine Name is written on one's skin, he must not bathe or anoint himself or stand in any unclean place. If he should turn out, however, to be required as a matter of religious duty to immerse in an immersion pool, he wraps a piece of reed around the spot and goes down into the immersion pool and immerses.

C. R. Yosé says, "In point of fact he may go down and immerse in an ordinary way, on condition that he not rub off the Divine Name." [Rabbis forbid indirectly causing the name to be erased, Yosé, only directly doing so.]

D. *That case is exceptional, for Scripture has said, "And you shall destroy their name out of that place, you shall not do so to the Lord your God" (Deut. 12:3-4) – it is a direct action that is forbidden, but an indirect action is permitted.*

E. Well, if so, here, too, it is written, "You shall not do any work" (Ex. 20:9) – *direct action is forbidden, indirect, permitted!*

F. *Since someone is excited about saving his property, if you permit him to do it that way, he will end up putting out the fire.*

G. *Well, then, if so, the positions of rabbis contradict one another: If in that case, even though someone is excited about saving his property, it is permitted, how much the more so here!*

H. *But does that stand to reason [that requiring the coverage of a reed is to prevent wiping away the Divine Name]? What situation do we have in mind? If the reed is wound tightly, it interposes; if not, the water will go in.*

I. *Now if you raise the question of interposition, then what about the ink itself?*

J. *It is wet ink, for it has been taught on Tannaite authority:* Blood, ink, honey, milk, mulberry juice, fig juice, sycamore juice, and carob juice, when dry, interpose, and when moist, do not interpose [T. Miq. 6:9D-F].

K. *Anyhow, there is a problem [with the reed].* [Freedman: This difficulty is raised to show that rabbis' view has nothing to do with the question of whether or not indirect action is permitted.]

L. *Rather, said Raba bar R. Shila, "This is the operative consideration in the mind of rabbis: They take the view that* it is forbidden to stand naked before the Divine Name."

M. *So does it follow that R. Yosé takes the view that* it is permitted to stand naked before the Divine Name?

N. *It would be a situation in which he puts his hand over the name.*

O. *Well, then, why not posit that from rabbis' perspective too, he puts his hand over the name?*

P. *Sometimes he may forget and take it away.*

Q. *Well, then, why not posit that from R. Yosé's view, sometimes he may forget and take it away?*

R. *Rather, if a reed is available, everyone will concur that it must be used [so that someone won't stand naked before the Divine Name]. But here with what situation do we deal? With whether or not it is necessary to go looking for a reed. Rabbis take the view that* [121A] *it is not required to have the immersion at its required time, so we do take time off to go looking for a reed, and R. Yosé maintains that immersion at the due time is required, so we don't take off time to go looking for a reed.*

S. *But does R. Yosé really maintain that it is a religious duty to have the immersion at the due time? And hasn't it been taught on Tannaite authority:*

T. A man afflicted by flux, a woman afflicted by flux, a man with the skin ailment [of Lev. 13-14] and a

woman with the same, a man
who has sexual relations with a
menstruating woman, and
someone unclean with corpse
uncleanness – they are to be
immersed by day. A woman who
has completed her menstrual
period and a woman after
childbirth may take their
immersion bath at night. A
person who is unclean by reason
of a seminal emission immerses
any time during the whole day.

U. R. Yosé says, "If the emission
took place from dusk onward, he
does not have to immerse"
[because immersion at a fixed
time is not obligatory].

V. *That represents the view of R. Yosé
b. R. Judah, who has said,* "The
immersion at the end suffices for
a woman after childbirth" [even
though that may not be the exact
time for the immersion, and
immersion when it becomes due
is not obligatory].

16:6

A. A gentile who came to put out a fire –
B. they do not say to him, "Put it out," or "Do not put it out,"
C. for they are not responsible for his Sabbath rest.
D. But a minor [Israelite child] who came to put out a fire –
E. they do not hearken to him [and let him do so],
F. because his Sabbath rest is their responsibility.

I.1 A. Said R. Ammi, "In the case of a
fire, sages have permitted one to
say, 'Whoever puts it out won't
lose.'"

B. *May we say that the following
supports his position:* A gentile
who came to put out a fire – they
do not say to him, "Put it out," or
"Do not put it out," for they are
not responsible for his Sabbath
rest? *So what we don't say to him
is, "put it out," but we may use the
language,* "Whoever puts it out
won't lose."

I.2 A. Our rabbis have *taught on
Tannaite authority:*

B.   There was the case in which a
fire broke out in the courtyard of
Joseph b. Simai in Shihin, and
soldiers from the garrison at
Sepphoris came to put it out,
because he was a royal agent, but
he didn't let them on account of
the honor owing to the Sabbath.
But a miracle was done for him,
and it rained and put out the
fire. In the evening he sent to
every one of them two selas, and
to the commanding officer five.
And when sages heard about it
they said, "He didn't have to do
it that way, for lo, we have
learned in the Mishnah: A
gentile who came to put out a
fire – they do not say to him, 'Put
it out,' or 'Do not put it out,' for
they are not responsible for his
Sabbath rest" [T. Shab. 13:9B].

II.1   A.   But a minor [Israelite child] who
came to put out a fire – they do
not hearken to him [and let him
do so], because his Sabbath rest
is their responsibility:

B.   *That implies that* should a minor
eat carrion, the court is
commanded to stop him.

16:7

A.   They cover a lamp with a dish so that it will not scorch a rafter;
B.   and the excrement of a child;
C.   and a scorpion, so that it will not bite.
D.   Said R. Judah, "A case came before Rabban Yohanan b. Zakkai in
Arab, and he said, 'I suspect [he is liable for] a sin-offering.'"

I.1   A.   *R. Judah, R. Jeremiah bar Abba, and*
R. Hanan bar Raba visited the
household of Abin of Neshiqqayya.
To R. Judah and R. Jeremiah bar
Abba [121B] *they brought couches,*
for to R. Hanan bar Raba they didn't
bring one. Now he found him
reciting to his son, and the
excrement of a child, *on account*
of the child [that he not cover
himself with the crap]. *He said to*
him, "Abin, only an idiot teaches his

son idiocy? Isn't the shit itself deemed fit for the dogs [and that is why it may be handled and disposed of, so there is no need to turn a dish over it anyhow]? *And should you say, it wasn't suitable for the dogs from the preceding day, hasn't it been taught on Tannaite authority:* Streams and springs that flow out – lo, they are in the status of whomever [takes their water] [T. Y.T. 4:8]"?

B. "*So how should I repeat the tradition?*"

C. "*Say:* They may cover chicken-shit because of the child."

II.1 A. And a scorpion, so that it will not bite:

B. Said R. Joshua b. Levi, "Whatever does injury may be killed on the Sabbath."

II.2 A. *A Tannaite authority repeated before Raba bar R. Huna,* "He who kills snakes or scorpions on the Sabbath – the spirit of the pious gets no pleasure from him."

B. He said to him, "Well, as to those allegedly pious men, the spirit of the sages gets no pleasure from them."

II.3 A. *Our rabbis have taught on Tannaite authority:*

B. If someone stumbles upon snakes or scorpions and kills them, it is certain that he was assigned to kill them. If he doesn't kill them, it is certain that they were assigned to kill him, but a miracle was done for him by Heaven.

II.4 A. Said R. Abba bar Kahana, "Once one of them fell in the schoolhouse, and a certain Nabataean student went and killed it."

II.5 A. *The question was raised: Is the meaning of,* He had already met upon one like it, *that he did well, or that he didn't do well?*

B. *Come and take note: R. Abba b. R. Hiyya bar Abba and R. Zira were in session at the gate of the household of*

> *R. Yannai. A question came up between them, and they asked R. Yannai:* "What is the law on killing snakes or scorpions on the Sabbath?"

II.6   A. *Abba bar Marta, a.k.a. Abba bar Minyumi, was being dunned by members of the household of the exilarch for money. They brought him before the exilarch, who so tortured him that he spat out some spit. The exilarch ordered,* "Bring a utensil and cover it over."

II.7   A. And said R. Abba bar Kahana said R. Hanina, "As to the candlesticks of the household of Rabbi [made in one piece], it is permitted to handle them on the Sabbath."

       B. Said to him R. Zira, "May they be handled with one hand or with two hands?"

II.8   A. And said R. Abba bar Kahana said R. Hanina, "The palanquins of Rabbi's household may be handled on the Sabbath."

II.9   A. And said R. Abba bar Kahana said R. Hanina, "R. Hanina permitted the household of Rabbi to drink wine carried in gentile palanquins, if they were sealed with one seal [not necessarily the normal two]. *But I don't know whether this is because he concurred with R. Eliezer [that only one seal is needed] or because of the fear of the household of the patriarch [that would prevent gentiles from touching the wine]."*

16:8

A. A gentile who lit a candle –

B. an Israelite may make use of its light.

C. But [if he did so] for an Israelite, it is prohibited [to do so on the Sabbath].

D. [If a gentile] drew water to give water to his beast, an Israelite gives water to his beast after him.

E. But [if he did so] for an Israelite, it is prohibited [to use it on the Sabbath].

F. [If] a gentile made a gangway by which to come down from a ship, an Israelite goes down after him.

G. But [if he did so] for an Israelite, it is prohibited [to use it on the Sabbath].

H. M'SH B: Rabban Gamaliel and elders were traveling by boat, and a gentile made a gangway by which to come down off the ship, and Rabban Gamaliel and sages went down by it.

I.1 A. *The several cases were necessary. For if we were told only the rule about the lamp, I might have supposed that the lamp is as good for a hundred people as for one, but as to water, I might suppose that it is subject to a precautionary decree, lest he come and add to the quantity drawn on the Israelite's account.*

I.2 A. *Our rabbis have taught on Tannaite authority:*

B. A gentile who gathered hay for his beasts – an Israelite may feed his beasts after him, but if this was for the Israelite, it is forbidden.

C. If he filled a bucket with water for his beast, an Israelite may give his beast water after him.

I.3 A. *Well, now, is that so? But didn't R. Huna say R. Hanina said, "A person may station his cattle on grass on the Sabbath, but he may not do so on fodder stored away for later use [which may not be handled on the Sabbath, for which it has not been designated]"?*

I.4 A. The master has said: Under what circumstances? When he doesn't know him, but if he knows him, it is forbidden –

B. *Lo, Rabban Gamaliel would refer to a case in which the gentile knew the Israelite [and yet this was permitted]!*

I.5 A. *Samuel visited the household of Abin of Toran. A gentile came and lit a lamp. Samuel turned away. When he saw that the gentile had brought a document and was reading it, he noted, "He lit it for himself," so he, too, turned toward the lamp.*

8

Bavli Shabbat
Chapter Nineteen

Folios 130A-137B

The remarks at the beginning of Chapter Three explain the work of this chapter as well. The results set forth at the end of Chapter Five are replicated in the foregoing repertoire of the chapter. Readers not interested in a detailed survey are advised to turn directly to the concluding chapter.

19:1

A. R. Eliezer says, "If one did not bring a utensil [used for circumcision] on the eve of the Sabbath, he brings it openly on the Sabbath."

B. And in the time of the danger, one covers it up in the presence of witnesses.

C. And further did R. Eliezer state, "They cut wood to make coals to prepare an iron utensil [for circumcision]."

D. An encompassing principle did R. Aqiba state, "Any sort of labor [in connection with circumcision] which it is possible to do on the eve of the Sabbath does not override [the restrictions of] the Sabbath, and that which it is not possible to do on the eve of the Sabbath does override [the prohibitions of] the Sabbath."

I.1 A. [He brings it openly on the Sabbath:] *The question was raised: Is the operative consideration behind the ruling of R. Eliezer special concern for that particular religious duty, or was it because of suspicion [that if the one who brought the knife*

219

did so surreptitiously, he might be suspect of violating the Sabbath]?

I.2   A.   It has further been taught on Tannaite authority:

       B.   "One brings it out in the open and doesn't bring it covered up," the words of R. Eliezer.

I.3   A.   *The question was raised: As to the witnesses that have been mentioned, does this mean him and one other, or him and two others?*

       B.   *Come and take note of the language:* **And in the time of the danger, one covers it up in the presence of witnesses.** *Now if you say that it means him and two others, there is no problem, but if you say it means him and one another, then how can we speak of "witnesses" here?*

II.1   A.   **And further did R. Eliezer state, "They cut wood to make coals to prepare an iron utensil [for circumcision]":**

       B.   *Our rabbis have taught on Tannaite authority:*

       C.   In the locale of R. Eliezer on the Sabbath they would cut wood to heat charcoal to forge iron [to make a circumcision knife, since in his view it was permitted to do everything that was required in connection with the rite]. In the locale of R. Yosé the Galilean, they would eat chicken meat with milk.

II.2   A.   *Levi visited the house of Joseph the fowler. They served him the head of a peacock cooked in milk. He didn't eat it. When he came before Rabbi, he said to him, "How come you didn't excommunicate them?"*

       B.   *He said to him, "It was the locale of R. Judah b. Beterah, and I thought, maybe he expounded for them [the rule] in accord with the position of R. Yosé the Galilean, for we have learned in the Mishnah:* R. Yosé the Galilean says, 'It is said, "You will not eat any sort of carrion," (Deut. 14:21), and it is said, "You will not seethe the kid in its* mother's milk" (Deut. 14:21). [The meaning is this:] What is prohibited on the grounds of carrion [also] is prohibited to be cooked in milk. Fowl, which is prohibited on the grounds of carrion, is it possible that it is prohibited to be seethed in milk? Scripture says, "In its mother's milk" – excluding fowl, the mother of which does not have milk' [M. Hul. 8:4F-H]."

II.3 A. Said R. Isaac, "There was a town in the Land of Israel, in which they acted in accord with R. Eliezer, and they died at the right time. Moreover, the evil kingdom made a decree against Israel in respect to circumcision, but in respect to that town no such decree was made."

II.4 A. *It has been taught on Tannaite authority:*

B. Rabban Simeon b. Gamaliel says, "Every religious duty that the Israelites accepted with joy, for instance circumcision, as it is written, 'I rejoice at your word, as one that finds great spoil' (Ps. 119:162), they still do with joy. Every religious duty that they accepted grudgingly, for example, the prohibition of consanguineous marriage, as it is written, 'And Moses heard the people weeping throughout their families' (Num. 11:10), that is, on account of the rules governing their families, they still do grudgingly" – *for there is no marriage contract that doesn't involve contention.*

II.5 A. *It has been taught on Tannaite authority:*

B. R. Simeon b. Eleazar says, "Any religious duty for which the Israelites gave up their lives unto death in the time of the government decrees, for instance, idolatry and circumcision, is still strongly confirmed in their possession, but any religious duty for which the Israelites did not give up their lives unto death in the time of the government decrees, for instance, phylacteries, is still infirmly held by them."

II.6   A.   *And what's the meaning of* Elisha, the man of wings?

B.   Once the wicked Roman government made a decree against Israel that whoever put on phylacteries – they would gouge out his brains. But Elisha put them on and went out to the marketplace. A detective saw him, so he ran away, and the other followed. When the other caught up, he took them off his head and put them in his hand. The other said to him, "What's this in your hand?"

II.7   A.   *And what differentiates* the wings of a dove from all other birds?

B.   Because the community of Israel *is compared to* a dove, as it is said, "as the wings of a dove covered with silver" (Ps. 68:14) – just as with a dove, its wings protect it, so Israel – religious duties protect them.

II.8   A.   Said R. Abba bar R. Adda said R. Isaac, "Once they forgot and didn't bring the knife on the eve of the Sabbath so they brought it on the Sabbath through roofs and courtyards [130B], contrary to the pleasure of R. Eliezer."

II.9   A.   R. *Zira asked R. Assi,* " A n alleyway in which the residents did not form a symbolic partnership [to create a single domain for purposes of carrying on the Sabbath] – what is the law as to carrying something in the whole of it [utensils present at the start of the Sabbath (Freedman)]? *Do we claim that it is comparable to a courtyard, so that, just as a courtyard, even though they have not formed a symbolic partnership, it is permitted to carry objects through the whole of it, so here, too, even though they did not form a symbolic partnership in it, it is permitted to carry through the whole of it? Or maybe there is no comparison to a courtyard, for a courtyard has four walls, but this doesn't have four walls? Or, also, a courtyard has tenants, but this has no tenants?"*

II.10 A. *It has been stated:*

B. Said R. Zira said Rab, "In an alleyway the residents of which did not form a fictive partnership they carry objects only four cubits and now more [as in public domain]."

II.11 A. Said R. Hiyya bar Abba said R. Yohanan, "Not for all purposes did R. Eliezer say, 'What is required to make it possible to carry out a religious duty overrides the restrictions of the Sabbath,' for lo, the two loaves represent the obligation of the day, and R. Eliezer derives the rule [that baking them overrides the restrictions of the Sabbath] only from an argument based on a verbal analogy [rather than holding that just as the duty is to put them out as an offering to the Lord, so baking them, necessary to carry out that duty, is permitted on the Sabbath as well]. *For it has been taught on Tannaite authority:*

II.12 A. *[With reference to R. Yohanan, "Not for all purposes did R. Eliezer say...,"], what did [Yohanan] mean to exclude? Should we say that it is to exclude the taking of the palm branch on Tabernacles that coincided with a Sabbath (Lev. 23:40)? But hasn't it been taught on Tannaite authority:* "The taking of the palm branch and everything having to do with preparing it override the restrictions of the Sabbath," the words of R. Eliezer?

II.13 A. "The taking of the palm branch and everything having to do with preparing it override the restrictions of the Sabbath," the words of R. Eliezer –

B. *How does R. Eliezer know this fact?*

II.14 A. "The taking of the palm branch and everything having to do with preparing it override the restrictions of the Sabbath," the words of R. Eliezer –

B. *How does R. Eliezer know this fact?*

II.15 A. "The unleavened bread and everything having to do with preparing it override the restrictions of the Sabbath," the words of R. Eliezer –

B. *How does R. Eliezer know this fact?*

II.16 A. "The ram's horn and everything having to do with preparing it override the restrictions of the Sabbath," the words of R. Eliezer –

B. *How does R. Eliezer know this fact?*

II.17 A. "Circumcision and everything having to do with preparing it override the restrictions of the Sabbath," the words of R. Eliezer –

B. *How does R. Eliezer know this fact? If it is from all of these others, then matters are as we have said. And furthermore, what distinguishes these other matters* [132A] *is that* if the time for doing them passes, they are annulled [which is not the case of circumcision]. *Rather, this is the scriptural basis for the position of R. Eliezer:* Scripture says, "And in the eighth day the flesh of his foreskin shall be circumcised" (Lev. 12:3) – even on the Sabbath.

II.18 A. *In any event rabbis differ from R. Eliezer* only with respect to what is required to carry out circumcision, but as to circumcision itself, all parties concur that it does override the restrictions of the Sabbath. So how we do know that fact?

B. Said Ulla, "It is a received law."

II.19   A.   And R. Yohanan said, [With reference to the verses, "You shall keep my covenant" (Gen. 17:9), "And in the eighth day the flesh of his foreskin shall be circumcised" (Lev. 12:3)], "Said Scripture, 'By day' – even [if the eighth day falls] on the Sabbath."

II.20   A.   R. Aha bar Jacob said, "Said Scripture, '...on the eighth day...' – even if it is the Sabbath."

         B.   *But this allusion to the eighth day is required to eliminate the seventh!*

II.21   A.   *It has been taught on Tannaite authority in accord with R. Yohanan and not in accord with R. Aha bar Jacob:*

         B.   "And in the eighth day the flesh of his foreskin shall be circumcised" – even on the Sabbath.

I.22   A.   *Said Raba, "Lo, as to the Tannaite authority before us, to begin with why was he satisfied, but in the end what troubled him?"*

         B.   *This is the sense of his statement:* "And in the eighth day the flesh of his foreskin shall be circumcised" – even on the Sabbath. And how do I interpret the statement, "And every one that profanes it shall surely be put to death" (Ex. 31:14)? That speaks of doing other aspects of the labor in connection with the rite of circumcision, other than the circumcision itself. *And as to circumcision itself, what is the basis in Scripture for the fact that it overrides the Sabbath?* It follows from an argument a fortiori based on the matter of the skin ailment of Lev. 13-14, which overrides the Temple service, [132B] and the Temple service overrides the restrictions of the Sabbath. And yet the rite of circumcision overrides the rules governing the skin ailment [since if there is a mark that may be the skin ailment, located on the penis, the

foreskin still is removed, even
though otherwise it is forbidden
to remove the mark of the skin
ailment]! So the Sabbath, which
is set aside by the requirements of
the Temple service, surely should
be set aside by the rite of
circumcision!

II.23   A.   *Our rabbis have taught on Tannaite
authority:*

B.   The rite of circumcision overrides
the rules of the skin ailment,
whether it is done at its correct
time or not at its correct time; it
overrides the restrictions of
festivals only when it is done at
its correct time [on the eighth
day].

II.24   A.   *What is the source of this statement?*

B.   *It is in line with that which our
rabbis have taught on Tannaite
authority:*

C.   "The flesh of his foreskin shall
be circumcised" (Lev. 12:3) –

II.25   A.   *Said Raba, "Lo, as to the Tannaite
authority before us, to begin with
why was he satisfied, but in the end
what troubled him?"*

II.26   A.   *That proof suffices for an adult, in
the context of which "flesh" is
written; so, too, in the context of an
infant "flesh" is written. But how do
we know that the same is the case for
one who is of intermediate age?*
[Freedman: We deal with these
three passages: "And the uncir-
cumcised male who is not
circumcised in the flesh of his
foreskin, that soul shall be cut off
from his people" (Gen. 17:14),
which applies to an adult; "and in
the eighth day the flesh of his
foreskin shall be circumcised"
(Lev. 12:3, speaks of the obligation of the father to circumcise the
son; "every male among you shall
be circumcised" (Gen. 17:10)
speaks in general, and we find
"flesh" in the first two but not in
the third, that is, the intermediate

age, between eight days and thirteen years and a day.]

II.27   A.   Raba said, "That circumcision at the proper time overrides [the restrictions of the skin ailment] *does not require a verse of Scripture, since that proposition derives from an argument a fortiori, as follows:* If circumcision overrides the restrictions of the Sabbath, which is the weightier matter, surely it should override the restrictions of the skin ailment."

       B.   *Said R. Safra to Raba, "So how do you know that the Sabbath is the weightier matter? Maybe the skin ailment is the weightier matter, since it overrides the restrictions of the Temple service, while the Temple service overrides the restrictions of the Sabbath?"*

II.28   A.   *And lo, the exchange of Raba and R. Safra* [133A] *represents a Tannaite exchange as well, for it has been taught on Tannaite authority:*

       B.   "'Flesh' – even if there is a mark of the skin ailment there, 'it shall be circumcised,'" the words of R. Josiah.

       C.   R. Jonathan says, "That is hardly determinative: For if circumcision overrides the Sabbath, which is weighty, shouldn't it override the skin ailment?"

II.29   A.   The master has said: "'Flesh' – even if there is a mark of the skin ailment there, 'it shall be circumcised,'" the words of R. Josiah –

II.30   A.   *There are those who repeat this exchange of Abbayye and Raba in reference to the following:*

II.31   A.   *Now as to Abbayye with reference to R. Simeon, how does he interpret the word "flesh"?*

II.32   A.   The master has said, "The rite of circumcision overrides the rules of the skin ailment, whether it is done at its correct time or not at its correct time; it overrides the restrictions of festivals only when

it is done at its correct time [on
the eighth day]" –

III.1   A.   An encompassing principle did
R. Aqiba state, "Any sort of
labor [in connection with
circumcision] which it is
possible to do on the eve of the
Sabbath does not override [the
restrictions of] the Sabbath, and
that which it is not possible to
do on the eve of the Sabbath
does override [the prohibitions
of] the Sabbath":

     B.   Said R. Judah said Rab, "The
decided law accords with R.
Aqiba."

19:2

A.   They do prepare all that is needed for circumcision on the
Sabbath:

B.   they (1) cut [the mark of circumcision], (2) tear, (3) suck [out the
wound].

C.   And they put on it a poultice and cumin.

D.   If one did not pound it on the eve of the Sabbath, he chews it in
his teeth and puts it on.

E.   If one did not mix wine and oil on the eve of the Sabbath, let this
be put on by itself and that by itself.

F.   And they do not make a bandage in the first instance.

G.   But they wrap a rag around [the wound of the circumcision].

H.   If one did not prepare [the necessary rag] on the eve of the
Sabbath, he wraps [the rag] around his finger and brings it, and
even from a different courtyard.

I.1   A.   [133B] *Now since the Tannaite
framer of the passages repeats each
item on its own, what is the
language,* all that is needed for
circumcision on the Sabbath,
meant to encompass?

I.2   A.   *Who is the Tannaite authority who
maintained,* Once he has
completed the rite, he may not
return to cut away those that do
not invalidate the circumcision?

I.3   A.   *Our rabbis have taught on Tannaite
authority:*

     B.   They trim the membrum, and if
one does not trim it, he is subject
to the penalty of extirpation.

I.4   A.   *Who is penalized in that way?*

     B.   Said R. Kahana, "The surgeon."

II.1   A. Suck [out the wound]:

B. *Said R. Pappa, "A surgeon who didn't suck out the wound – that is a source of danger, and we throw him out."*

III.1   A. **And they put on it a poultice and cumin:**

B. *Said Abbayye, "Mother said to me, "A salve for all pains is seven parts of fat and one of wax."*

IV.1   A. **If one did not pound it on the eve of the Sabbath, he chews it in his teeth and puts it on:**

B. *Our rabbis have taught on Tannaite authority:*

C. Things that are not done for circumcision on the Sabbath are done for it on the festival day: they crush cumin, beat up wine and oil together, on its account.

IV.2   A. *Said Abbayye to R. Joseph, "What differentiates the matter of crushing cumin on festivals? It is because it can be used in a recipe. But wine and oil are suitable for a sick person on the Sabbath, for it has been taught on Tannaite authority:* They don't beat up wine and oil for a sick person on the Sabbath. R. Simeon b. Eleazar said in the name of R. Meir, 'They may even beat up wine and oil on the Sabbath.' Said R. Simeon b. Eleazar, 'One time R. Meir had a bellyache, and we wanted to beat up for him some wine and oil, but he didn't let us. We said to him, 'Your ruling will be nullified in your own lifetime.' He said to us, 'Even though I say that it may be done, and my colleagues say that it may not be done, in my whole life my heart never so swelled up with pride as to permit me to go against the opinion of my colleagues.' *So he was strict with himself but for everybody else it is permitted."*

IV.3   A. *Our rabbis have taught on Tannaite authority:*

          B.   They don't strain mustard through a mustard strainer, nor do they sweeten it with a glowing coal.

IV.4   A. *Said Abbayye to R. Joseph, "What differentiates the matter from the following, which we learned in the Mishnah:* And they put an egg into a mustard strainer [M. Shab. 20:2C]?"

IV.5   A. *Said Abbayye to R. Joseph, "What differentiates roasting meat on coals [which may be put out by the gravy]?"*

IV.6   A. *Said Abbayye to R. Joseph, "What is the law on cheesemaking on a festival?"*

V.1   A. And they do not make a bandage in the first instance. But they wrap a rag around [the wound of the circumcision]:

          B. *Said Abbayye, "Mother told me, 'The side selvedge of the infant's bandage should be uppermost [facing outward], lest a thread stick and the infant end up with a penis that has been cut off.'"*

19:3

A.   They wash off the infant,

B.   both before the circumcision and after the circumcision,

C.   and they sprinkle him,

D.   by hand but not with a utensil.

E.   R. Eleazar b. Azariah says, "They wash the infant on the third day after circumcision [even if it] coincides with the Sabbath,

F.   "since it says, 'And it came to pass on the third day when they were sore' (Gen. 34:25)."

G.   [If the sexual traits of the infant are a matter of] doubt, of [if the infant] bears the sexual traits of both sexes, they do not violate the Sabbath on his account.

H.   And R. Judah permits in the case of an infant bearing the traits of both sexes.

I.1   A. *First you say,* They wash off the infant *[meaning in the normal manner, but then* by hand but not with a utensil]! *Both R. Judah and Rabbah bar Abbuha say, "The intent of the Tannaite formulation is to explain, how do they do it, namely:* They wash off the infant, both before the circumcision and after the circumcision: how so? They sprinkle him by hand but not with a utensil."

B. Said Raba, "But the language that is used is, They wash off the infant [and sprinkling is not washing]!"

I.2 A. Someone came before Raba. He ruled for him in accord with his view [that the infant may be bathed on the first day, the Sabbath as it happened, in the usual way. Raba got sick. He said, "What business did I have with the interpretation of the elders?"

B. Rabbis said to Raba, "But has it not been taught on Tannaite authority in accord with the position of the master?"

I.3 A. When R. Dimi came, he said R. Eleazar [said], "The decided law accords with R. Eleazar b. Azariah."

B. In the West they reflected on that matter: Does that mean, washing the whole body or just the place of the circumcision?

I.4 A. So, too, it has been stated:

B. When Rabin came, he said Abbahu said R. Eleazar [said], and some say, said R. Abbahu said R. Yohanan, "The decided law accords with R. Eleazar b. Azariah, with respect to both water that was heated on the Sabbath and hot water that was heated before the Sabbath, whether with respect to washing the whole body or with respect to washing the wound of the circumcision, because it is a danger to the infant."

I.5 A. Reverting to the body of the foregoing:

B. Said Rab, "They do not withhold hot water and oil from a wound on the Sabbath."

I.6 A. Our rabbis have taught on Tannaite authority:

B. They put on a wound on the Sabbath dry wadding or a dry sponge, but not a dry reed or dry rags.

II.1   A. [If the sexual traits of the infant are a matter of] doubt, or [if the infant] bears the sexual traits of both sexes, they do not violate the Sabbath on his account:

         B. *Our rabbis have taught on Tannaite authority:*

II.2   A. The master has said: But in a case of doubt, then the rite does not override the restrictions of the Sabbath – *covering what case?*

II.3   A. *It has been stated:*

         B. Rab said, "The decided law is in accord with the initial Tannaite authority."

II.4   A. *R. Adda bar Ahbah: To him was born an infant who was circumcised. He made the rounds of thirteen circumcisers [to bring out a drop of blood for the sake of circumcision, but they refused to do so on the Sabbath], so he himself did it and [botching the job,] cut off his penis. He said, "May such and so come upon me, for I have violated what Rab said."*

II.5   A. *Said R. Joseph, "On what basis do I make that statement? Because it has been taught on Tannaite authority:* R. Eliezer Haqqappar says, 'The House of Shammai and the House of Hillel did not dispute about the case of an infant born circumcised, that it is necessary to draw a drop of blood as the mark of the covenant.   Concerning what did they differ? Whether or not it is permitted on that account to desecrate the Sabbath.   The House of Shammai say, "On that account they do desecrate the Sabbath."   And the House of Hillel say, "On that account they do not desecrate the Sabbath."' *Doesn't it follow that the first Tannaite authority maintains,* they do desecrate the Sabbath on his account?"

II.6   A. Said R. Assi, "Any infant whose mother is unclean by reason of childbirth is circumcised on the eighth day [but it is done immediately], and any whose mother is not unclean by reason of childbirth is not circumcised on the eighth day: 'If a woman conceive seed and bear a male child, then she shall be unclean...and in the eighth day the flesh of his foreskin shall be circumcised' (Lev. 12:2-3)."

II.7　A.　*It is in accord with a conflict among Tannaite authorities:*

B.　There is a slave born in the master's household who is circumcised on the first day and there is one circumcised on the eighth day; there is a slave bought with money circumcised on the first day and there is such circumcised on the eighth day.

II.8　A.　*It has been taught on Tannaite authority:*

B.　R. Simeon b. Gamaliel says, "Any human offspring that survived for thirty days is not classified as a miscarriage, as it is said, 'And those that are to be redeemed of them from a month old shall you redeem' (Num. 18:16). Any animal that lives for eight days is not classified as a miscarriage, 'and from the eighth day and henceforth it shall be accepted for an offering' (Lev. 22:27)."

II.9　A.　*Said Abbayye, "It is in accord with the following Tannaite dispute":*

B.　"Of which you may eat":

C.　This encompasses an embryo at eight months, indicating that an act of slaughter [of the mother] does not render it clean. [If the mother is slaughtered, the embryo eight months old is not affected by the act of slaughter, but if born dead, is regarded as carrion.]

D.　R. Yosé b. R. Judah and R. Eleazar b. R. Simeon say, "As to the embryo at the age of eight months, the act of slaughter does render it clean [so that if it is properly slaughtered before it expires, it is not deemed carrion]" [Sifra CXX:III.1].

E. [Abbayye continues:] *"Isn't this what is subject to dispute: The one authority holds that it is classified as a living creature [which is therefore made clean by slaughter, like any other animal], and the other authority maintains that it is classified as dead?"*

II.10   A. *The question was raised: [With reference to the statement,* R. Simeon b. Gamaliel says, "Any human offspring that survived for thirty days is not classified as a miscarriage, as it is said, 'And those that are to be redeemed of them from a month old shall you redeem' (Num. 18:16). Any animal that lives for eight days is not classified as a miscarriage, 'and from the eighth day and henceforth it shall be accepted for an offering' (Lev. 22:27)"], *do rabbis differ from Rabban Simeon b. Gamaliel, or do they not differ from him? If you should conclude that they differ from him, then is the law in accord with him or is the law not in accord with him?*

II.11   A. Said Abbayye, "If an offspring fell from the roof or is eaten by a lion, all agree that it was viable. [We assume it might have lived; hence if the child survived the father, however briefly, the mother is exempt from levirate marriage; in the case of an animal, if slaughtered before it is eight days old, it may be eaten; we assume it was viable (Freedman).] *Where there is a difference, it concerns a case in which* it gasped and died *[naturally, in a thirty day period]. The one authority maintains that it is classified as having lived, the other takes the view that it is classified as having died."*

II.12 A. If an offspring fell from the roof or is eaten by a lion, is it the fact that all agree that it was viable?

B. *But lo, R. Pappa and R. Huna b. R. Joshua visited the household of Rab the son of R. Idi bar Abin, and he made for them a third-born calf on the seventh day after it was born. They said to him, "If you'd waited until evening, we would have eaten it. But now we won't."*

II.13 A. *The son of R. Dimi bar Joseph: To him was born an offspring, which died within thirty days. He sat in mourning for him. Said his father to him, "Do you want some dainties [as a sign that mourning is not appropriate, since he wasn't viable]?"*

II.14 A. *R. Ashi visited the household of R. Kahana. A mishap happened within thirty days [his child died within thirty days after birth]. He saw him sitting in mourning for him, and said to him, "Doesn't the master concur with what* R. Judah said Samuel said, 'The decided law accords with Rabban Simeon b. Gamaliel?'"

II.15 A. *It has been stated:*

B. If the offspring died within thirty days and the mother [widow of the deceased father] went and got betrothed [assuming that she no longer had a levirate obligation] – Rabina in the name of Raba [136B] said, "If she is the wife of a member of the Israelite caste, she undertakes the rite of removing the shoe, but if she is the wife of a member of the priestly caste, she does not even have to do that.'"

III.1 A. **And R. Judah permits in the case of an infant bearing the traits of both sexes:**

B. Said R. Shizbi said R. Hisda, "It was for not all purposes that R. Judah permitted in the case of an infant bearing the traits of both sexes, for if you take that

position, the offspring also would
be subject to a vow of valuation."

19:4

A.   He who had two infants, one to circumcise after the Sabbath and
      one to circumcise on the Sabbath,
B.   and who forgot [which was which] and circumcised the one to be
      circumcised after the Sabbath on the Sabbath,
C.   is liable.
D.   [If he had] one to circumcise on the eve of the Sabbath and one to
      circumcise on the Sabbath,
E.   and he forgot and on the Sabbath, circumcised the one to be
      circumcised on the eve of the Sabbath,
F.   R. Eliezer declares him liable to a sin-offering.
G.   And R. Joshua exempts him.

> I.1   A.   [He who had two infants, one to
>   circumcise after the Sabbath and
>   one to circumcise on the
>   Sabbath, and who forgot [which
>   was which] and circumcised the
>   one to be circumcised after the
>   Sabbath on the Sabbath, is
>   liable:] R. Huna repeated, "He is
>   liable."
>   B.   R. Judah repeated, "He is exempt
>   from liability."

19:5

A.   An infant is circumcised on the eighth, ninth, tenth, eleventh or
      twelfth day [after birth],
B.   never sooner, never later.
C.   How so?
D.   Under normal circumstances, it is on the eighth day.
E.   [If] he was born at twilight, he is circumcised on the ninth day.
F.   [If he was born] at twilight on the eve of the Sabbath, he is
      circumcised on the tenth day [the following Sunday].
G.   In the case of a festival which falls after the Sabbath, he will be
      circumcised on the eleventh day [Monday].
H.   In the case of two festival days of the New Year, he will be
      circumcised on the twelfth day [Tuesday].
I.   An infant who is sick – they do not circumcise him until he gets
      well.

> I.1   A.   [An infant who is sick – they do
>   not circumcise him until he gets
>   well:] Said Samuel, "Once a fever
>   has left the child, he is given
>   seven full days of recovery."
> I.2   A.   *The question was raised: Do we
>   require a full twenty-four hours of
>   recovery?*

19:6

A. These are the shreds [of the foreskin, if they remain] which render the circumcision invalid:

B. flesh which covers the greater part of the corona –

C. and such a one does not eat heave-offering.

D. And if he was fat [so the corona appears to be covered up], one has to fix it up for appearance's sake.

E. [137B] [If] one circumcised but did not tear the inner lining [the cut did not uncover the corona, since the membrane was not split and pulled down], it is as if he did not perform the act of circumcision.

I.1 A. [Flesh which covers the greater part of the corona:] Said R. Abina said R. Jeremiah bar Abba said Rab, "It is the flesh that covers the greater part of the height of the corona."

II.1 A. And if he was fat [so the corona appears to be covered up], one has to fix it up for appearance's sake:

B. Said Samuel, "An infant's penis that was overgrown with flesh, we look into the case. So long as, when he has an erection, he appears circumcised, it is not necessary to circumcise him, but if not, it is necessary to recircumcise him."

III.1 A. [If] one circumcised but did not tear the inner lining [the cut did not uncover the corona, since the membrane was not split and pulled down], it is as if he did not perform the act of circumcision:

B. *Our rabbis have taught on Tannaite authority:*

C. He who performs the rite of circumcision says, "Blessed...who has sanctified us by his commandments and commanded us concerning circumcision."

9

Decoding the Talmud's Exegetical Program

I. From Detail to Principle in the Bavli's Quest for Generalization

Let us now review that which we have sought, with such paltry results. In a propositional document made up of examples, such as we find in the Mishnah and propose to find in the Talmud, a case bears implications for a principle or premise, and one important source of exegetical inquiry will derive from the comparison of cases and premises. Let me begin by restating what we find occasionally, namely, a good example of the way in which the Talmud occasionally moves from a case to a principle – rapidly and without fanfare.

Our case takes us through two levels of generalization in approximately two sentences. The first asks whether an action done by indirection is classified as is an action done directly and effectively. If I accomplish a goal that a given action attains, but do so not in the ordinary way in which that action is done, is the result (for example, the consequence as to culpability) the same that it would be if I accomplished that same goal in the ordinary way in which that action is done? The still more remote issue is, the status of indirect causation, as distinct from direct causation. Both of these abstract principles are contained in the following rather simple exposition.

20:5
A. The straw which is on the bed –
B. one should not shift it with his hand.
C. But he shifts it with his body.
D. And if it was food for a beast, or if there was a cushion or a sheet on it, he may shift it with his hand.

    E.   A press used by householders do they loosen but do they not tighten.

    F.   And one of laundrymen one should not touch [at all].

    G.   R. Judah says, "If it was untied on the eve of the Sabbath, one may untie the whole thing and remove [clothing from] it."

I.1   A.   *Said R. Nahman, "As to a radish, if it is right side up, it is permitted, if it is upside down, it is forbidden [because carrying indirectly is not classified as handling]."*

    B.   *Said R. Adda bar Abba, "They said in the household of Rab, 'The Mishnah rule does not accord with R. Nahman:* The straw which is on the bed – one should not shift it with his hand. But he shifts it with his body. And if it was food for a beast, or if there was a cushion or a sheet on it, he may shift it with his hand. *This proves that indirect handling is not classified as handling."*

    C.   *Sure does.*

The issue of indirect carrying, that is, doing something in an unusual way, is explicit; the further issue, the status of the result of an indirect cause, is the most general way of framing the foregoing.

Now what I wish to find out is how the Mishnah exegetes knew what they wanted to know about a given passage. Specifically, can we find out whether or not the chapters we have surveyed contain principles of a general order, abstract generalizations for instance, that instruct an exegete of a particular passage concerning what he wishes to investigate in that passage? For that purpose we review the on-site results of the substantive chapters.

II. The Premises of the Exegesis of the Mixed Grid

1. Bavli-Tractate Shabbat Chapter Three

These are the principles that I have identified in the survey of the chapter at hand:

    1.   Am I penalized for inadvertently violating the law? Am I penalized in the way I would be if the violation were deliberate?

    2.   In any case in which you find two authorities at odds and one taking a mediating position, the decided law accords with the position of the one who takes the mediating position, except in the case of the catalogue of lenient rulings that pertain to rags [catalogued at B. Shab. 29A], in which case even though R. Eliezer takes the strict position and R. Joshua the lenient, with R. Aqiba mediating, the decided law does not accord with the mediating position.

3. The issue that follows gives us a fine example of how through a particular case a principle of broad general interest and applicability is set forth. It is whether the effect of an action is affected by the intention of the person who does it. Here it is expressed in this language: If there is a result that is not intentional, the act is permitted [on the Sabbath]. The upshot is that we take an action to bear consequences only if it is done with full intentionality.

4. The exegetical distinction that follows is a fundamental and important one, between doing something in a routine manner, and doing it in an unusual way. If something is done in an ordinary way, then it falls under the ordinary restrictions, for example, of the Sabbath; if it is done in an unusual way, then the action is governed by other (more lenient) considerations. There is no more generative a distinction than the one at hand. The Mishnah rule itself makes the point that if one does a permitted action and it produces results that one wants, without one's doing a forbidden action, there is no objection to that fact. But that principle does not generate the one that I find operative here.

This presence of the principle I allege to be present is made explicit: Which authority stands behind the rule? It cannot be R. Simeon, who rejects the conception of not using what has not been designated prior to the Sabbath for use on the Sabbath. It cannot be R. Judah, for so far as he is concerned, what does it matter if one doesn't intend to capture the bees, since he holds that an unintentional act is forbidden anyhow.

5. Another recurrent principle is whether or not one may touch on the Sabbath what one may not use. That is certainly a problem that pertains to a broad variety of cases. In the most general terms, it represents whether and how we erect barriers against the possible violation of the law, by preventing even the possibility of violating the law.

6. By contrast, the next item is absolutely basic: How do we assess indirect or secondary cause? If something is done that, by indirection, produces a result, am I culpable because of what happens not because of what I have done, but because of the result of what I have done? This issue is expressed in concrete terms.

2. Bavli-Tractate Shabbat Chapter Seven

1. How and whether we differentiate a variety of actions by reference to whether or not one knew what one was doing yields the deeper concern in intentionality, and the governing principle is, one is guilty for an act done in full awareness that the act is wrong and in entire intentionality to violate the law. So within that principle we generate a variety of secondary questions on the interplay of knowledge and intentionality, on the one side, and prohibited actions, on the other.

2. What follows asks about the differentiation of like things and introduces an extrinsic principle of differentiation. This represents an example of the notion that taxonomic classification rests not only on the traits of things, as generally is the theory of the Mishnah, but also, or only, on the taxic indicators supplied by Scripture itself. But it seems to me difficult to find many sustained exegetical exercises that are provoked by that principle.

3. All of these rules have been stated only relative to the condition of those who are storing things [so that there is no fixed rule deriving from general practice, but we assess each situation in terms of the intent of him who is doing the storing; a rich person would store more, a poor person, less, each valuing things in his own terms (Freedman).]

4. The following raises a very interesting question, which is certainly subject to application to a variety of cases and problems. Do laws apply without regard to circumstance, or do we accommodate the rule to the situation? That issue may be expressed in the case of taking account of personal preference or attitude when we deal with a general rule, for example, on how much of a volume of a substance will be taken into account by a person, so that that volume involves liability in the present context. One person may take account of more, another of less, for example, a poor person may regard as useful a much smaller volume of a substance than a rich person.

II.1   A.   **And whatever is not suitable for storage, which people generally do not store in such quantity as one has taken out on the Sabbath – only he is liable on its account who stores it away [and who then takes it out]:**

B. **[76A]** *Said R. Eleazar, "This does not accord with R. Simeon b. Eleazar, for it has been taught on Tannaite authority:* A governing principle did R. Simeon b. Eleazar state, 'In the case of anything that is not regarded as suitable for storage, the like of which in general people do not store away, but which a given individual has deemed fit for storage and has stored away, and which another party has come along and removed from storage and taken from one domain to another on the Sabbath – the party who moved the object across the line that separated the two domains has become liable by reason of the intentionality of the party who stored away this thing that is not ordinarily stored.'"

The issue is clearly and explicitly drawn.

3. Bavli-Tractate Shabbat Chapter Eight
I found nothing relevant in this chapter.

4. Bavli-Tractate Shabbat Chapter Nine
I found nothing relevant in this chapter.

5. Bavli-Tractate Shabbat Chapter Eleven

1. When we have to sort out the rule, among intersecting ones, that governs a given situation, do we turn only to the principal component of the situation or do we take account of a subsidiary one? Here is a marvelous example of the intersection of two distinct grids: the rules that govern what is primary, or the different, now intersecting, rules that govern what is subsidiary.

I.6 A. *Said Raba, "It is clear to me:* Water that is lying on water – lo, that is a situation in which it has come to rest. A nut that is lying upon water – lo, that is **[100A]** not a situation in which it has come to rest."

B. *Raba raised this question: "A nut that is lying in a utensil, and a utensil is floating on water – do we invoke the criterion of the situation of the nut, in which case it has come to rest, or do we go by the criterion of the utensil, which, being unstable, has not come to rest?"*

C. *The question stands.*

The issue here is subject to generalization: Do we invoke as our criterion the principal object or the subsidiary one?

2. The next item is a fabricated case that permits us to explore the principle that intentionality must govern at all phases of an action. Here the generalization is offered at the outset, and it clearly governs a wide variety of cases. Then we are

given a concrete case, but it is framed to allow us to consider all of the intricacies of uniform intentionality.

II.1   A.   This is the governing principle: All those who may be liable to sin-offerings in fact are not liable unless at the beginning and the end, their [sin] is done inadvertently. [But] if the beginning of their [sin] is inadvertent and the end is deliberate, unless at the beginning and at the end their [sin] is inadvertent:

   B.   *It has been stated:*

   C.   If the object traveled for two cubits when the one who threw it did so inadvertently, but the next two cubits of the voyage were subject to his deliberate will, and then two more cubits unwittingly –

   D.   Rabbah said, "He is exempt."

   E.   Raba said, "He is liable."

   F.   Rabbah said, "He is exempt" – *even in the opinion of Rabban Gamaliel, who said,* "If one is aware of half of the requisite measure only, that is null" [Freedman: it does not separate two acts of eating, when in each case only half the standard quantity to create liability is consumed], *that is the case in that situation, because, when he completes meeting the requisite standard for culpability, he completes it entirely inadvertently, but here, he completes the requisite standard deliberately, so that would not apply.*

6. Bavli-Tractate Shabbat Chapter Sixteen

   1.   The issue of indirection causation is articulated in the following, and that differentiation between direct and indirect cause forms a considerable source of differentiation in topical exegesis.

II.1   A.   And they make a partition with any sort of utensils, whether filled [with water] or empty, so that the fire will not pass. R. Yosé prohibits doing so with new clay utensils filled with water, for they cannot take the fire, so will split open, and [the water within them] will put out the fire:

   B.   *Does that bear the implication that rabbis hold,* indirectly causing a flame to go out is permitted, *and R. Yosé maintains,* indirectly causing a flame to go out is forbidden? *But lo, we have a tradition that reverses the positions, for it has been taught on Tannaite authority:*

   C.   People may make a partition of empty bottles and full ones not likely to burst; and what are full ones not likely to burst? Metal utensils.

   D.   R. Yosé says, "Also utensils made in Kefar Shihin and Kefar Hananiah are not likely to burst" [he, too, permits only utensils not likely to burst].

   E.   *And should you say, reverse our Mishnah formulation, well, while R. Yosé of the rule formulated external to the Mishnah argues within the position of the rabbis,* [Freedman: even if they are likely to burst, he will permit utensils, but even on the more stringent view of rabbis, utensils such as those of the specified villages should be permitted too], *well, now, can you really reverse these positions at all? And hasn't Rabbah bar Tahalipa said in the name of Rab, "Who is the Tannaite authority who holds, indirectly causing a flame to go out is forbidden? It is R. Yosé"?*

F. *In point of fact, do not reverse the positions, but the whole of the Tannaite formulation external to the Mishnah belongs to R. Yosé, but the version is flawed, and this is the proper Tannaite formulation of the matter:* People may make a partition of empty bottles and full ones not likely to burst; and what are full ones not likely to burst? Metal utensils. And also, utensils made in Kefar Shihin and Kefar Hananiah are not likely to burst. For R. Yosé says, "Also utensils made in Kefar Shihin and Kefar Hananiah are not likely to burst."

The clear intent is to differentiate what one actually causes by his action from what is a subsidiary result of what one has caused, that is, indirect causation.

7. Bavli-Tractate Shabbat Chapter Nineteen

I found nothing relevant in this chapter.

III. The Code: How Prominent? What Lies Undecoded?

The upshot of this probe may be stated in a brief way. There is no doubt that some general considerations governed inquiry into some Mishnah passages. But I see no governing general consideration, no proposition that at a high level of abstraction encompasses the bulk of the concrete inquiries that bear philosophical implications or rest on philosophical premises (philosophy here meaning simply, what is subject to generalization and extension to a variety of cases). I think there is no doubt that the Talmud's sages reading the Mishnah's and associated statements asked questions about intentionality and awareness or consciousness of what one is doing, causality, differentiation between ordinary and extraordinary forms of the same action, whether we accommodate the law to individual tastes and preferences (which is, intentionality in a different form), the distinction between what is primary and what is subsidiary (which is the issue of causality once again), and the like. What holds these several principles together seems to me a single common trait: we make distinctions between this and that, and when distinctions do not lie on the surface of a problem, we introduce them from some other source than the details of said problem. All of this adds up to considerably less than a code, a source of generative inquiries, a guide that operates throughout to what is important in diverse and unrelated problems.

Shall we then conclude that the Bavli's authors or authorships consulted a primary and a priori set of principles when reading the Mishnah? Yes and no. Clearly, from time to time, as the circumstances warranted, they did. But, equally obviously, for the bulk of their reading of the Mishnah, they did not. And, more to the point, even when a case was read as though it contained a code to be identified and decoded, the code that served in one case was not the same as the code that served in some other – so the results now surveyed show, in my opinion, beyond much doubt. So if the entire code, in all cogency and coherence, consisted of the principle that we make distinctions between this and that, then the code is obvious, trivial, and merely instrumental. Not only so, but if so ineffably general a principle is in play, it makes only a negligible impact on the whole – which does not even respond to that principle in any considerable measure, over much of the surface of the writing. In detail do we see the working of my general notion that the Bavli's framers form of a two dimensional grid a cubic one, that is, bringing into relationship two, three, or even four taxic structures and uncovering their interstitial relationships? Not very often. To what extent is a sizable sample of the Bavli accurately characterized by my allegation as to its intellectual quality? To no appreciable extent. And, of great interest, what proportions of the document are formed in the way I claim they are, and what proportions are not? Neglible proportions. The code – if it is a code at all – is not prominent.

Then what lies undecoded? The answer is, Why the Bavli? For, it is clear from the formal studies of mine that I cited in the Preface, most of the Bavli forms a cogent and unified commentary to the Mishnah; the document speaks in a single way about some few things. Where the authors or authorships undertake their vast, secondary inquiries into the theory of things in general, as they certainly do, these exhibit in common no proposition, no goal of argument, no determined truth to be demonstrated in detail after detail, in the way in which the framers of the Mishnah set forth in tens of thousands of details the basic proposition that all things properly classified form a hierarchy, everything rising to one thing, all things deriving from one thing. That is not how the Bavli works, that is not what the Bavli is. The Talmud then is not a propositional document, it is only a document that sets forth and demonstrates propositions – a very different thing. Then is everything reduced to method, and is the argument the main point of this writing? That is the proposition presented in a recent monograph, and, since the proposal is current, let me repeat my argument against it, concluding with a brief response to the negative results that are now in hand.

IV. The Method and the Message: The Talmud's Exegetical Program and the Bavli's Theological Formulation of Religious Truth

It would appear that all we have is method, no message: numerous examples of no determinate proposition. Then all that would appear to matter in the Bavli is the method, the argument, the way we reach conclusions – but there are no encompassing conclusions to be drawn. And that is precisely a position taken just now by David Kraemer in his *The Mind of the Talmud: An Intellectual History of the Bavli.*[1] There he claims to "trace the development of the literary forms and conventions of the Babylonian Talmud and analyze those forms as expressions of emergent rabbinic ideology." In his view, that "ideology" (an eighteenth century word surely out of place in a seventh century document, a secular word surely inappropriate for a religious writing, hence, substitute: "theology") expresses the conviction of "the inaccessibility of perfect truth," and concluding that [not the determination, but the mere] "pursuit of truth...becomes the ultimate act of rabbinic piety," Kraemer spells out his program in these terms: "[The book is]...a literary history. It traces the development of the literary forms and conventions by which rabbinic sages...recorded their opinions and rulings. What motivates this examination is the assumption...that literary conventions are reflections of ideological [better: theological] choices and that by tracing the history of literary developments we can say something of the history of ideas. This is also, therefore, intended as an intellectual history of the Jews who produced the Bavli."

He alleges that the anonymous and commanding discourse of the document concerns not conclusion but argumentation. While received materials (Kraemer: "for the Amoraim") contain "both brief and discursive" writing, "conclusion and argumentation," for the unattributed and definitive discourse ("for the stam" not italicized, a foreign word meaning, "what is not attributed to a named authority") *"there is only argumentation."* In the words he has italicized is Kraemer's principal descriptive allegation. All else rests upon that characterization. The relevance of Kraemer's proposition to the present monograph is clear. I have not been able to show that a cogent set of principles animates argumentation, such that conclusions in respect to how these principles govern particular cases form the cogent center of the document. On the contrary, I have found codes but no code, various operative principles but no prevailing principle. So would this not yield the conclusion that method is the thing – method, not meaning,

---

[1]New York: Oxford University Press, 1990.

argument, not upshot? So have I not lent powerful support to Kraemer's view of matters?

Now it is certainly the fact that on occasion derivative cases are set forth, sometimes at great length, to put forward theoretical possibilities on sorting out conflicting principles, and these not uncommonly conclude, "The question stands." The argument then is the main thing: conflict of principles, left unresolved. So there is ample anecdotal material in the document – we know not the proportion or place in the composition of the whole – to validate Kraemer's claim in detail. But the passages that present conundrums invariably attend to interstitial issues, and none of them, so far as I have observed, present without resolution the conflict of fundamental principles (for example, contradictions between the premises of two distinct Mishnah paragraphs are never left in conflict but always harmonized). So that phenomenon, which does conform to Kraemer's description, is not primary to the document, its modes of thought and argument.

Kraemer adduces in evidence of his claim that the document concerns itself with argument, not decision, by showing a variety of specific traits characteristic of what he calls the anonymous layer of the writing. He finds, for instance, that the redactor will "extend the range of the original argumentation" (p. 80). "The authors of the gemara also saw fit to create argumentation out of amoraic sources that were originally not argumentational" (p. 84). They created "fictional argumentation" (p. 87), "argumentation for its own sake" (p. 90). He then claims to have illustrated the point that "the Babylonian gemara is, at the level of its anonymous composition, an uncompromisingly deliberative/argumentational text." He properly compares this Talmud to the other one, the Talmud of the Land of Israel (a.k.a., the Yerushalmi) and finds that a principal difference is that the Yerushalmi reaches conclusions, the Bavli does not.

A considerable problem in assessing his evidence, argument, and therefore proposition, has to be specified here. All of these cases are treated as exemplary, but, unfortunately, Kraemer never tells us what proportion of the document as a whole, or of some sizable sample thereof, is comprised by them. So we have argument from anecdote and episode, without any sustained demonstration of the determinate characteristics of the writing as such. Kraemer would have done well to learn from my example: I do not generalize and give three instances of my generalization; I survey entire bodies of data. Having given his paltry set of instances, Kraemer regards it as established fact that the Bavli has been given "an argumentational form." The remainder of the book is devoted to "the indeterminability of truth," an issue that the document under discussion on its own terms hardly portrays as urgent.

Indeed, I am inclined to suspect the authors of the Bavli will have been amazed to be told that their document was more interested in argument than in "truth," meaning, determinate conclusions. To the contrary, since, as a matter of fact, the Bavli forms a highly systematic representation of a complete, proportionate, and authoritative system, Kraemer seems to wish to answer a question the document itself does not require that we ask.

What apparently has happened is that Kraemer has evidently found compelling a couple of philosophical books on the subject of the indeterminacy of truth and has identified his philosopher's stone. So he finds in the issue (his idiosyncratic reworking of the claims, along these same lines, of the literary critics of the deconstructionist school) a basis on which to explain the traits of the document in terms that are intellectually generally accessible, a worthwhile exercise, if carried out in a somewhat mechanical manner. If, then, the meaning is indeterminate, as deconstructionism wants us to believe, so, too, must be the message, Kraemer wishes us to conclude; all that is left is process. Now no one would reject the notion that process is critical; that is, indeed, the very burden of this book of mine. But Kraemer seriously misrepresents the document by misunderstanding the process, missing the point that, the way people think and set forth their ideas itself constitutes a medium for the communication – through the medium itself – of a message that is repeated everywhere and all the time. The entire history of the reception of the Bavli testifies that the document was meant to teach truth, not merely exemplify process. But the implausibility of Kraemer's result does not form an important reason to disbelieve his book.

Rather, let us ask ourselves whether, in his representation of the document, Kraemer has accurately described its paramount traits. It seems to me that, to do so, he will have wanted to answer a variety of fairly basic questions. The first must be, Does the document seen in the aggregate repeatedly utilize a few fixed forms and time and again take up a few determinate intellectual initiatives? If it does, then we may speak, as Kraemer does, of "the Talmud," and if not, we may not. Second, if it can be shown that the document is cogent, saying the same thing of many things, then what is the principal focus of the document? I am inclined to wonder whether Kraemer's characterization will stand up to the scrutiny made possible by the answers to these questions. For from Kraemer's description of the Bavli, we should hardly know the simple fact that, while cogent and coherent as he claims, the rhetorical focus of coherence is upon a prior document, the Mishnah. My analysis of eleven tractates, presented in *The Bavli's One Voice: Types and Forms of Analytical Discourse and Their Fixed Order of Appearance* (Atlanta, 1991: Scholars Press for South Florida Studies in the History of Judaism), has shown that the Bavli is set forth in a systematic way as a commentary to the Mishnah, and, depending upon the tractate, from 85 percent to 97 percent (by my admittedly rough and ready reckoning) of the whole serves as Mishnah commentary. Kraemer does not deal with that fact, to which his characterization of the writing is monumentally irrelevant.

Further, from Kraemer's description, we should hardly have realized that the Bavli does set forth a highly propositional program, which it repeats time and again throughout. The allegation that the purpose of the document is to represent argument, not conclusion, contradicts that fact, spelled out both in these pages and in my *The Bavli's One Statement. The Metapropositional Program of Babylonian Talmud Tractate Zebahim Chapters One and Five* (Atlanta, 1991: Scholars Press for South Florida Studies in the History of Judaism). In other words, it is difficult for me to identify, in the terms of Kraemer's description, the paramount literary and propositional program of the Bavli, as sustained and not merely episodic and exemplary analysis has shown it to be. So not only is his proposition on the indeterminacy of truth on the face of it implausible, his characterization of the document as a matter of fact simply fails to encompass the document's fundamental and indicative traits, since he has not bothered to tell us what he thinks the Bavli is. I hasten to add, in Kraemer's defense, that the results to which I have alluded are very recent, so he is not to be blamed for not knowing what, when he was writing his book, no one knew. But my characterization of the Bavli, even before Kraemer produced his book, did not end with my *Judaism: The Classical Statement. The Evidence of the Bavli* (Chicago, 1986: University of Chicago Press), and *The Bavli and Its Sources: The Question of Tradition in the Case of Tractate Sukkah* (Atlanta, 1987: Scholars Press for Brown Judaic Studies), two books of mine that Kraemer does know and utilize.

But, as a matter of fact, there were two other works that take up precisely the same problem of description as the one treated in the second half of Kraemer's book, in print when he was at work. These are *The Making of the Mind of Judaism* (Atlanta, 1987: Scholars Press for Brown Judaic Studies) and *The Formation of the Jewish Intellect. Making Connections and Drawing Conclusions in the Traditional System of Judaism* (Atlanta, 1988: Scholars Press for Brown Judaic Studies). In these two works I formulated precisely the same question that Kraemer's book asks, but I framed it in terms and categories quite different from his. The results were what led me precisely to the results, as to the overall characteristics of the writing, set forth just now: we deal with a sustained and systematic commentary to the Mishnah, and the problem of the intellectual history of the document is to be defined in the framework of a writing in exegetical form, but with a well-framed propositional program. Of all of this Kraemer knows nothing. How might he have framed his research, had he chosen to see the document as a whole from the perspective of the writing at the end of its formation? For one thing, he will have dropped the words "history" and "historical" from the numerous sentences in which they occur, beginning with the title. But that hardly forms a weighty flaw in his work. In my view the intellectual interest of his inquiry will not have greatly suffered, given the rather formidable chasm that separates the first half of the book from the second (for instance, the authorities who take a principal place in the first four chapters play a negligible role in the final three, where philosophers, not Talmudists, predominate in the footnotes). Indeed, I am inclined to think he can have written Chapters Five through Eight without the results of Chapters One through Four.

But the accuracy of the description of the document that Kraemer puts forward will have gained. A brief account of how I have defined the task will explain why I think the flaws in his description are formidable. In the former work I describe the distinctive modes of thought that produced a kind of writing in Judaism quite different in the basic structure of its mentality and interior traits of logic and, especially, the formation of large-scale structures of knowledge, from the kind of writing carried out by contemporary Christian theologians – even on the same questions. I then described and analyzed, in the context of the concrete expression of mind provided by principal canonical writings, the four critical processes of thought, which I call logics, as I see them, three being propositional logics, the philosophical, teleological, and metapropositional, and one a nonpropositional logic, the logic of fixed association. In this description of the modes of coherent thought and cogent argument, I was able to characterize precisely what Kraemer claims to describe, namely, the intellectual traits of the writing. I cannot point to a single passage in his book in which he tells us not about "truth" (for example, "truth in the classical philosophical tradition," p. 175) but logic in the framework of intelligible thought. Telling about "truth" leads us to attend to mere propositions, for example, this is so, that is not so. But a description of the intellectual processes of a piece of writing should tell us about modes of thought: what is plausible and why, what is found cogent, how are connections made, for instance.

In the latter work, turning to the larger tasks of comparison and contrast of documents, where reliable intellectual history *is* possible (as what I call "the documentary history of ideas"), I claimed to account for how Judaic system builders framed their systems by comparison to the modes of cogent discourse characteristic of prior ones, beginning with the pentateuchal system of Judaism. "The formation of the Jewish intellect" interprets the word "formation" in two senses. The first is "formation" as the ways in which that intellect formed a Judaic system, and the second is, "formation" as an account also concerning the structure of that intellect, that is, of what modes of thought that intellect was formed. First I set forth the order, proportion, structure, and composition of a Judaic system, that is, a worldview and way of life addressed to a defined social entity called (an) "Israel." Second, I explained how framers of such a system made connections and drew conclusions in the setting up of their system. The order was deliberate. *For the order of the formation of the intellect is from the whole to the parts.* The reason is that it is the systemic statement that to begin with defines the logic needed to make that statement. The manner of making connections and drawing conclusions – the true life of intellect – does not percolate upward into the framing of the systemic statement.

What Kraemer has said about the traits of the Bavli therefore is not only dubious as a characterization of the writing as a whole. It is also monumentally beside the point, if the issue is the intellectual structure (if not history) of the Bavli. In this rather facile, shallow, and private work, therefore, Kraemer has presented an intellectual history which is neither historical nor intellectual, since what he describes as the indicative intellectual traits of the document prove in fact to be subordinate and contingent, not systemic, not typical, and not determinative. Would that we could argue only from example, select evidence and ignore whether it is representative, characterize what may not be characteristic at all! But plausible propositions rest upon a thorough and accurate knowledge of the document as a whole and in its parts. Kraemer simply has not done the slow, hard work of adducing literary evidence in behalf of the task of the description, analysis, and interpretation of "the mind of the Talmud." Whether or not the Bavli really favors argument over conclusion because its authors believe that truth is indeterminate simply is not settled in these pages.

True, it can be shown that Kraemer is wrong as to the facts on every point he wishes to make about both the method and the propositional program of the document. But at issue here is not whether he is right or wrong, but only whether he has composed at least what we may judge to be a plausible, if arguable, case for his proposition, and I do not think he has done his homework adequately or set for himself a sufficiently rigorous challenge, involving thorough research. The book misses the mark because the first part – the historical – has evaded the problem of historicity, the second – the literary – has substituted argument by example for systematic research, and the third – the philsophical – fails to present an accurate description of the document's program of logic and its metapropositional consequences. It is not merely that the book lacks its own point (*iqqar haser min hassefer*). It is that Kraemer really doesn't see the point of the document at all. Here I have said what that point is, through two stunning chapters of what I claim is one of the world's genuinely remarkable intellectual achievements. Readers can then judge for themselves whether my examples persuasively show the intellectual character of the writing – and compare my mode of formulating and solving the problem of description with the one that, in its errors, persuaded me to spell out things I had had in mind but thought a bit routine. Only when I see how someone misses the point that strikes me as obvious am I able to persuade myself that what is self-evident in the writing has still to be spelled out. The character of the Bavli is formed out of distinct components, one of them an exegetical program, another of them an intellectual program. The generative problematic formed out of the formation of mixed grids imparts to the Bavli a principal component of its intellectual program.

Having argued that Kraemer has not shown the argument is the main thing, but having failed to find any other generative problematic governing large stretches of the Bavli's discourse, where do I find myself? It is with the problem of how the method of the document constitutes its statement of meaning. I have formed the answer to that question, but to spell it out, I have first to continue my description of the Bavli. It would be premature to say what I think the Bavli accomplishes until I have demonstrated what the Bavli is. And to do that, it is clear, we must find a mode of description that does not paraphrase discussions and call the result philosophy, as I have tried to do. The description of the Bavli, not as to its external form but as to its internal program, will derive only when we have compared this Talmud to the other one. What has gone wrong? It is my description of the Bavli. My method until now has been to try to describe the Talmud of Babylonia in its own terms, wholly inductively, without a comparison and contrast with some other piece of writing of the same genre. If we had no other talmud, then the word Talmud would be a proper noun, speaking of only one, and no comparison would serve. But the genus, talmud, covers two species, that is, there are two Talmuds, the one of the Land of Israel, the other of Babylonia. So definition of either of the two Talmuds can be conceived without a systematic work of comparison and contrast with the other one: What is this? is a question we can answer only when we can say, Why this, not that? So that is what is to be done, and then, and only then, shall we know not only how the Bavli differs from the Yerushalmi, but also, what is the Bavli. By showing what the Bavli is that the Yerushalmi is not, and by showing what the Yerushalmi did not do that the Bavli did, I shall accomplish the necessary description of the Bavli.

Then the plan and intent of the Bavli – its intellectual program – will be reliably described, and, of course, in the description, fully characterized and explained as well. It goes without saying that, at the end – perhaps a dozen monographs into the future – the Bavli, along with its associated Midrash compilations, will be seen as the restatement of religion as theology. Then, it will further emerge, we shall see the formation of Judaism as the working of a thesis, an antithesis, and a synthesis: the philosophical system of the Mishnah, the counterpart, the religious system of the Talmud of the Land of Israel and associated Midrash compilations, and the upshot, the theological system of the Talmud of Babylonia and its associated Midrash compilations, that is to say, philosophical method brought to bear upon a religious message. But, as I said, to unpack that conception and to show how the documents yield it will require some more probes, some more monographs.

Index

South Florida Studies in the History of Judaism